New Methods for
Old-Age Research
Strategies for Studying Diversity

Christine L. Fry
Jennie Keith
& Contributors

Bergin & Garvey Publishers, Inc.
MASSACHUSETTS

First published in 1986 by
Bergin & Garvey Publishers, Inc.
670 Amherst Road
South Hadley, Massachusetts 01075

6789   987654321

Printed in the United States of America

Library of Congress Cataloging-in-Publication Data
Main entry under title:
New methods for old-age research.
    "Based on Workshop on Cross-Cultural Research on
Old Age, held at Loyola University in May 1980"—Pref.
    Bibliography: p.
    Includes index.
    1. Aged—Cross-cultural studies—Congresses.
2. Old age—Research—Congresses. I. Fry, Christine L.
II. Keith, Jennie. III. Workshop on Cross-Cultural
Research on Old Age (1980: Loyola University of Chicago)
GN485.N49   1986   305.2'6   85-26792
ISBN 0-89789-063-9
ISBN 0-89789-034-5 (pbk.)

Cover photo: Nancy Clark

With respect, gratitude, and affection,
this book is dedicated to

M. MARGARET CLARK

CONTENTS

Preface

Many of the chapters in this book are based on earlier versions presented at the Workshop on Cross-Cultural Research on Old Age, held at Loyola University in May 1980.* Since that time, interest in comparative and qualitative methods for the study of age has increased greatly, leading to new and more refined questions, and necessitating innovative modes of research. For this publication, all the papers from the workshop have been revised and brought up to date, with special attention given to bibliography. An entirely new chapter on measurement of age, by Nancy Howell, presents the most recent perspectives on this issue. Historical demography is discussed in a new chapter by David Kertzer and Andrea Schiaffino, and the significance and measurement of ethnicity are discussed in a chapter by Linda Cool. The ritualization of the life course is now the subject of a full chapter by John Himmant. The contributions of Rosamond Vanderburgh, who has extensive field experience with native Americans, are added to those of Gelya Frank in a chapter on life histories.

We are encouraged by the interest in comparative and qualitative methods that has stimulated this book. We believe as strongly as ever that the data obtainable only through such methods are essential to understanding the aging process and the significance of age in human social life.

The original papers presented at the Workshop were available in book form by Loyola University in 1981.

Christine L. Fry
Jennie Keith

*The Workshop was sponsored by a National Institute of Aging grant (No. AG02268-01). The Editors are very thankful to Mrs. Shirley Bagley of NIA for her assistance in planning the workshop. They would also like to thank David Gutman of Northwestern University, Margaret H. Huyck of Illinois Institute of Technology, and Charlotte Ikels of Harvard for their helpful participation in the workshop. We also wish to thank Lauree Garvin and Deborah Vandenhoonard for their assistance in bringing the manuscript to book form.

Introduction

CHRISTINE L. FRY
Department of Sociology &
Anthropology
Loyola University, Chicago

JENNIE KEITH
Department of Sociology &
Anthropology
Swarthmore College

The origin of this book is our conviction that comparative and qualitative methods are greatly needed in research on old age. The book's goal is to develop that conviction into strategies for collection of qualitative and comparative data about aging. Information about the qualtity and meaning of older people's lives is often called for, as is information about the situation for the elderly in various cultural settings (see e.g., *Our Future Selves*, National Advisory Council on Aging 1978). The empirical base of gerontological generalization will not be adequate without these kinds of data. Having participated loud and long in such exhortations, we decided it was time to move away from preaching and toward practice.

Specification of the kinds of information most needed and strategies for obtaining it in various cultural contexts will provide both a stimulus and a guide for future research. The first step toward creating such a guidebook was a Workshop on Cross-Cultural Research on Old Age, sponsored by the National Institute on Aging, to bring together researchers experienced with anthropological methods in gerontology. The major challenge of comparative cross-cultural research is to obtain data that are at once comparable across cultures and valid within cultures. Comparability requires a common guide to methodology, while validity prohibits standardized measurement across cultures. The bridge linking these two requirements is a common *strategy* for measurement, which promotes comparability but stops short of standardization.

Each chapter argues for the significance of a specific kind of data for understanding aging and old age, then offers strategies for obtaining that kind of information in various cultural settings. A persistent theme is that comparative and qualitative methods, and the data they produce, are needed not only in exotic settings, but also at home. The cultural diversity of most modern industrial societies is great, and qualitative data about the meanings older people give to their own lives are, if anything, more scarce for complex than for simpler societies.

This is a guidebook, not a cookbook. Its goal is not to provide lists of specific questions or measures, but strategies for discovering the appropriate questions and measures of old age in different cultures. More qualitative and comparative data must be available for adequate generalizations about the processes and experiences of aging. Our hope is that, like our own favorite guidebooks, *New Methods for Old-Age Research* will offer temptation as well as direction into more adventurous explorations of old age.

RESEARCH DESIGNS: THE COMMUNICATION OF METHODOLOGY

Discovery and verification may be the intent of all research designs, but they also have other functions. It is through our methodology that we communicate with peers. Peer review occurs at two critical points. The first is a review of a grant application in which an investigator presents a plan of research with the intent of receiving the resources to do the research. The second peer review is when research results are submitted for publication. Unless a researcher presents a research design well, effectively addressing the basic issues that peers use in evaluating the work, that work will not be funded or published. Presentation of research design might consequently be considered an important ingredient of our methodology. Although research designs are the backbone of both proposals and final publication, we will focus here on the necessary first step of communication about research: presentation of a research design in a proposal for funding.

A scientific enterprise, and the research design that serves as its map, have three major components: theory, data-collection procedures, and a plan for data analysis. The chapters in this book focus on the data-collection procedures, as these are often inadequately described for qualitative and comparative data. However, in a complete and balanced research design, these procedures must be presented in the context of both theory and plans for analysis. Perhaps the most common failure in research proposals is imbalance. Depending on the applicant's skills and tastes, one component may be presented brilliantly, while the others get only minimal attention.

Theory

If a research design should be a complete and well-balanced "meal," then what constitutes an adequate portion of these three essential ingredients? The theory integrates the process, justifying both data collection and analysis. A theory is a set of related statements that attempt to explain some aspect of reality. The basic elements in that domain, as well as the relationships among them, are defined. Given these basic definitions, certain questions are reasonable, certain others are not. If the model of reality constructed by a theory assumes a functional interrelationship among subparts, then reasonable questions will address how one part affects another. If the model assumes stimulus-response learning processes, then questions about innate sources of behavior are not likely to arise.

There are many types and levels of theory. "Grand" theory attempts to explain a very large area of reality; lower-level or middle-range theories focus on more restricted domains. Marx, Durkheim, and Parsons are often called grand theorists, while writers such as Rosow (on age and roles) and Lawton (on age and environment) are in the process of developing theories that have more specific explanatory goals. Many types of theories can form a framework for research. Essential to research design are explicit statements of the theoretical framework within which the research problem will be defined. For example, the design for research on social ties among old-age peers might begin within the grand theoretical framework of Durkheimian propositions about the bases of integration in social life, or of middle-range propositions about adult socialization.

Kinds of Models

The intent of all models whether folk or scientific, is to generalize. The way generalizations are made varies. Scientific models differ from old models in that they are subject to a spiral of theory testing. Ultimately scientific generalizations are retained or revised through empirical evaluation of their explanatory power. Scientific models are not alike. Within anthropology at least four kinds of models are in use (Naroll & Cohen 1970:33-49): descriptive models, associational models, functional models, and system models. These models differ by level of generalization; what the model is trying to accomplish; and adequacy criteria.

Descriptive models are at the simplest level of generalization, describing regularities among a group of people. This kind of model involves the most heterogeneous research strategies and criteria for empirical verification. This can range from exemplification of the pattern to the formal eliciting frames of ethnosemantics and the computer-aided modeling of cognitive structures. *Associational models* are those in which variables are shown to vary with respect to each other. Quantification ultimately is involved, since verification rests on counts of "more" or "less" of a variable. *Functional models* are at a higher level of generalization. In addition to dealing with questions of covariance of correlation, the intent is to deal with issues of cause. Finally, *systems models* are models in which an entire set of variables are theoretically related to one another. Boundary maintenance and feedback relationships are common to these models as variables must be linked to a context and the problems of circularity resolved.

In presenting a research design, it is essential to know the kind of model involved. If the model is descriptive, the researcher does not want to present it as associational . The effects of this are only to "call up" the wrong set of adequacy criteria for evaluation. Research designs should be presented in a way that addresses the issues of the established tradition for the kind of model the researcher is using.

Topics vs. Researchable Problems

A critique that an application is atheoretical doesn't always mean that theory is lacking. It may mean that the theory is not well presented or is underdeveloped, or that the investigator has not narrowed the topic to a researchable problem. Selection of a topic is a very necessary first step. However, topics usually are in and of themselves not researchable. The links between the topic of interest and the theoretical framework must be thoroughly and explicitly presented. A useful rule of translation from topic to researchable question is to ask the question: "Under what conditions? With what consequences? And so what?" For example, if the topic is peer ties among older people, applying this rule leads to statements of hypotheses about the factors promoting or obstructing such ties, about their relationship to various aspects of older people's lives, and to a statement of the theoretical and practical significance of such ties. What the theory predicts, or how the model might be generalized, must be stated in terms that can guide the practical steps of research. Hypotheses, for example, have several requirements.

Falsifiability

A hypothesis must be falsifiable. It must be possible, logically, to find evidence for and against it. On the other hand, a hypothesis should not be trivial or obvious: "People who speak the language are more likely to ineract than people who do not." Hypotheses should also not be circular or tautological, i.e., true by definition: "People who have lived a greater number of years are older than those who have lived a lesser number of years."

Measurability

Each concept in a hypothesis or question must eventually be translated into measurable terms. Questions or hypotheses must be stated in conceptual terms, and then each concept "operationalized" or made measurable. As Cool discusses, for example, ethnicity may be conceptually defined in various ways, each of which may in turn be measured in various ways. Measurement is the synaptic point between theory and evidence. The measurement problem for any researcher is what specific kinds of evidence will best represent the concepts of the hypotheses or questions. Measurement is too often equated with counting, and simply not considered by those who collect qualitiative information. In fact, measurement is the crucial link between the general question and the specific case, and must be adequately defined in any research design. If life histories will provide evidence for major themes in older people's perceptions of their lives, then the researcher needs to explain what about the life histories will be interpreted in what ways to obtain that evidence.

Keith proposes that in some research situations the discovery of appropriate measures may be a major activity of earlier stages of fieldwork. The essential requirement is that the measurement *issue* be addressed in the research proposal, even though in many cases complete definition of measures would be a serious scientific error. If ability of older poeple to participate fully in the daily life of their communities is an important variable in the research questions, then an appropriate measure for that ability must be discovered. However, if the research is cross-cultural, it may be dangerously misleading to define the measure too early. What should be presented in the research design is the strategy through which that definition will be made, e.g., through a preliminary stage of participant observation, or of ethnosemantic eliciting, focused on community member's differentiation of full and impaired participation.

Generalizability

For practical reasons, when we want to bring empirical data to our model, seldom can we use the whole world. One of the broadest questions about measurement and evidence is, from where, and from what population, should data be collected? Immediately we are faced with the question of generalizability of the units from which we are collecting data. First, what is it about the people in a particular location (tribe, neighborhood, retirement community, census tract, etc.) or people sharing a certain characteristic (ethnicity, age, race, sex, social class, etc.) that will enable us to evaluate the hypotheses or answer the questions derived from the model and to what extent will these results be generalizable to the whole or similar units? Explicit statements on the selection of the units and how they are salient to the model are necessary. Also, unless the units selected are small enough that a total sample is feasible, a sampling procedure should be included. This outlines the steps taken to identify and select those individuals who will provide data. These procedures may either be designed to minimize unknown selection biases on the part of the investigator and/or to make explicit the selection criteria so that the biases are known. Since no research design is totally generalizable., the limits on generalization become one factor that must be addressed and considered in the evaluation process.

It is toward the adequacy and presentation of measurement strategies that the chapters of this volume are directed, with the goal of strengthening and enriching research designs on aging. Five chapters address the significance and measurement of specific groups of variables: functionality (chap. 1, Beall & Eckert) age (chap. 2, Howell), morale (chap. 9, Nydegger), social networks (chap. 10, Sokolovsky), and ethnicity (chap. 11, Cool). Existing strategies are presented along with discussions of potential problems. Two chapters focus on the problems of working with certain data sets: historical demograghy (chap. 4, Kertzer & Schiaffino) and the holocultural research using Human Relations Area Files (HRAF) data to examine treatment of older people (chap. 1, Glascock & Feinman). A complex phenomenon, the life course, is the material examined through specific conceptual problems: age transitions (chap. 6, Nydegger) and rituals of the life cycle (chap. 7, Hinnant). Finally, three chapters are concerned with discovery procedures extensively used in anthropology that are particulary suited to collection of qualitative data, and notoriously difficult to present in research designs: participant observation (chap. 1, Keith), ethnosemantics (chap. 5, Fry), and life histories (chap. 8, Frank & Vanderburgh). Each chapter provides guidelines for development and presentation of a research strategy that is appropriately complete and explicit.

Administrative Issues

Research activities for any project change through time from start-up through data collection, analysis and wrap-up. Attention should be given to projecting the sequence of research activities in a schedule of research. A chart that presents various research activities in monthly units is a very useful part of a proposal. (See fig. 1.1 for an example). Also, projects usually involve a staff of researchers with a division of labor. If there is a division of labor, this should be explicitly demarcated, along with a plan of training of the partially or untrained staff. Information on the administrative component of the project and the schedule of research gives evidence tht the project can be done in the amount of time projected and within the amount of funds requested.

Plans of Analysis

Of all components of a research design, analysis is the most conditioned by the other two. Analysis is the bridge between theory and data. Levels of measurement (categorical, ordinal, interval, or ratio) limit the statistics that can be appropriately used. Different kinds of models call for different analytic procedures. For instance, an ethnosemantic descriptive model can use fairly specialized procedures such as multidimensional scaling or cluster analysis (see chap. 5). A statistical model, on the other hand, has a wide variety of statistical frameworks that are readily accessible through such software packages as SPSS, SAS, or BMD. The generalizable point is that there must be an explicit plan of analysis. It should present clearly and thoroughly what will be done with the various types of information collected, and why. If life histories are recorded, then the plan of analysis must explain how those complex documents will be stored, coded, and interpreted in order to answer the research questions. As with measures, coding schemes for labeling various topics or themes may not be definable at the stage of research design. However, the strategy through which this definition will take place must be included. If coders will read the histories, progressively noting more-refined themes and testing their scheme on new sections or new histories, then this activity should be described and justified, and money and time budgeted to carry it out.

NEW METHODS FOR OLD-AGE RESEARCH

Our "new methods" are rooted in well-established anthropological practices that include the use of culture as an important variable, a comparative strategy, the search for emic or system-specific meanings, and a holistic perspective. Our "old-age research" has several foci: (1) physical aspects, including functionality assessment, measurement of age, and utilization of demographic data from historic contexts; (2) cultural defintions of age, age transitions, and the life course; (3) subjective aspects of aging obtained from life histories and the measurement of well-being; (4) social networks; and (5) cultural factors, including the measurement of ethnicity and the treatment of older adults.

Physical Aspects

Biological and cultural factors are nearly impossible to separate. Age, sex, and health are basic characteristics of people in any social and cultural arena. Major research concerns are the health status and abilities of older people to maintain themselves as independent adults. Functionality (chap. 2, Beall & Eckert) is an important variable in that it is among the most predictive of the quality of life of those who have grown old. Yet, functionality has its cultural side in that the tasks of adult life are defined and conditioned by cultural responses to basic life issues, including increased dependency. Although physical functioning has measures that can be directly observed and monitored, these are best interpreted in the cultural context in which they occur. Also, demographic factors, age, and sex distributions are familiar variables to those who study old age. Vital statistics indicate dependency ratios and in some ways reflect societal priorities and needs. Demography is a well-developed science among the industrialized nations of Europe and North America. But in Third-World countries and smaller scaled societies, vital statistics are problematic or nonexistent (chap. 3, Howell). Even when taking your own census, age often cannot be measured directly, as birth records may not be kept and age is not reckoned in calendar years. Strategies to pinpoint and translate approximate age into Western calendar years are multiple and by necessity must use the meaningful events and sequences in the local culture.

   When research on the life course is extended into the historical dimension, as described in chapter 4, a variety of archival sources are available (census reports, vital registration records, population registers), each of which has its own strengths and weaknesses. Kertzer and Schiaffino present a scheme for recording and analyzing data from Italian population registers that has allowed them to use computers for a statistical analysis of patterning in the occurrence of life events such as widowhood and remarriage.

Cultural Definitions

Age is a much-respected and much-used variable because of its exactitude. However, precision in the measurement of time tells us very little about the meaning of age and actually hides more than it measures. When directed to aging, techniques from cognitive anthropology, (chap. 5, Fry) probe the semantic organization and the defining features of age (chronology, roles, statuses or other salient dimensions) in a culture. Sorting techniques facilitate the documentation of intracultural variation and are frames of reference for eliciting data on age norms, boundaries, and the qualities of relationships within and between age grades. Such techniques elicit cultural data on aging which are normative, ideational, and definitional. These norms, as used in negotiating real situations, present a more complicated web to disentangle.
   Age is intertwined with roles, which, in turn, are the patterned components of the life course. Age, role transitions and cohort effects (chap. 6, Nydegger, & chap. 4, Kertzer & Schiaffino) are confounded variables. Careful attention should be paid to un-tangling such terms in a research design involving age. Perhaps the most extreme case of cultural definition of the life course appears in the age- graded societies discussed by Hinnant in chapter 7. He presents strategies for collection of information about the rituals through which individual social behavior is linked to this formal system of age categories and norms. As in many "extreme case" analyses, there is much that is vividly clear in his report that may help illuminate the influential but less obvious systems of age categorization and expectation in other societies.

The Subjective Side

Subjectivity has its role in aging research, especially since much of our research has been directed toward understanding how older people feel about themselves and their lives. Life-history research, developed in the 1930s and 1940s, has produced many fascinating documents of experience and culture. Life histories (chap. 8, Frank & Vanderburgh) encourage a review and interpretation of a life or an exploration of a life in process. By encouraging the subjective and idiosyncratic, life histories document individuals' management of their sources of contentment (discontentment), self-esteem, and evaluation of that life. Measuring the happiness and well-being of old people is the intent of many standardized morale scales (chap. 9, Nydegger). With so many to choose from, how can we select the most appropriate measure? These are major issues currently being sorted out by researchers. An even bigger question concerns the possibility that the values "happiness" and "morale" represent a culturally restricted concept of Western civilization. In light of the difficulties in measuring well-being and quality of life, alternate strategies are in order. Self-report data, self-evaluation, alternate data sources, and elicitation procedures to probe the dimensions of well-being are especially useful in comparative research on psychological variables that are conditioned by cultural context.

Social Networks

Interaction and the articulation of older people with their society is another major research focus. What roles do the old play, and with whom do they interact? What is the quality and the quantity of these interactions? Social network mapping (chap. 10, Sokolovsky) is an anthropological technique especially well suited to answer these questions. This strategy examines the contacts a person maintains and the qualities of those relationships (e.g., duration, content, frequency, intensity, reciprocity). In resolving some of the problems associated with data collection and management, Sokolovsky has developed a network profile. Only after the initial phases of participant observation are complete can a culturally sensitive profile be constructed to elicit the data on an older individual's interactions in differing domains. The profile serves both as a categorical guide to dimensions and qualitative variables of interaction and as an abbreviated coding sheet.

Cultural Factors

An initial question logically asked of ethnographic accounts about older people is, How are they treated? In fact, this is the longest standing issue in the anthropology of aging, dating to the 1940s. Treatment is not a simple and singular variable (chap. 12, Glascock

& Feinman) to be scaled "good," "okay," or "bad." A comparative analysis, using a standard sample from the Human Relations Area Files, reveals that we must carefully sort through differences in attitudes, as opposed to behavior. It also must be remembered that treatment can be of many kinds and that there may be the more than one category of old. Thus, a major issue becomes creation of more meaningful, manageable, and measureable variables. Measurement, however, entails a wide range of techniques, including all those we examine in this volume.

Ethnicity may be the cultural variable par excellence, as it is often defined in part by the sharing of a common culture. In chapter 11, Cool discusses the various conceptual definitions of ethnicity and their implications for relationships between ethnicity and satisfaction with life in øld age. This chapter also describes the requirements of multiple measurements for any multidimensional phenomenon (such as ethnicity) which includes cultural, behavioral, and personal components.

ANTHROPOLOGICAL ALTERNATIVES

Anthropological methodology is replete with many alternatives. With a global perspective, method and theory are continually challenged. In grappling with the issues of diversity and comparability in comparative research, anthropologists have created their distinctive methodology. Throughout the chapters of this book, we find the features of this perspective expressed in the concerns of "emics and etics," "holism," real vs. ideal culture, and in qualitative and quantitative research.

Emics and Etics

Data are not just plain data and facts are not simple facts. Culture filters out what is important and has meaning. But, whose culture are we using? "Etic" refers to the culture of science, e.g., of anthropology or gerontology. "Emic" is the inside view of another culture, using its language and the judgments of informants in ascertaining the dimensions of the issues being investigated. Emics and etics are equally important, but it is the emic that offers the greater challenges and insights. Emic research strategies not only lead us to new meanings and different assumptions about reality, but they enable us to create instruments which appropriately measure culturally significant variables.

Holism

Life is lived as a whole, not in bits and pieces or shreds and patches. To understand lives and the daily business of living, anthropologists emphasize their entire context. Behavior, attitudes, aspirations are all examined with reference to their particular sociocultural and physical environment. Interactions between culture-specific variables and their meanings are understood *before* we abstract selected aspects for statistical evaluation of our hypotheses. As a result, theory is firmly grounded in a context and more adequately represents that context.

Real and Ideal Culture

Culture is the code guiding people's lives. It charts the good and the bad. Usually we seek the positive, but obviously the ideal is not always attainable. When given a choice, most people will present themselves in the best possible manner. Data from a singular, brief interview encounter or a questionnaire are notably distorted toward the ideal. Long-term field research (at least one year or even longer) serves as a check on this normative bias. Continued involvement with informants, and the knowledge of their culture as revealed through participant observation, permit insights into the compromises people make. Also, the researcher has opportunities to see how the ideal, including both the positive and negative, is used to sanction and motivate behavior.

Qualitative and Quantitative Research

Quality and quantity are not as diametrically opposed as we often suggest when we discuss research. They are different, but they are also a part of the same process. Before we can ask, How much? we must ask, . . . of what? Quality comes before quantity. The call is for new variables and for refinement of the variables we already have. Above all, it is a call for variables founded in the experiences of the people we study. Emic, holistic, qualitative research, without a normative bias, is essential to the development of gerontology. The anthropological alternatives presented here should help provide the data to promote understanding of old age at home and in its widest cultural diversity. We cannot know one without the other.

NOTES

Naroll, Raoul, and Ronald Cohen. 1970. "The Logic of Generalization." In A Handbook of Method in Cultural Anthropology, ed. Raoul Naroll and Ronald Cohen, New York: Columbia University Press, pp. 25-50.

1
Participant Observation

JENNIE KEITH
Department of Sociology & Anthropology
Swarthmore College

Participant observation is not often placed first in an inventory of research methods.[1] However, in a volume dedicated to research on old age, first place is entirely appropriate. The holistic and qualitative data this method can provide about the lives of older people are urgently needed. So little is known about the quality or the insider's view of those lives that many other research methods cannot be used before preliminary participant observation discovers reasonable questions and answers. With emphasis on old-age research, this chapter describes the situations in which participant observation is most needed, and the strategies through which it is most productively presented, carried out, and analyzed.

Anthropologists do participant observation much better than they talk about it. The complexities of its techniques and its data are usually hidden behind a brief reference to "the anthropological method" or "standard ethnographic techniques." We need to do for ourselves what we have done for many others, i.e., make explicit the shared understandings embedded in this important term from our professional culture. By "going native" in this positive sense, we will make our culture more accessible to significant outsiders such as users of our data, others who wish to use participant observation, and granting agencies that support research. The goal in this chapter is less to tell anyone how to do participant observation than to suggest how to talk about it better.

Participant observation means what it says. It is distinguished by active participation as a means of observing the setting under study. There are many degrees of participation (Gold 1958), but the observer's personal involvement in a research setting is always a central means to understanding it. Rather than using a research instrument, the participant observer becomes one.

STAGES OF PARTICIPANT OBSERVATION

Participant observation refers to several distinct activities that are carried out by a researcher during distinct stages of a study. A most important step toward better understanding of the scientific merits of this method is to make explicit these stages, each with its own goals, activities, and resulting data. Table 1.1 presents a sample outline of the stages of participant observation in the research project "Age, Generation and Experience" (NIA No. AGO 3110--principal investigators, Fry & Keith).

Stage 1: Introduction

The goal of Stage 1 is a basic map of the research setting, including definition of a role for the observer that will give him or her a place on the map. Data at this stage are field notes kept in a daily journal: activities are characteristically multiple and nonstop. The researcher participates in all accessible activities, at first predominately public, which gradually lead to invitations or at least permission to share in more private encounters . A simple census is a good way to visit every household or a sample of them. Regardless of the information it produces, census taking introduces the fieldworker and the project to a large number of people. When census material is already available, other strategies for initial contacts must be invented. Early in my research in a French retirement residence, I offered people copies of photographs taken at a community party. Delivering the pictures gave me a reason to visit every apartment, as well as an opportunity to hear comments about the individuals and activities in the photos (Keith 1982).

The map to be charted in Stage 1 must include the cast of characters, important territories, temporal divisions, conflicting issues, major past events, types of contexts, and major categories of activity. As the researcher tries to move more or less appropriately through a daily round, listening to and watching everything possible, tentative patterns will begin to emerge from the wearying confusion. As insights become reinforced into hypotheses about the way things work here, key informants can be asked to verify the patterns. In other words, when the observer knows enough to form a coherent question, preliminary lines on the map can be checked out with individuals who seem perceptive about their community and willing to talk.

At the Residence Les Floralies in Bagnolet, France; this re-seacher ate in the dining room every noon, attended the sewing club and the pottery class, watched movies and television, worked in the laundry and the kitchen, made Christmas decorations, and played *belote*. Gradually, "the lady with the cane" and "the man in the white cap" acquired names; shoes vs. carpet slippers signified formal events; Christmas decorations were identified as a Communist task; seats in the dining room were understood as permanent, personal territory. This mixed bag of discoveries must be emptied every day into the fieldworker's notes. At this point, dumping out the day's events is an accurate image, since there is not yet a basis for sorting. This makes it especially important not to impose any gratuitous order. Notes should describe at this stage, with any tentative judgments clearly separated. Behavior, dress, and speech should be reported, not evaluated or summarized. (Pelto 1978:93-94 gives good examples of the contrast between the two.) If only the judgment is in the notes, the observation can never be retrieved. As the fieldworker learns more about the settings, quite different interpretations might be made of the same details--if they are still available (see Spradley 1980:73ff on descriptive recording).

The other major task of Stage 1 is to establish a role that is comfortable and consistent enough for both researcher and com-munity members to facilitate a lengthy and intense relationship. The first choice point is whether to take a role that exists in the research setting or to attempt to define a new one; second, the role may be more central or more peripheral. The existing role may be very appealing because it exists; it requires no effort of definition and persuasion. There may also be pressure from authorities who see such roles as desirable constraints on the fieldworker. The researcher should consider carefully, however, if an existing role can meet the criteria of comfort and consistency. Is this a role you want to live in for a year? Can you live in it comfortably enough to put others at ease as well as yourself? Does it allow you access to a wide enough range of people and situations that it will be satisfactory throughout the field study, or will you need to change roles later? Major inconsistency in social identity during the research produces at least puzzlement and possibly suspicion or anger.

Defining a new role at the beginning of research is difficult, but once it is done the fieldworker can relax into an honest identity, and appropriately concentrate on the business of research, which may be unfamiliar to this community, but is now by definition "what researchers do." Fieldworkers often agonize about the rogues' gallery of possible misinterpretations of this role: are they spies? tax collectors? exposé seekers? Unless special circumstances conspire to make a community particularly sensitive about strangers, it is probably more often the hierarchical implications of studier-studied that make direct presentation of a research role painful. Many fieldworkers are delighted and relieved at acceptance of the idea that they want to learn something about a group of people, and that the best way to do that is to spend a great deal of time with them. Most people are too busy with their own lives to spend long worrying about the motivations or activities of a researcher. We should be more concerned about being seen as minor nuisances than as major threats--and should remember that, humbling as it may be, a degree of ignorance and powerlessness may be useful fieldwork tools.

Central vs peripheral role is another choice for the participant observer. Although participation in central activities, such as decision-making councils, offers access to interesting information, it may also lead to highly visible identification with elites or factions. The cost may be loss of entree into other groups whose members may be fearful or suspicous.

At Les Floralies I was strongly encouraged by retirement-fund authorities to take the existing role of waitress. Since I decided to try to define a more flexible and comfortable role as a researcher, I was introduced to the residents committee, who agreed that it made sense to study a "model home" such as theirs, and that living with them was a reasonable way to learn about it. As I realized the one-sided role of the committee in the factionalized world of the residence, however, I carefully balanced my introduction through this central group with visible participation in the more peripheral activities of the opposing faction.

Stage 2: Focused Research

The first problem in participant observation is drawing a map; the second problem is drawing it too well. The transition to the focused inquiry of Stage 2 is difficult because few researchers ever believe they have enough basic information about a setting. Most fieldworkers are prodded into Stage 2 by someone else: letters from a dissertation adviser, a visit from a colleague, comments from a resident companion. The prod consists of questions like, "What do you want to know all this for?" Once the fieldworker lifts his or her gaze above the details, a temporary separation from the research setting is often useful for focusing distance. Many experienced fieldworkers have reported that they left their research sites at what is here described as the transition from Stage 1 to Stage 2. Those planning to use this method should consider including this transitional period in their research schedule, so that time and funding needs can be anticipated.

At this point the task shifts from general mapping to investigation of specific questions. The major concepts in hypotheses from the research design or formulated in the field must be measured in Stage 2. The liminal period away from the research context and activities is needed to rediscover the research design, to sort through its hypotheses in light of what is known about the setting, to refine them, and very likely to add new ones. A common discovery in Stage 1 is a variety of intervening variables that complicate the original hypotheses. One of the great contributions of long-term, contextual research using participant observation is the discovery of mechanisms to explain relationships discovered through other methods. The activities of this stage are more focused, directed to collection of information to measure specific concepts and to refinement of hypotheses into testable form (Spradley (1980:100ff and McCall & Simmons 1969:142-228 discuss transition to Stage 2). The results of Stage 2 are operationalized hypotheses, ready for testing.

In this author's research at Les Floralies, Stage 2 involved focusing on socialization of new residents and on political factions. The original research design centered on the process of community creation. One hypothesis was that homogeneity of residents in characteristics other than age would promote development of we-feelings. Discovery during Stage 1 that the residence was highly factionalized introduced two intervening variables. First, the factions seemed to be important channels for socialization of new arrivals, and second, factional conflict seemed to promote rather than weaken commitment to the community. Stage 2 for me therefore began with the decision to focus my observations on socialization of new residents and on conflict.

Activities in Stage 2 are more specialized. At Les Floralies, for example, this researcher went with the driver to pick up every new arrival, and spent a great deal of time with these people during the first weeks at the residence. Any hint of conflict was pursued by spending time with the protagonists, hearing various sides, keeping alert to how far the reverberations spread into conversations at meals or in the lounges, attending resident committee meetings in case the problem was discussed. As is usual in Stage 2, these more specialized observations took time that, in Stage 1, had been used for more diffuse participation. No longer could every meeting of the sewing club, pottery class, and

Christmas decoration group be attended, no longer could the researcher play *belote* after lunch, watch movies every Wednesday, or work in the kitchen, garden, office, and laundry. This transition had to be explained to community members, since those activities were, of course, just as important to them as ever. The efforts spent establishing a research role paid off at this point because the change in behavior could more easily be explained.

Recording of data also becomes more focused in Stage 2. Field notes continue to include a journal of daily activities, but this will be much briefer, mainly because many routines have been recognized by now. Most notes will be on specialized topics. Word-processing or data-management programs for a microcomputer make possible indexing entries and creation of subfiles for various topics at the time observations are being recorded. Since battery packs now make possible use of a microcomputer in almost any setting, most budgets for research that includes extensive participant observation should include a microcomputer and appropriate software. At Les Floralies, during this phase, extended cases of conflicts were recorded, and the details of arrival for each new person, as well as their informal contacts, formal group participation, and contacts with the outside. In addition to narrative journal entries, the more focused topics as well as the "map" available from Stage 1 make possible more precise recording of data. Because the repertory of activities available to residents was known to the researcher, a code sheet was created to record participation of each individual. A simple list of names and activities (both formal and informal) became a tool for recording observations systematically, in numerical form, and for every resident. Any "missing data" was immediately pursued. This was an important check against the participant observer's pitfall of learning a lot about only the most visible or talkative members of a community (see Spradley 1980:82-83 for a "descriptive question matrix"). In addition, during Stage 1, the predominant significance of seating in the dining room was demonstrated. Since the residents chose their own seats, and changed them only under pressure of strong attraction or rejection, a map of the tables was a natural sociogram, which charted both the incorporation of new members, and the factional "purification" of meeting groups over time. Once the reseacher had memorized the seating arrangements, changes could be noted once a week on a mimeographed chart (see Webb et al. 1966 for a discussion of unobtrusive measures).

Stage 3: Evaluation of Hypotheses

The systematization of Stage 2 may not sound like the impressionistic image of the participant observer soaking up atmosphere and simmering with insights. Because participant observation is done more systematically than it is talked about, many nonanthropologists identify the technique entirely with Stage 1. Stage 3 moves even farther away from the stereotype. This is the phase of hypothesis testing. Hypotheses must now be stated precisely, so that data can be collected for their evaluation. Proper nouns-- persons, places, events--must be translated into variables (Przeworski & Teune 1970; chap. 1). At Les Floralies, for example, the dining room "nomads" who never found a permanent place at a table, or in the social organization, suggested the hypothesis that the lower the level of political identity, the lower the level of social participation in the residence.

Stage 3 is also the time to consult other studies or theoretical literature that will stimulate translation of patterns observed in this setting into more general explanatory hypothesis. Research on utopian experiments, for instance, suggests that communal work leads to higher levels of commitment. Since members of one faction at Les Floralies were, for ideological reasons, more likely to work than members of the other faction, patterns of loyalty to the residence might be explained by this broader hypothesis. Evaluation of one hypothesis that individuals who worked at residence jobs would have higher levels of loyalty to the residence than those who did not required attitudinal data collected by questionnaire in addition to observations and inquiries about work roles.

Data collection in Stage 3 is both more specific and more diverse. With hypotheses stated and with an inventory of measures appropriate to the setting, it is possible to construct various research instruments: questionnaires, card sorts, network profiles. Either natural or constructed experiments may be carried out in the field (Campbell & Stanley 1963; Sechrest 1970). There is no *one* best measure for anything. Multiple measures are always the preferred strategy (cf. Campbell & Fiske, 1959; Le Vine 1970), and by Stage 3 it is possible to create them.

The fact that participant observation falls into at least three stages, each with distinctive goals, activities, and results, has important implications for the way it is presented and justified as a method in research designs and grant proposals. *All* the stages, goals, activities, and expected data must be presented. Even though the *content* of the measures to be defined in Stage 3 cannot be stated ahead of time, the goal of defining them can. The same is true of the general map in Stage 1, and the focused research of Stage 2. The concepts for which measures will be needed can be derived from the preliminary hypotheses; examples of activities and types of data can be taken from other studies. A detailed schedule of research should be diagrammed on a time chart, such as Table 1.2. (See Bohannan 1981 for another example.)

RESEARCH CONDITIONS
REQUIRING PARTICIPANT OBSERVATION

Reasons for choosing participant observation as a method must be detailed as clearly as the procedures involved in its use. Observers must talk about *why* as well as about *what* they are doing. There are several research conditions for which participant observation is the best, or even the only, method. First, settings and/or topics about which little or nothing is already known require preliminary participant observation for definition of appropriate measures for existing concepts as well as discovery of new questions. Participant observation was invented in the exotic field sites that made it necessary. Its virtues make it just as necessary now in many situations about which we know far less than their surface familiarity might suggest.

In gerontology, participant observation was first used to study old people in age-homogeneous communities (Keith 1982a; Marshall 1975; Fry 1979). The activities and attitudes of old people *among themselves* were as unknown as any unexplored tribal village. The qualitative aspects of older people's lives in any setting are still exotic data, as cross-cultural information about old age is rare (Keith 1980, 1982b, 1984). Ethnographers concerned with age also need to follow the footsteps of many fieldworkers who have gathered their courage to move out of neatly bounded little communities into the interesting complexities of modern, urban existence. Participant observation will be needed to discover both measures and questions for topics such as the meaning of friendship and kinship, preparation for death, the structure of daily routine beyond work, the salience of age in social interaction--because we don't yet know enough about these issues, especially in cross-cultural terms, to use other techniques.

A second condition requiring participant observation is sensitivity of topics or respondents. Some topics may be seen as inappropriate when raised through direct questions, either because of their substance or because of attributes of the person doing the asking. In addition, some respondents may be unable or unwilling to cooperate with researchers using more explicit techniques. Sexuality and death are topics of concern to many older people that may be difficult to explore adequately in a cross-age interview, because of a cultural context that defines them as taboo. Reporting on these is distinctly different when participant observation has been employed (Marshall 1975; Keith 1982a) than when researchers have relied on more explicit questioning (Byrne 1971; Jacobs 1974).

At Les Floralies, the significance of either sex or death could not be avoided no matter how difficult it might have been to administer a questionnaire on these subjects. (Note: this is not a suggestion that awkwardness is always on the side of the respondent or that it is even mutual.) After many months of fieldwork, a questionnaire was prepared for use in Stage 3. One of this researcher's most memorable field experiences was an interview in which a woman *told* the lurid details of her sexual history, punctuated by protestations that she could *never* put such information on a piece of paper (Keith 1982a:32).

Because thus far, older people have less formal education, on the average, than younger people, they may often feel less comfortable than younger respondents with formal instruments that resemble tests. Participant observation may be an alternative to other methods, or a preliminary tool that will assist in the development of more appropriate formal strategies, as well as a rapport between researcher and subjects that will make them more likely to try an unfamiliar and slightly threatening task. The old people at Les Floralies disliked "papers" intensely. They were also puzzled as to why the researcher needed to ask these questions, "since you already knew all these things," as they said. However, they indulgently answered the questionnaire. An explanation of the researcher's need for their help was a *precis* of the persuasiveness of quantitative data to scientists and policy-makers. "People won't believe me if I just say so," is a sincere response and the residents were willing to help. In addition, the months spent in Stages 1 and 2 made it possible to write questions that the respondents perceived as reasonable and real.

Informants' inability or unwillingness to report accurately is a third reason for choosing an observational method. There are many factors influencing adequacy of self-reports: memory, fear, distractions, idealization toward norms. As Beatrice and John Whiting wisely point out, however, the researcher should no more assume that people *cannot* report accurately than that they can (1970:284ff). Since observation is "labor-intensive," it is worth some checking to see if it is really necessary. The researcher should observe the behavior in question, then later ask the participants to report what happened. If there are discrepancies, they should be discussed with the informant. On the basis of several tests like this, the situations in which observation is needed should be distinguished.

Short-term memory loss might make older people unable to report on their activities. Idealization may interfere with their willingness to tell about some behaviors or beliefs. Information about the significance of peers that has been received through report, has been very different than that which has come from observations. Old people who say what perhaps a modern industrial context encourages them to say about other old people--i.e., that they are depressing and boring--can be observed nonetheless in active, powerful, warm, interesting interaction with age-mates. Another example is the vehement "loners" of single-room occupancy hotels who protect their ideal of independence by asserting that they have no friends and receive support from no one. Participant observers, however, have discovered the personnel, locations, and content of the social supports that are necessary, in fact, to maintain this perception of independence (Eckert 1980; Sokolovsky, chap. 10 in this volume). Relations with children are also subject to reporting skewed by what old people wish for or by what they think they ought to say. As a group, people, no matter what age, might be expected to report inaccurately about some key topics. The Whitings' advice is excellent: check to see how accurate your informants are on various topics. First of all, you will know where observation is needed; second, you will learn about sources and patterns of misrepresentation (theirs and yours) through discussing discrepancies.

Collective or emergent realities also require observation. The dynamics of an age-homogeneous vs. an age-heterogeneous group cannot be captured adequately through an aggregation of individual reports. The shared understandings about appropriate behavior when younger people were or were not present, as well as the sanctions imposed for deviance, are aspects of the collective reality of Les Floralies about which I could learn only through observation and comparison over time.

Finally, as important as what the researcher does is how it is explained. The reasons for choosing participant observation must be clearly presented. The general principles I have outlined along with references to what has and has not been done in previous work with old people, should provide a persuasive rationale.

SAMPLING

With whom, when, and where to use participant observation are the next significant questions. They raise the issue of sampling. Participant observation may precede or follow sampling procedures. It may be an important part of defining a sample, or a sample may define the units to be observed by a participant researcher. The goal of probability sampling is to select for observation units which are representative of a population. If every unit in the population has an equal chance to be selected for the sample, then the characterisitics of the sample may be generalized to the total population.

Participant observation may be needed at several points in a sampling process. First, a *sampling frame* must be discovered, i.e., an enumeration of units in the population, from which every nth one, or each one corresponding to numbers read off a random number table, may be drawn. If the population is already enumerated--in terms of the characteristics of interest to the researcher--then the frame is available, e.g., in a census. The population of older people in a particular society has often not been counted, however, so that identification of an appropriate frame requires considerable ingenuity. The initial mapping of Stage 1 may reveal various sources of information for a sampling frame, as well as the likely differences between the frame and the population, which must be explicitly reported (see Honigmann 1970 for a discussion of sampling in anthropological fieldwork).

A researcher interested in all old people in a community as the research population may face a serious challenge in constructing a frame. If the frame is not obvious at the beginning of fieldwork, then the research design should include a clear statement that a major goal for the first stage of participant observation will be identification of sources for it. Discovery of age-grading in associations or collective celebrations of decade birthdays, for example, might provide lists of older people from which a sample could be drawn.

Second, when it is not possible to create an adequate frame for the entire population to which the researcher wants to generalize, *cluster sampling* may be appropriate. In this technique, the population is divided into roughly similar groups (clusters) for which sampling frames can be established, from which random samples can then be drawn. For example, if there is no list of old people in a community, but there is a list of households, the households would be sampled, then in each household in that sample, the old people would be listed, providing a final sampling frame of old people from which individuals could be selected randomly (see Brim & Spain 1974:84-86). Cluster sampling obviously requires identification of appropriate subunits, another task for Stage 1 of participant observation.

Third, if certain bases of heterogeneity in a population seem to the researcher likely to have significant relationships to variables in the study, then it is important that this diversity be adequately represented in the sample. To make sure all the theoretically interesting diversity appears in the final sample in substantial numbers, the sampling frames may be *stratified*, i.e., samples drawn from subcategories in the population. They may be sampled proportionate to their numerical status in the population, or over-sampled because of the researcher's special interest in their characteristics. If black old people are a very small proportion of a community, for example, a researcher interested in ethnic differences might oversample from the black subpopulation ("stratum").

Once again, it is clear that strata must be discovered through initial social mapping of the research site. The collection of information on which to base decisions whether or not stratified sampling is needed, and if so, how the strata should be defined, is an additional appropriate goal for Stage 1 participant observation. Explicit statement of those goals indicates a rigorous intention for a research site whose uncharted condition may make the research initially as difficult to describe as it is necessary.

Finally, although any sample consists of *units,* what those should be is not a given, but a major decision. Should they be individuals or families? families or households? households or networks? Without the map provided by Stage 1 observations, the researcher cannot make an informed decision about which units are meaningful for the intended research questions. If the study concerns allocation of resources to old people, for example, then the appropriate sampling units will be those social groups in which decisions about resource allocation are made. This is an emic (system-specific), not an etic (standard), unit; it must be discovered, not predefined.

Units for a sample do not consist only of humans, either. Events, times, contexts for observation should also be chosen in principled ways. Frames for these can only be established through initial exploration of behavioral, temporal, spatial, and situational categorization meaningful in a specific social context (see Spradley 1980:82-83; Whiting & Whiting 1970:289-290; Forgas 1976; Frederiksen 1972). These emic categories, necessary for adequate sampling procedures, are often only available after a long seige of Stage 1 participant observation, and should be explicitly stated as goals of that phase of research (see Honigmann 1970 for discussion of situations when probability sampling is impossible, and of possible alternative sampling strategies).

ANALYSIS OF DATA
FROM PARTICIPANT OBSERVATION

The final question about participant observation, as about any method, is how to make use of the data it produces. This is an aspect of research design about which those using participant observation are seldom adequately explicit. There are two ways in which we can be more precise. First, the specification of stages already clarifies for both researchers and readers of research designs or reports the fact that this method produces various kinds of data. Each type of anticipated data should be described in the research proposal along with planned techniques of analysis. The coding matrix from my Stage 2 observations at Les Floralies, for instance, included numerical scores that could be analyzed correlationally. Extended, open-ended interviews produce texts that can be coded thematically through a version of content analysis (cf, Clark & Anderson 1967:76-77, 173-206). Systematic observation of times and places should produce numerical data that can be analyzed by many statistical techniques. For example, multiple observations of the ages and activities of individuals using various public spaces would provide data that could be analyzed by cross-tabulations and a measure of significance such as chi-square. Results of a card sort can be analyzed through a technique suited to nominal data that require visual presentation, e.g., multi-dimensional scaling or a cluster analysis (see Fry, chap. 5 in this volume, and 1980; also Romney 1980). The most problematic data for analysis are the hundreds of pages of field notes recorded throughout participant observation research. These must be indexed and cross-referenced so that patterns can be discovered. Whyte (1955) describes an indexing system; Spradley (1980:155) proposes a system for making a "cultural inventory" from field notes. Becker (1969:252) demonstrates how to analyze negative cases. The software available for microcomputers offers many options for indexing and creation of subfiles in narrative texts.

Research designs should be well balanced between descriptions of how the data will be collected and what will be done with them later. How the data will be analyzed should have as strong an influence on how they are collected as the theoretical reasons for posing certain questions. The intent and the techniques for whatever means of data storage and manipulation are planned should be presented in the research design. It must be clear what kind of data, e.g., numerical or narrative, are going to be stored and analyzed using what techniques. If absence of any discussion of data analysis is the most common error in research designs, including participant observation, then the second worst sin is probably the casual mention of an analysis technqiue that is inappropriate for the type of data the research described in the design will produce. If narrative text is going to be transformed into numerical codes that can be factor analyzed or cross-tabulated, then the goals and strategies of the coding process need to be presented. It is quite legitimate not to be able to create a detailed codebook for an exploratory project. However, it is imperative to present the techniques through which the codebook *will* be created once the texts are available. For example, coders may read texts looking for important themes, assign these numbers, and proceed until they find no more themes requiring codes; or a computer program can count word frequencies to suggest clues about important topics requiring codes. The two techniques might be combined to have the human coders choose key words that could then be located and counted by computer. The research design should include all the stages from note taking to analysis so that all the required time and activity, both human and mechanical, can be scheduled and budgeted. An excellent principle is that any researcher should know how data will be *analyzed* before they are recorded (see Whiting & Whiting 1970:291 for a very helpful discussion of the relationship between recording and analysis).

Very little is known about the quality of older people's lives, about the mutual influence of the old and various cultural contexts, about older people's own views of the world. Old age is for many individuals, and in many contexts, a sensitive topic. Participant observation, in all its stages, will be needed to chart and decipher the interrelationships of age, society, and culture. The contribution of participant observers to our understanding of old age will depend on both how well we use the method, and how well we learn to talk about it.

NOTE

1. Basic ideas in this chapter first appeared in Ross and Ross (1974).

TABLE 1.1   Participant Observation (P.O.) Protocol (Project A.G.E.)

Stage	Goals	Major P.O. Activities	Parallel Research Activities	Types of P.O. Data
I. Introduction (Month 1)	Define Research Role	Publicize project through appropriate local channels	None	Extensive fieldnotes, detailed description, little evaluation or summary. (See Pelto 1970:93-94; Spradley 1980:73ff). Special attention to indicators of salience or social significance of age, e.g., in speech, dress, nonverbal communication, formal leadership roles, participation in community conflicts, etc.
	Establish Research Station	Discuss project with Community leaders		
	Identify Key Informants	Rent and furnish research station		
	Chart Basic Map of Community: Social Categories, Formal Associations, Public Spaces, History, Conflict Issues and Alignments	Attend all meetings and events open to the public		
		Attempt to make informal ties		
		Read archival materials		
	Define Sampling Frame for Probability Samples of Adult Population, and of 65+ Population	Collect demographic data from existing sources or conduct household census		Demographic statistics
	Define Sampling Frame for Formal Associations			General photographs of community
	Define Sampling Frame for Observation Times in Public Spaces			Detailed photographs of public spaces
II. Focused Observation (Months 2 & 3)	Identify Patterns of Age Relations in Selected Groups, Spaces	Observation of age relations in selected spaces and groups	General life stage interviews with key informants	Field notes: more focused more hypotheses about patterns in observations
	Identify Measures for Functionality, Network Links, Card Sort, Life History Coding	Observation of typical days of selected individuals of different culturally defined age and social categories	20 Questions and Make-a-Person with key informants	Tape recordings of conversations
			Cards for "Age Game" defined in consultation with key informants	
			Samples drawn	

TABLE 1.1 Participant Observation (P.O.) Protocol (Project A.G.E.)

Stage	Goals	Major P.O. Activities	Parallel Research Activities	Types of P.O. Data
II. (Continued)	Indicators of Affect Intensity and Direction Significance of Types and Levels of Material Support	Recording dimensions used in spontaneous conversation to evaluate persons, relationships, and situations, e.g., positive-negative direction, intensity, integration or meaningfulness, dependence-reciprocity, etc.		
III. Specific Coding (Month 4)	Definition of Dimensions for Systematic Coding of Observations: Situations, e.g., formal-informal, age homogeneous-heterogeneous-hierarchical-egalitarian (See Forgas 1976; Fredricksen 1972) Spaces, e.g., public-private, specific function-diverse, sacred-profane Age Relations, e.g., degree of age salience, degree of age explicitness degree of sub-grouping by age degree of age conflict/harmony	Code observations in terms of dimensions (See Keith 1982:31-2)	Formal instruments administered: "Age Game," "Network Profiles," "Age Evaluation."	Quantitative coding of age relationships in various contexts Focused field notes

TABLE 1.2   Research Schedule for Project A.G.E.

RESEARCH ACTIVITY	0	1	2	3	4	5	6	7	8	9	10	11	12
Participant Observation	Stage I (Introduction) _____			Stage II (Focused) _____				Stage III (Specific Coding) _____					
Card Sort Construction with Key Informants:													
General Life Stage Interview	_____												
20 Questions and Make-a-Person	_____												
Random Generation of Personal and Key Informant Ratings	_____												
Instrument Finalized and Pretested	_____												
Sample Drawn	_____												
Instrument Administered To:													
Adult Community Sample				_____ ----------								
Older Adult Sample					----------- -------							
Intensive Data Collection													
Older Adult Sample:													
Life Histories									_____				
Network Profiles									_____				
Networks of Significant Others										_____			
Observational Information													
Coded on Group Structure Recruitment and Formation	_____												

NOTE: Chart of sequenced research activities for each field site projected over the 12 months of data collection (__ is intensive activity; --- is less intense or continued activity).

BIBLIOGRAPHY

Becker, Howard. 1969. "Problems of Inference and Proof in Participant Observation." In Issues in Participant Observation, ed. George J. McCall and J. L. Simmons, Menlo Park, Calif.: Addison-Wesley.

Bohannan, Paul, J. 1981. "The Unseen Community: The Natural History of a Research Project." In Anthropologists at Home: Toward an Anthropology of Issues in America, ed. Donald A. Messerschmidt, New York: Cambridge University Press.

Brim, John A., and David H. Spain. 1974. Research Design in Anthropology, New York: Holt, Rinehart & Winston.

Byrne, Susan. 1971. "Arden: An Adult Community." Ph. D. diss. University of California.

Campbell, Donald, and D. W. Fiske. 1959. "Covergent and Discriminant Validation by the Multitrait-Multimethod Matrix." Psychological Bulletin 56:81-105.

Campbell, Donald, and J. C. Stanley. 1966. Experimental and Quasi-Experimental Design for Research. Chicago: Rand McNally.

Clark, Margaret, and Barbara G. Anderson. 1967. Culture and Aging: An Anthropological Study of Older Americans. Springfield, IL: Charles C. Thomas.

Eckert, Kevin. 1980. The Unseen Elderly. San Diego: Campanile Press.

Forgas, J. P. 1976. "The Perception of Social Episodes: Categorical and Dimensional Representations in Two Different Social Milieus." Journal of Personality and Social Psychology 34:199-209.

Frederiksen, N. 1972. "Toward a Taxonomy of Situations." American Psychologist 27:114-23.

Fry, Christine L. 1979. "Structural Conditions Affecting Community Formation among the Aged." In The Ethnography of Old Age. ed. J. Keith. Anthropological Quarterly 52:7-18.

Gold, Raymond. 1958. "Roles in Sociological Field Observations." Social Forces 36:217-233.

Honigmann, John. 1970. "Sampling of Ethnographic Field Work." In Naroll and Cohen 1970.

Jacobs, Jerry. 1974. Fun City: An Ethnographic Study of a Retirement Community. New York: Holt, Rinehart & Winston.

Keith, Jennie. 1980. "'The Best Is Yet to Be:' Toward an Anthropology of Age." In Annual Review of Anthropology, ed. Bernard J. Siegal, Palo Alto, Calif.: Annual Reviews.

_____. 1982a. Old People, New Lives: Community Creation in a Retirement Residence. Chicago: University of Chicago (Phoenix paperback ed. of Ross (1977)).

_____. 1982b. Old People as People: Social and Cultural Influences on Aging and Old Age. Boston: Little, Brown.

_____. 1984. "Anthropological Research on Aging." In Handbook on Aging and the Social Sciences, ed. Robert S. Binstock and Ethel Shanas. New York: Van Nostrand.

Le Vine, Robert. 1970. "Research Design in Anthropological Field Work." In Naroll and Cohen 1970.

Marshall, Victor. 1975. "Socialization for Impending Death in a Retirement Village." American Journal of Sociology 80:1124-44.

McCall, George J. and J. L. Simmons, eds. 1969. Issues in Participant Observation. Menlo Park, Calif.: Addison-Wesley.

Myerhoff, Barbara, 1978. Number Our Days. New York: Dutton.

Naroll, Raoul, and Ronald Cohen, eds. 1970. A Handbook of Method in Cultural Anthropology. New York: Columbia University Press.

Pelto, Pertti. 1978. Anthropological Research: the Structure of Inquiry, 2d ed. Cambridge University Press.

Przeworski, Adam, and Henry, Teune. 1970. The Logic of Comparative Social Inquiry. New York: Wiley.

Romney, A. Kimball. 1980. "Multidimensional Scaling Applications in Anthropology." In Numerical Techniques in Social Anthropology, ed. J. Clyde Mitchell. Philadelphia: ISHI.

Ross, Jennie-Keith, and Marc H. Ross. 1974. "Participant Observation in Political Research." Political Methodology 1:63-88.

Ross, Jennie-Keith. 1977. Old People, New Lives: Community Creation in a Retirement Residence. Chicago: University of Chicago Press.

Sechrest, Lee. 1970. "Experiments in the Field." In Naroll and Cohen 1970.

Spradley, James. 1980. Participant Observation. New York: Holt, Rinehart & Winston.

Webb, Eugene J., Donald T. Campbell, Richard D. Schwartz, and Lee Sechrest. 1966. Unobtrusive Measures: Nonreactive Research in the Social Sciences. Chicago: Rand McNally.

Whiting, Beatrice, and John Whiting. 1970. "Methods for Observing and Recording Behavior." In Naroll and Cohen 1970.

Whyte, William F. 1955. Street Corner Society: the Social Structure of an Italian Slum, 2d ed. Chicago: University of Chicago Press.

2
Measuring Functional Status Cross-Culturally

CYNTHIA M. BEALL AND J. KEVIN ECKERT
Department of Anthropology
Case Western Reserve University

Measuring functional status cross-culturally is a complex and multi-faceted task necessitating ingenuity and innovation on the part of the researcher. This chapter will address some of the ways in which functional status has been conceptualized in the past and how it might be expanded upon in the future. Before selecting a particular approach to measuring functional status, the researcher must consider several basic issues. First, clarity regarding the focal research question is central to the selection of measurement tools and instruments. For example, if the intent is to study normative patterns of biological aging, various physiological measures gathered for descriptive and comparative purposes would be more appropriate than measures designed to assess the capacity to perform everyday activities. If the intent is to study an individual's ability to live alone, then the capacity to perform everyday activities may be the appropriate measure. Similarly, if health status is the outcome of interest, then the particular level or dimension of health must be decided upon. Second, the unit of analysis in the study must be defined. Is the focus on an individual/clinical assessment, on specific social groups or environments (e.g., nursing home, rural village, widow vs the never married), or on larger population groups (e.g., all Japanese, all males)? The emphasis on the representativeness of the sample and validity of the measuring instruments will vary depending upon the unit of analysis. Finally, the validity and reliability of the specific measurement instruments in the cultural context under study must be considered very carefully. Ethnographic understanding of the particular individual, group, or population is the only way to answer or address this issue.

This chapter is divided into four sections: (1) the importance of the functional perspective in cross-cultural studies of aging, (2) cross-cultural measurement of health status, with emphasis on functional adequacy, (3) the assessment of habitual activity, and (4) the assessment of biological capacity.

THE IMPORTANCE OF THE FUNCTIONAL PERSPECTIVE

The concept of functional status encompasses an extremely broad range of meaning (see, e.g., Kane & Kane 1981). For example, those working in the area of providing services tend to focus on functional health status and to refer to the degree of disability that interferes with or prevents undertaking the so-called activities of daily living. Others, more concerned with factors influencing "normal" variation, refer to observations of habitual activity or to measures of an individual's biological capacity. These latter two measures emphasize the assessment of function using observation and standardized testing procedures whose relationship to the performance of specific tasks is not always known, i.e., the etic perspective of functional capacity (see p. 34 for a definition).

Anthropologists feel that both etic and emic viewpoints are critical to an understanding of biocultural systems. On the one hand it is important to describe roles and age-related variation in the physiological, economic, and social resources upon which people may draw and upon which productive and self-maintenance activities are based. On the other hand, it is important to understand the cultural definitions and cultural setting in which the measures are taken. The perception and evaluation by the elderly (and others) of the processes and statuses which the measures reflect are important considerations. The etic view suggests that time-related morphological and biological involution may ulti-mately preclude the performance of certain tasks and that a time may occur when capacity has declined to a point where some activities are not feasible and an individual must alter his or her activity because it presents an excessive physiological strain. The emic view considers the meaning and importance attached to the function by the individual involved.

Functional capacity has been a topic of research for several reasons. First, functional health assessment seeks to measure the level of biological fitness and ability to perform self-maintenance activities rather than the extent of pathology. This is essential information for evaluating the need for various kinds of living arrangements, social and medical services. It is estimated that in the U.S. roughly 93 percent of the people over 65 report the presence of at least one chronic condition and, of these, approximately half experience some limitation of their daily activity (USDHEW 1972). Comparable data are not available for the developing countries and they are needed. It is estimated that as many elderly now live in the Third World as in the developed countries, and the numbers there are ever increasing (UN 1980). It is imperative to know if a similar prevalence of impairment exists in the Third World, since increasing numbers and proportions of impaired elderly would increase the demands upon social and medical services.

Second, function (in terms of daily activity, social and psychological competence) relates directly to the issues of dependence and need.

Third, objective assessment of biological capacity is desirable in order to understand the pattern of age-related biological change, variations in this pattern, and the way this is handled in particular cultural settings.

CROSS-CULTURAL MEASUREMENT AND FUNCTIONAL ADEQUACY

There are at least three ways in which individual health status can be evaluated: (1) by a physician or other trained professional in a physical examination; (2) by a person's self-report; (3) by how a person behaves (Shanas et al. 1968). Together, these three types of assessment provide an important composite of an individual's health status. Separately, they describe health status from both objective and subjective perspectives.

Many different instruments have been developed to measure the concept of general physical health. The kinds of items that have been used to assess general physical health include the following (Kane & Kane 1981):

1. physician's rating of health
2. signs on a physical examination
3. symptoms indicative of a health problem
4. disease/diagnosis
5. pain or discomfort
6. permanent impairment (e.g., paralysis, amputation, loss of vision, hearing, speech)

7.   number of visits to a physician over a specified period of time
8.   number of days spent in a hospital over a specified period of time
9.   days in which normal activities are restricted due to a health problem
10. days spent in bed
11. self-ratings of health

Before discussing specific instruments for assessing general health status, it should be noted that there are a number of ways in which the listed items could be adapted for use in cross-cultural research. Some of these suggestions are taken from an excellent paper by Lawton, Ward, and Yaffee (1967).

1.   Questions designed to elicit symptoms in cross-cultural situatons must tap culturally relevant symptoms (i.e., symptoms recognizable to the interviewee as well as to the interviewer and not those based solely on biomedical criteria).
2.   Self-ratings of health are subject to distortions and biases ranging from individual characteristics such as denial or hypochondriasis to cultural norms prohibiting one from discussing certain health problems or parts of the body.
3.   Listing diseases and diagnoses found upon physical examination is an inadequate index of individual general health status, since the range of severity of impairment within a diagnosis is often greater than among diagnoses.
4.   A permanent impairment such as loss of vision, speech, or hearing may have very different implications and consequences among different cultural groups. These differences should not be ignored.
5.   Treatment by a physician is highly influenced by ability to pay, availability and accessibility of the physician, and emotional state of the respondent. Furthermore, in cross-cultural research it is imperative to consider treatment by indigenous and culturally relevant healers.
6.   For the same reasons, the number of hospital days is too gross an indicator of health for cross-cultural studies of the general aged public.
7.   Days spent in bed could be expanded to include days in which the respondent was confined to quarters (e.g., room, hut, village). Simply asking a person the number of days spent in bed could be too restrictive in some cross-cultural situations. Questions about the number of days confined are usually linked to a fixed period of time. On many instruments the question reads, "How many days have you spent in bed during the past year?" Adaptation of this question for cross-cultural research might read, "How many days

did you stay in the courtyard when others went to work during the barley harvest?" in another instance, it may be more appropriate to ask the number of days confined since a culturally significant occasion (e.g., Ramadan, or last full moon). The reliability of answers to this question is very much influenced by respondent's ability to recall (which may vary with age and mental status and with the importance attached to the event).

8. Finally, Lawton, Ward, and Yaffee (1967) note that an inverse relationship exists between the objectivity of a health measurement and its comprehensiveness as an indicator of functional ability. For example, an objective and reliable laboratory test may have almost perfect validity as an indicator of a diagnosis but poor validity as an indicator of functional level. Because functional level may be better predicted by a composite of items including diagnosis, self-rating and physician rating of health, and fulfillment of personal and social roles, more opportunity for error is introduced into the comprehensive measure.

Operationally, behavioral functioning assesment (or what some refer to as health status) consists of at least two components: one tapping the construct of general physical health or absence of illness, and one tapping the ability to perform basic or elemental self-care activities or activities of daily living. Scores of instruments and scales are available for each component. In this review, however, discussion will be limited to the most widely known instruments and approaches and those that show promise for use in cross-cultural studies. At all times the researcher must be mindful that the operationalization and interpretation of measures used by each approach requires a considerable understanding of the particular cultural context under consideration. Readers are encouraged to refer directly to the instruments mentioned here and to an excellent critical summary (Kane & Kane 1981) for a full appreciation of their complexity, applications, and limitations. The present review suggests possibly useful assessment tools and their modifications and strategies for measuring functional adequacy.

Measures of General Health

As the somewhat lengthy list just stated illustrates, physical health status is not a unidimensional concept (Hickey 1980; Kane & Kane 1981); many different techniques have been used to measure it and commonly used indicators do not always yield identical results. For example, measures of health status in many studies are based on the self-perceived judgment of the respondent. Such self-ratings have been shown to differ substantially from physician ratings (Maddox 1962), with individuals rating themselves more positively than their physicians (Tissue 1972). While the interchangeability of self-perceived health and more objective medical assessments has been challenged (Haberman 1969), research has shown self-assessment of health to be important and valuable in answering certain research questions about human development, particularly in the later years. When viewing health as an interactive process between the person and his or her social and physical environment, "the subjective belief that one is healthy or ill may be more important than actual medical status in predicting an individual's general emotional state and behavior" (Maddox & Douglas 1973:88).

The following instruments are widely accepted general-health-assessment tools, with tested reliability and validity for populations in the United States and other western developed societies. Using these instruments with culturally diverse populations would require considerable adjustment, adaptation and testing. However, they remain excellent starting points.

The OARS Index. The OARS (Older-American Resources Survey index (Duke University 1978), which enjoys wide use in the United States, is based on the assumption that one must take a comprehensive approach when assessing the elderly. Its design permits comparison of individuals against summary data from a reference population. As such, it is useful for research at the individual, small group, and population levels. A major goal of the OARS is to assess overall functional health of the elderly in terms of five domains: social and economic resources, activities of daily living, mental health, and physical health during an interview. This is accomplished through the (SEMPA) scale; which includes basic social and demographic information similar to other scales. The mental health component of the index covers basic mental functioning related to memory, anxiety, depression, life satisfaction, and perceived mental health.

The physical-health section includes items on doctor visits, sick days, hospital days, nursing-home days, alcohol problems, and participation in various exercises. Checklists are provided for eighteen categories of medication use, twenty-six illnesses, three impairments, and use of ten prosthetic devices. Likert scales are used to rate overall health, relationship of present to past health, and the degree to which health problems stand in the way of desired activities.

After collecting all the information on the five separate domains of the OARS questionnaire, the interviewer scores the respondent from 1 (excellent functioning) to 6 (totally impaired) in each domain. These five ratings, one for each domain, can then be combined in a variety of ways. For example, the six-point scale can be collapsed to a dichotomous scale where individuals rated from 1 to 3 are considered to be functioning adequately and those rated 4 to 6 are considered to be impaired for the dimension. A cumulative impairment score can be derived by adding the impairment score for each of the domains to yield a range of from 5 (no impairment on any dimension) to 30 (totally impaired on all dimensions). The OARS is well designed and comprehensive in its approach. While it would require significant alterations for cross-cultural application, it provides a model of a fairly representative index of a wide range of functional levels in many different areas of life.

The Sickness Impact Profile (SIP). The SIP was developed by an interdisciplinary team as a measure of behavioral functioning in the clinical practice of medicine (Bergner & Gilson 1981). Three important assumptions underlie the development of the SIP: (1) The SIP deliberately measures the impact of sickness on behavior; (2) in so doing it focuses on performance, what a person does rather than potential ability or capacity for behavior (while this imposes limits, it provides for a sounder and more reliable and valid instrument than one based on a combination of performance and capacity); (3) the SIP measures *sickness* rather than health or wellness, i.e., health-related behavioral change. In this way the instrument is sensitive to the impact of sickness on the individual's ability to fulfill social roles in society.

The SIP contains 136 statements or items about health-related dysfunction; it may be administered by an interviewer in twenty to thirty minutes or may be self-administered. To complete the SIP the respondent is asked to check only those statements that describe him or her on the test day and are related to health. The items on the SIP fall into twelve domains: sleep and rest, eating, work, home management, recreation and pastimes, ambulation, mobility, body care and movement, social interaction, alertness behavior, emotional behavior, and communication. The inclusion of multiple domains allows one to comprehensively assess the impact of sickness on a person's behavior.

Scores can be computed for the overall SIP or for the separate categories of information. The overall score for the SIP is computed by summing the scale values of all statements checked by the respondent and dividing the sum by the grand total of all statement values. This ratio is then multiplied by 100 to convert it to a simple percent. Similarly, scores can be computed for each of the SIP categories.

The SIP has been shown to be a highly reliable and valid health status outcome measure for populations in the United States. Its validity as a health-status measure for the general population suggests its potential for use by anthropologists interested in human development and health status. The developers of the SIP (Bergner et al 1976a, 1976b) anticipate that the SIP will be useful in assessing the impact of chronic conditions in which the most precise laboratory and clinical measures often do not correlate well with observed levels of functioning.

Focusing on Specific Systems

Another group of measures are symptomatology questionnaires focusing on individual's reports of symptoms relating to particular physiological systems such as the pulmonary or cardiovascular (Stuart-Harris et al. 1965; Rose & Blackburn 1968). These may be used alone or in conjunction with physiological tests or physical examinations. Aging studies may find those designed to assess mental status most pertinent. The following discussion of techniques to measure mental status and dementia is limited to measures of cognitive (and not affective) functional status.

The study of the epidemiology of dementing illness is complex in Western settings and its cross-cultural extension requires care. Dementing illness may be produced by a number of disease states. The research interest may lie simply in ascertaining the prevalence of dementing illness or more specifically those due to specific causes such as organic brain disease, reversible nutritional deficiencies, etc. In either case, documenting current status and whether or not it represents a change from a priori status are initial steps (Schoenberg 1981; Mortimer, Schuman & French 1981). A number of mental status questionnaires have been developed for use in Western settings. Each includes items dealing with orientation as to time, place, and person (e.g., age, date, location, season, last meal) and memory for immediate and remote events (e.g., examiner's name, names of current and past presidents or political events). Other test items may investigate mathematical skills and practical and perceptual ability. Examples of these tests include the VIRO Orientation Scale (Kastenbaum & Sherwood 1972), the Mental Status Questionnaire (Kahn et al. 1960), the Short Portable Mental Status Questionnaire (Pfeiffer 1975) and the Mini-Mental State Examination (Folstein, Folstein & McHugh 1975). They are fully discussed and evaluated elsewhere (Kane & Kane 1981; Butler & Lewis 1982). They are brief (some only eight or ten questions), easily administered tests that yield quantifiable scores. Although many specific items are culture bound (such as mother's maiden name, current telephone number) it appears easy to develop appropriate parallel questions for cross-cultural use (e.g., current cost of rice, name of current and past headman). It should be kept in mind that if a particular task is patently absurd or a question wholly inappropriate in a given cultural setting, then an individual's failure to complete the test may not reflect poor mental status.

Some tests of mental status which seem minimally culture bound include the Face Hands (Fink, Green & Bender 1952; Kahn et al. 1960), the Visual Counting (Fishback 1977), and the Set Test (Isaacs & Kennie 1973). The Face Hands test simply assesses the accuracy of reporting touches on the face and on the back of the hands, while the Visual Counting requires that the individual count the number of fingers extended by the interviewer and the Set Test asks the subject to name examples of animals, fruits, colors, and towns.

Questioning other people in order to verify the accuracy of data obtained from a respondent through use of such questionnaires provides several useful additional pieces of information. It ascertains whether others familiar with the individual recognize any deficiency. An opinion may be solicited as to whether current performance is consistent with past performance or represents a change, an important facet of assessing mental status that may be difficult in the absence of medical, educational, or other written records. The locally perceived cause of any change may be elicited. If an individual's behavior changes markedly after being cursed, for example, it may be more appropriate to consider that individual in a special category.

Interpreting the meaning of an absence or high prevalence of dementing illness must take into consideration that dementia is most prevalent in the numerically smaller, older age categories and even then in relatively small proportions. This may be especially problematic in small communities where small numbers of people are at risk.

A strategy for devising culturally sensitive tests may begin by exploring local definitions of senility, age-appropriate and age-inappropriate behavior, and capacity. This plus a knowledge of reasonable items to use to assess orientation, memory, and various other skills will enable construction of culturally meaningful questionnaires and tests parallelling those described. The extent to which the local definitions and the developed questionnaire overlap in identifying the most extreme cases of dementing illness may provide a useful internal check on the questionnaire. Validity, in the sense of correlation with biomedical diagnosis of various types of dementia, will be unknown unless a special effort is made. It may be unimportant depending upon the research question, which may, for example, deal with various aspects of a demented individual's social situation and may not be concerned with the ultimate underlying causes.

Elemental Activities of Daily Living (ADL) or Physical Functioning

Unlike the general-health-assesment measures cited earlier, ADL measures tap the practical dimension of how well an individual performs activities necessary to maintain personal independence. Hickey (1980) suggests that an individual's behavior in a particular context may be a more meaningful indicator of health status than a physician's or the individual's own evaluation. An understanding of the social and cultural norms and expectations concerning older persons is essential to assessing the extent to which an individual's behavior is appropriate, expected, excusable, etc.

Indices of ADL are based on the notion that "the presence of a particular disease does not necessarily indicate for any given person inhibition of activity which results from it" (Townsend 1963: 272). For example, Townsend's approach focused on the consequences of disease and injury and the kinds of activities an old person in England or the United States would have to perform to live alone.

The most widely used approach for assessing functional capacity of the elderly relies on either questionnaire-based measures of performance (as in the Shanas et al. 1968 study or in the OARS Multidimensional Functional Assessment Questionnaire) or on ratings made by trained observers. Simple dichotomous measures and more complex trichotomous measures are used in both the questionnaire and provider's evaluations to rate the respondents on predetermined mobility and self-help functions relevant to daily living in the cultural setting. Bathing, dressing, toileting, feeding, and ambulatory ability are among the most frequently measured activities. The evaluation of one's ability may be self-reported or independently assessed by an observer, more often the latter.

Ratings can be made on the basis of immediate observation at a particular point in time or on the basis of performance during a specified period of time. The latter approach creates a problem in that average levels of performance over time are difficult to determine, and Kane and Kane (1981) suggest that "best performance" may have more precision. A retrospective time frame creates the problem of dependence on the memory and judgment of the rater, while here-and-now evaluation may produce results that are not a valid reflection of performance apart from the test situation.

Scoring Functional Capacity. Scores on ADL are based on the degree of independence the individual demonstrates on each function. For example, on the index of functional status used by Shanas et al. (1968), in their cross-national study of aging in the

United States, Great Britain, and Denmark, the older person was required to answer six questions: (1) Can he/she go out of doors? (2) walk up and down stairs? (3) get about the house? (4) wash and bathe himself/herself? (5) dress himself/herself and put on shoes? (6) cut his/her own toenails? The individual was asked if he/she could do each of these tasks without difficulty and without assistance; with some difficulty, but still without the help of another person; and, finally, with difficulty and only with the help of another person. As a functioning member of the community a person of any age in nearly all cultures must be able to leave the house and interact with the surroundings to some degree. Walking out of doors and up and down stairs and caring for personal needs are usually necessities for continued independent life in the community.

The ability to perform a task without any restriction was assigned a score of 0, the ability to perform a task only with difficulty was assigned a score of 1 and complete inability to perform a task was assigned a score of 2. The scores for the six tasks were summed, producing a range of physical incapacity from 0 to 12. A score of 1 meant that five of the tasks could be performed without difficulty, but one could not. A score of 7 or more indicated a serious degree of difficulty with several activities and dependence in at least one of the six activities.

Dichotomous criteria for functional assessment provide a simple measure of a person's performance of mobility functions, such as movement from supine to upright position, and in general are used to determine if a patient is disabled and in need of services. Like clinical diagnostic categories to define illness, dichotomous measures provide a one-dimensional description of an individual's status. These measures define disability in terms of performance or nonperformance of delineated activities.

A limitation of simple dichotomous scales is that they mask the more complex decision processes involved in rating an indivdual's ability to perform or not perform a given function. For example, an elderly person's functional status may be influenced by short-term fluctuations, which are nevertheless recorded in an absolute score. As noted by Kaufert et al. (1979), by using threshold or critical points, a dichotomous system tends to force absolute decisions about a person's ability to perform a given function when in fact ability fluctuates. Another limitation of dichotomous systems is that they cannot control for the impact of aids, adaptations, and helpers.

One way of compensating for some of the limitations of a dichotomous approach has been to develop more complex measures, which summarize functional status in terms of three or more levels of performance. Multi-level measures of functional ability are sensitive to the influence of aids and helpers on a person's performance. They may also control for the level of difficulty encountered and the consistency of performance. For example, a trichotomous rating system used to score questionnaire data may generate three alternative classifications of disability. One score summarizes unassisted function cases wherein the individual consistently performs the function with little or no difficulty--without aids, adaptation, or assistance from another person. The second score summarizes assisted function cases wherein the individual performs functions with difficulty or is able to perform the function only at certain times--with the help of aids, adaptation, or another person. The third score rates functional ability by whether the function is actually performed by the person himself--cases wherein the individual does not perform the function himself, even with the help of aids or adaptation. These three categories summarize the individual's need for assistance, use of aids, consistency of performance and level of performance, and level of difficulty.

Limitations. Existing functional capacity measures require modification in order to be truly anthropologically sensitive. For example, the study reported by Shanas et al. (1968) did not include any measure of sensory impairment or biological function. As well, it can be expected that conditions vary widely in the countries considered, and no measure was included of the ability of the old person to perform complex activities of daily living such as the ability to use a telephone, manage money, or use public transportation. Since the study was dealing with industrialized countries, it did not deal with the sorts of problems faced when comparison is made with Third World or developing countries. For example, the sorts of elemental activities included in the study are based on emic categories relevant to western modes of life, that is, going up and down stairs or putting on shoes. In some cultural settings activities relevant to continued independent living may be quite different, i.e., fetching water from a stream, chopping and carrying home firewood, walking to a river for bathing. On an etic level, the biological resources required for independent living (e.g., strength) may vary greatly among cultures, and this may especially be true when contrasting the developed countries with the Third World. What is necessary, then, is the discovery of culturally relevant activities and categories and the construction of appropriate indices. Another consideration is that inability to do an equivalent activity in two different cultures may have very different meanings, in terms of the values attached to the activity and its relationship to dependency. An emic understanding is necessary for relating functional capacity to social consequences.

Constructing Indices of Functional Capacity. While the following measures of self-assessed or rater-assessed functional ability are in one sense etic measures, they require cultural specificity and sensitivity in their construction. Such approaches must be based on activities that members of a society see as appropriate and necessary for people to perform. The activities may or may not vary on the basis of such variables as sex, age, and status. However, this can only be learned through systematic observation and interviewing.

In assessing the functional capacity of older persons based on questionnaires or rater judgments, several steps should be followed. Approaches to the assessment of activity-based functional capacity need certain modifications in order to be useful in different cultural contexts. The following brief research sequence will provide a beginning for both an "emic" interpretation of activity and an "etic" assessment of performance.

Step 1: Initial Participant Observation and Key Informant Interview of Older Persons

The researcher needs to observe the sorts of activities which older persons perform in various social contexts. Individuals then need to be interviewed as to the significance, meaning, and value of these activities. For example, the researcher studying functional status of older persons in a West African village should observe older persons in various settings in which they habitually participate, e.g., home or compound, on the farm or in the garden (coffee and cocoa plantation), in voluntary associations. As well, one needs to determine the activities associated with sex, status, and stage in life cycle within the particular cultural milieu. Systematic ethnographic interviewing and participant observation (Spradley 1979, 1980) could provide the research with a model for eliciting and attaching meaning to culturally relevant activities.

Step 2: Constructing an Index

After initial participant observation and ethnographic interviewing, the researcher could construct indices of activities of daily living relevant to the cultural setting. The individual items included should reflect the sorts of activities and demands actually placed on the older person. Such indices might contain universal criteria such as ability to transfer from supine to upright position, ambu-late indoors or outdoors, dress, and bathe oneself. As well, it should contain items relevant to the particular cultural setting, e.g., can the individual carry his or her own firewood. The per-formance of activities must be sensitive to the cultural distinctions that emerge through participant observation. For example, fetching firewood or washing clothing may be considered women's work, while being able to accurately recount parables and proverbs may be considered an important activity for men. In constructing indices of appropriate activities, the reseracher must decide how functional ability will be scaled. The decision to utilize dichotomous or multilevel scales rests with the research problem, time considerations, and other factors. As mentioned earlier, the advantage of trichotomous scales is that they are sensitive to the adjustment, accommodations, supports, and aids that people receive when they are unable to perform activities unassisted. Questions such as these are extremely important for an understanding of cultural response to disability and incapacity.

Step 3: Scale Use

After constructing an appropriate functional assessment scale and pilot-testing it with a small sample of persons, the researcher can attempt its use with a larger sample of persons. The manner in which the scale is administered (whether in questionnaire form or independently rated) will depend on the literacy of the population and/or their accessibility for systematic observation.

THE ASSESSMENT OF HABITUAL ACTIVITY

The Etic Approach

The assessment of habitual activity is another approach to measuring function. Habitual physical activity is defined as the physical workload to which a person is usually subjected during work and leisure. For such assessments, both the total workload and the pattern of activity are important (WHO 1968:24).

The two basic methods of assessing habitual activity levels are (1) observation and (2) direct physical measurement. Observational techniques include retrospective questionnaires and interviews, prospective diaries, time-motion studies, and cinematography. Direct-measurement techniques include monitoring heart rate and movement, oxygen consumption, and food intake. Each of these techniques has drawbacks with respect to accuracy, feasibility, convenience, expense, applicability to large groups, level of behavioral and physiological detail, and--critically--social and cultural acceptability. In general, combining observation with direct measurement enhances accuracy (Weiner & Lourie 1969; WHO 1968). Several of these methods have been used to study the habitual activity of older adults.

Various retrospective-interview techniques have been used to obtain data on the occurrence and duration of certain broad activity categories. One way in which the studies vary is the length of time between the recalled events and the interview. This ranges from one year to one day. The Baltimore Longitudinal Aging Study utilized a recall-activity inventory for the year previous to the interview to examine activity participation and satisfaction among a sample of several hundred men between the ages of twenty and ninety (McGandy et al. 1966; Stone & Norris 1966). A community survey of male activity levels in Tecumseh, Michigan, supplemented a recall-activity inventory with interviews to examine occupational and leisure-time activity levels during the previous year (Cunningham et al. 1969).

Shorter periods of recall may yield greater accuracy and a finer level of detail. It is often convenient to limit recall to the previous twenty-four hours, taking into consideration the possibility of unusual activity patterns associated with weekends, festivals, etc., and perhaps adjusting the interview schedules and/or analysis accordingly. Dichotomizing activities into work/leisure or obligatory/discretionary may be useful (Moss & Lawton 1982). Obtaining a sequential recounting of tasks jogs the memory and may provide an approximation of the amount of time devoted to each activity, even if the subject did not clock his or her activities. An effective technique for eliciting this in societies where Western time concepts and watches are not prevalent structures interviews around the local patterns of eating. Thus, the subject is asked about his activities between arising and taking the first meal, between the first and second meals, etc. These data may yield an estimate of the frequency with which certain tasks are undertaken and/or the amount of time allocated to certain tasks (Beall & Goldstein 1982; Moss & Lawton 1982; Nag, White & Peet 1978). For example, a twenty-four-hour time budget obtained for entire households in an Islamic Bangladesh village demonstrated that as women advance in status and age within the household, their average daily hours of labor decline (Cain, Khanam & Nahar 1979).

Successful use of the recall technique requires verification of the activities reported and their duration. Since it is likely that the subject's and the investigator's emic activity categories do not completely overlap, the latter must become familiar with the possible range of activities and must be aware of the steps entailed in a particular reported activity (e.g., does making tea entail fetching firewood). Once this is done, a checklist of standard activities may be developed for use in conjunction with the recall data to further jog the memory and to enhance the accuracy and level of detail. It may include an inventory of activities of daily living modified for the appropriate cultural setting as indicated earlier. Verification of the length of time will probably be rough and may derive from the investigator's general knowledge of the culture. However, because of the likelihood that individuals of different age-sex categories structure activities differently, observation of bouts of activity is preferable.

Even with a short period of recall and sequentially structured interviews, limited information can be obtained from recall techniques, and therefore prospective approaches may be undertaken. The prospective-diary technique of habitual activity assessment depends upon diligent cooperation and literacy. The general approach is to provide a recording form divided into short time intervals one, two, or five minutes, usually covering an entire week during which the participant records his ongoing activities. The elapsed time may then be categorized in a number of ways, including (1) according to posture, i.e, sitting, standing, lying, stooping; (2) according to the amount of physical effort (calories expended or heart rate level attained); (3) according to class of activity: productive, active leisure, housework, etc. This technique has been used in conjunction with measurement techniques such as heart-rate monitoring or oxygen-consumption measurement.

Heart-rate monitoring eliminates inaccuracy in reporting and may provide a global measure of total activity and, if monitored continuously, on patterns throughout the day (Salvosa, Payne & Wheeler 1971). Used alone, this provides data on heart rate and on the physiological strain of the activities, but not on categories of activities such as cooking, walking, etc. Interpretation is, however, based on the problematic assumption that observed heart rates are the result of activity rather than emotional stress. Better is a combination such as that in a study of a group of elderly Canadian men and women enrolled in a preretirement exercise program, who prospectively completed diary cards and also wore SAMIs (socially acceptable monitoring instruments) to record total heartbeats and another device to continuously record heart rate. This protocol yielded two independent measures of activity level and revealed the average time engaged in any activity producing a heart rate over 120 beats per minute (the level at which physical training effects begin) and the distribution of minutes of activity in a number of categories (Sidney & Shephard 1977).

A seven-day prospective-diary technique to elicit activity patterns has been used in conjunction with oxygen-consumption measurement of the principal activities and food intake in order to measure energy balance (Durnin, Blake & Brockway 1957, 1961; Durnin et al. 1961). The results of these studies focusing on activity among the elderly offer some guideline for designing new studies. With rare exceptions, people over the age of sixty appear to engage in only a few minutes of moderate activity each day, and activity variation between individuals is generally quite large (Durnin 1966, Durnin & Passmore 1967). This emphasizes the need for an adequately large sample of individuals (preferably *not* self-selected) and a sufficiently short recording interval, plus, a long-sampled time span, in order to encounter the total range of variation.

These requirements may be met using another prospective-observation technique, the time-motion study. This provides very accurate descriptions of activity but is costly in terms of observer effort and time, generally requiring one observer per subject. It entails continuous observation of subjects, noting the duration, nature, and context of each activity. While this may eliminate problems of inaccurate reporting by subjects, it may introduce bias due to the observer's presence until the subject has been habituated. Some researchers have tried to lessen these difficulties by suggesting that its use be limited to observations of groups (Weiner & Lourie 1969). Time-motion data may be reported in terms of minutes per day of certain specific activities or types of activities. This technique may be supplemented by measures of energy expenditure determined by measurement of oxygen consumption (Norgan, Ferro-Luzzil & Durnin 1974) or by heart-rate measurement. Together, these techniques produce data that may be reported in terms of minutes per day of activities at certain levels of physiological strain (e.g., heart rate or caloric expenditure) as well as by activity category.

Another variant focuses on a specific task or set of tasks of interest for some theoretical reason and assesses variation in the way in which they are completed (e.g., different postures, frequencies of motions). Another variant of the time-motion technique is the random-visit or instantaneous-scan sample. Using some sampling strategy, the activity of randomly selected individuals or individuals within households at randomly selected times is observed and a frequency distribution of activities produced (Montgomery 1978; Montgomery & Johnson 1977). An early version of this technique found that men and women over the age of sixty in a Mayo village spent about half their time in leisure (Erasmus 1955). As with standard time-motion techniques, this random-visit method may then be combined with calorimetry to obtain estimates of energy expended. A limitation of the technique is the large number of observations necessary to arrive at reliable estimates (Cain 1977) and the difficulty in isolating individual variation.

Additional techniques that may prove helpful in analyzing habitual physical activity include the use of pedometers and acclerometers (Saris & Binkhorst 1977a and 1977b). Both record movement and can be useful in obtaining gross quantitative measures of activity (Edgerton et al. 1979).

While most of these techniques can be used alone to produce measures of habitual activity, combinations may provide optimum accuracy and detail and focus on certain aspects important for theoretical reasons or for research design implementation.

The Emic Dimension

In addition to the observation and measurement of activities from the observer's viewpoint, the meaning of these activities for the individual participants is important information. Embellishments of the bare bones of the observations may provide important insight into the quality, context, or selection of activity. An example is the subjective evaluation of the meaningfulness of particular activities (Moss & Lawton 1982). Further examples include considering whether or not the individual feels his activity status corresponds with other dimensions of status such as economic, health, or authority. Whether he feels they are appropriate to someone in his perceived situation may be critical to emotional and psychological adjustments.

Strategies

The following tentative guidelines are presented to illustrate one way of organizing a cross-cultural study of aging using a habitual-activity method for measuring function. Such a study would likely begin with a combination of twenty-four-hour-recall interviews and random-visit observations. The recall interviews provide entree to the subject's own terminological and conceptual activity frameworks as well as an opportunity to obtain other sociodemographic data and to develop and administer an appropriate ADL schedule. Partial assessment of the individual's status may begin at this time. A series of dimensions of status, such as biological, health, activity, economic, household, psychological, and social status may be defined operationally and may be investigated etically as well as emically. To use recall or prospective-diary techniques, some direct observation is essential in order to understand what each activity actually entails. The particular research question will determine the sort of direct observation technique selected.

Several points to consider in the protocol design include the period over which the observations will be made. The time covered by the period of random-visit observations must be sufficiently long to encounter the entire range of variation and to obtain a sufficient number of observations. For example, in some settings, the work week plus weekend probably encompass the complete range, while in others it may be necessary to observe a full agricultural or annual cycle. When data are obtained by direct observation, the activity, posture, location, and context should be noted. Once these are gathered, frequency distributions of activity according to several different criteria can be constructed. For example, activity may be categorized to indicate the percent of observations when certain kinds of individuals engaged in field work, handicrafts, child care, etc. Similarly, the percentage of observations when individuals were lying, stooping, kneeling, etc., may provide an index of level of activity and exertion. The physiological stress may be further described by the size of loads carried or implements wielded relative to body size. Or it may be more elaborately described by heart rate or oxygen consumption or pedometry. Reporting the age and sex and activity of other people in the vicinity of the person being observed helps describe the social context. To answer certain research questions or fulfill certain research design, it may be desirable to structure the sampling scheme in such a way as to ensure sufficient representations of particular sociodemographic or other categories of individuals (e.g., caste, class). Altmann (1974) presents a detailed discussion of sampling methods for the observational study of behavior.

Another point to consider is the desirability of sampling a broad versus a narrow age range. Selecting a broad age range (such as all adults) and a broad range of household sizes is desirable in order to understand what factors influence habitual activity within as well as between age categories. It is essential to identify intracultural sources of variation such as class and caste and not to assume *a priori* that the elderly undertake a unique set of tasks. These types of data will reveal whether certain activities are age graded or whether assignment of tasks is primarily influenced by other considerations such as sex, social status, physical work capacity, or health.

Selecting among observational techniques also requires decisions regarding the level of detail. For example, the instantaneous-scan technique provides relatively little information about a single bout of activity and relies upon large numbers of observations. An alternative, completely task-oriented approach to assessing activity and workloads could be structured by observing naturally occurring situations such as the water tap or agricultural field, and recording the age, sex, rate of work, size of load relative to body size, posture, heart rate, heart rate elevation, or number of motions of everyone who engages in that behavior over a sampling period. In this case one may focus on activities with known social, economic, or survival importance or on those known to be especially strenuous. A disadvantage lies in preselecting the activities for observation. This should be done after a thorough knowledge of the range of activities is obtained. Another point is that this samples only those engaged in the particular, therefore, some attention to the difference between those who do and do not engage in that activity may be essential.

Another approach combines focal-individual and task-specific sampling to provide more detailed information on the way in which activities are carried out and their effects on the actor. A study of a carefully stratified sample engaged in a series of set, culturally appropriate tasks may be the most efficient means of obtaining detailed measurement of the workload. The subsample should contain a range of ages throughout adulthood and ideally the selection of tasks should include activities normally undertaken by the entire age range (although this may not always be possible). Observation during spontaneous occurrences of these activities should yield a picture of the actual strain which an individual experiences during his own structuring of his daily activities. Alternatively, observer-structured situations, such as carrying specified loads over certain distance, may be preferable. These would yield data in a more standardized format for intergroup comparisons and would perhaps yield insight into why certain individuals structure their activities as they do. There are several ways of translating these data into measures of physiological strain. These include the heart rate, weight of a load relative to the body weight or muscular strength of the individual, length of time required, and efficiency. The specific tasks and settings selected for analysis will vary according to the cultural settings and the hypotheses being tested. For a given task, the posture, intensity, duration, efficiency, heart-rate elevation, and level of accuracy of an activity may vary by age or sex or by other criteria. For example, do people in their seventies harvest as many rows of radishes per hour, take more rests, kneel more frequently than they stoop from the waist, overlook more radishes, achieve higher heart-rate elevation, or take fewer steps during radish harvesting than people in their twenties or forties?

The foregoing presented several strategies for use in describing habitual activity and its amount of physiological strain. If a measure of energy expenditure is desired, then oxygen consumption would be measured. The method of indirect calorimetry used by several investigators requires measurement of oxygen consumption for each person in the major postures or during the major activities; this information is used in conjunction with the time budgets to obtain an estimation of energetic output. An alternative is use of published standard energy values for many values for many activities (e.g., Durnin & Passmore 1967).

Socioeconomic and demographic data are also necessary. Information on whether or not the individual is self-sufficient (or receives food or money from someone, and, if so, from whom), with whom he lives, who his relatives are and where they live, and economic status is critical to understanding the situation of the elderly and interpreting the data on habitual activity.

THE ASSESSMENT OF BIOLOGICAL CAPACITY

The assessment of biological function represents a third approach to evaluating function. This approach produces objective assessment of biological capacity without special consideration of the extent to which the capacity may be utilized or required in the execution of habitual activities. The relationship between a particular functional measure and the ability to carry out a wide range of tasks is often not known, although in the case of certain functional measures, such as physical work capacity or visual acuity, it may be precisely known. The general model underlying this approach to function is the hypothesis that the morphological involution and the decline of biological function with age may proceed to the point where certain tasks are too great a strain to be sustained or performed in the standard fashion or are no longer feasible. The nature and rate of these aging changes vary greatly among individuals and populations, a phenomenon called differential aging (Bourliere 1970).

There are a number of reasons for objective assessment of this type, including the interest in (1) documenting the age-related changes in different individuals, populations, and environments, to provide normative and comparative data; (2) factors influencing these changes and the differential aging phenomenon; (3) understanding the relationship between the changing capacity and changing habitual activity patterns and performance of activities of daily living; and (4) analyzing the potential for training or rehabilitation.

The concept of biological, as opposed to chronological, age, referring to the degree or stage of some developmental process attained by an individual, is often appropriate for use in these studies. Measures of biological age are widely used in analyzing child growth and development to measure the extent of an individual's progress toward an endpoint, generally, mature size or function. Unfortunately for methodical research, development after maturity does not proceed along universal, clearly defined stages. It is often unclear what common changes are time-related pathologies (such as osteoporosis and arteriosclerosis) or disease-related pathologies and what are inevitable consequences of the passage of time (such as loss of height). Therefore, selection of measures is troublesome. Because most people do undergo involution and loss of function and adaptability, the common approach has been to undertake a diverse battery of tests to describe the aging of the whole organism (e.g., Borkan & Norris 1980; Bourliere 1970). Not all of these tests are appropriate for use by anthropologists in a field situation, where medical facilities and expertise, electricity, and refrigeration may be unavailable or the test unacceptable to the local culture. The monograph by Bourliere entitled *The Assessment of Biological Age in Man* (1970) is a highly recommended discussion of measuring differential aging, as are the reviews by Rossman (1977, 1979).

Table 2.1 presents a series of measures of biological age. The breakdown into simple and complex is pragmatic and in this context corresponds roughly with the expertise required to perform and interpret the test (which is generally correlated with the technological sophistication of the instrumentation) and to the level of the subject cooperation and understanding essential for obtaining reliable measurements. There is emphasis on objective measurable indicators whose assessment involves minimal interpretation and thus may be especially valuable in cross-cultural studies. Many measurements are applicable over a broad range of ages, but others are more relevant to the biological characteristics of the diminished capacities of the elderly. An example of the latter is the checklist of impairments that is part of a comprehensive patient-classification protocol (Jones, McNitt & McKnight 1973). Comfort has developed a test battery specifically to measure physiological age, which includes a number of additional items. To varying degrees, these measures provide a measure of resources, reserves, and capacities, regardless of the extent to which they are actually used.

Criteria for selecting measures appropriate for these assessments include the need for simple, reliable measures, inclusion of a wide range of morphological and functional systems, and measures which change sufficiently with age (in some populations at least), to detect differences over five- to ten- year spans (Bourliere 1970; Shephard 1978). Under appropriate circumstances, it may also be desirable to investigate adaptation to a particular environmental feature such as thermal or attitude stress. The selection of specific measures may vary depending upon the hypothesis to be tested and the environmental and cultural setting. In some cases a single measure, such as visual acuity or pulmonary function, is sufficient. In other cases a broad range of measures may be desirable. Discussions about the strategies of measurement (Baker 1976, 1977) and the many techniques themselves (Weiner & Lourie 1969) are available.

In addition, presentation of the data in some meaningful way in terms of central tendencies, frequencies, trends, indices, or profiles in order to compare individuals, subpopulations, and populations is essential. An initial step may be examination of age differences within a population; another useful method is comparison and presentation of data with reference to some reference or well-studied population such as the United States. Points to consider during analysis include the observation that variation generally increases with age and that on some brief scales, many elderly may fall into the "worst" or lowest functional category and thus the variation within that category may be masked. Another method is the use of multiple regression techniques to obtain a single estimate of biological age based on one or more measurements. A useful critique of the biological age concept has been offered by Costa and MacRae (1980). An additional method is to construct a profile utilizing a number of measures and using percentile scores (Heron & Chown 1967) or standardized residuals of each of a series of age-related variables (Borkan & Norris 1980a,b; Beall & Goldstein 1982b). For example, a profile of twenty-four physical parameters was used to demonstrate that men in the Baltimore Longitudinal Aging Study who were classified as looking older than their age were biologically older on the profile of parameters (Borkan & Norris 1980a,b). In another example, a profile was constructed for elderly Sherpa in order to test the hypothesis that those who live with family members are biologically older than those living alone (Beall & Goldstein 1982b). The advantage of a profile is that each variable may be considered separately as well as in relation to the others and to any specific activities under consideration. A disadvantage is the requirement of a large number of observations on each individual.

Assessment of nutritional status may be desired as well. Various techniques and guidelines are available (Weiner & Lourie 1969; Garn 1980), and some special problems and considerations involved in studies of nutritional status of the elderly have been discussed (e.g., Exton-Smith 1982; Rivlin 1981).

Health status may temporarily or permanently affect both biological capacity and habitual activity (in both emic and etic aspects). A variety of approaches to assess the health status of a community was discussed earlier. The interpretation of measures of habitual activity and biological function depends upon the cultural context in which these occur.

SUMMARY

A recent review of functional assessment commented that "the intertwining of physical, psychological and social well-being in the elderly makes independent measurement of physical functioning difficult" (Kane & Kane 1981:25). The assessment and measurement of functional capacity in research on aging can be approached from three interrelated and complementary perspectives: the assessment of health status and functional adequacy, the assessment of habitual activity, and the assessment of biological function. The three approaches differ from one another along several important dimensions. The first approach focuses on what people cannot do, i.e., it assesses function in terms of impairment and incapacity; the second approach focuses on what people can actually do; and the last approach focuses on what people could do--the biological potential for activity. Another difference between these approaches is that the first usually relies on the self-reports of respondents and, in that sense, is a more subjective assessment of capacity than the other two approaches. While each approach differs as to what is measured and the techniques used for measurement, they are alike in that none can be interpreted independently of the cultural context in which they are applied. With an approach combining etic measurement and emic sensitivity we may achieve a truly biocultural understanding of functional capacity and aging.

Table 2.1

Simple Observations, Tests, and Measures of
Biological Function With Special
Relevance to the Study of Biological Aging

Simple Observations	Simple Tests, Measures, and Assessments	More Complex Tests and Measures	Special Tests for Certain Environments
Greyness	Joint contracture	Serum immunoglobulin levels	Adaptation to thermal, disease, altitude stress
Wrinkles	Joint mobility impairment and range of motion	Pulmonary function	
Arcus senilis		Heart-rate response to exercise task	
Facial hair	Dentition--tooth loss	Maximal and submaximal physical work capacity	
Diagonal ear crease	Pupil response to light and accommodation	Symptomatology questionnaire--Cornell Medical Index, chronic bronchitis, angina	
Palmar and finger varicosities	Grip strength	Bone mineralization and bone loss	
Posture	Respiratory impairment	Glucose tolerance	
	Morphological change--height, weight, anteroposterior, chest depth		
	Posture--kyposis		
	Body composition change--skinfolds		
	Special senses: vision, taste, hearing, smell, touch, vibration		
	Blood pressure		
	Hemoglobin and hematocrit		
	Menopause and associated symptomatology		
	Falls and accidents		
	Mental status		

Sources: Goldman 1979; Heron & Chown 1967; Howell 1949; Montoye, Willis & Cunningham 1968; Damon et al. 1972; Rossman 1977, 1979; Jones 1973; Snider et al. 1959; Bourliere 1970; Cole 1971.

BIBLIOGRAPHY

Altmann, J. 1974. "Observational Study of Behavior: Sampling Methods." Behavior 49:277-67.

Baker, P. T. 1976. "Research Strategies in Population Biology and Environmental Stress." In The Measures of Man: Methodologies in Biological Anthropology, ed. E. Giles and J. S. Friedlaender. Cambridge, Mass.: Peabody Museum Press, pp. 230-59.

_____. 1977. "Problems and Strategies." Human Population Problems in the Biosphere: Some Research Strategies and Designs, ed. P. T. Baker. MAB Technical Notes No. 3. Paris: UNESCO.

Balinsky, W., and R. Berger. 1975. "A Review of the Research on General Health Status Indexes." Medical Care, 13:283-93.

Beall, C. M. and M. C. Goldstein. 1982a. "Work, Aging, and Dependency in a Sherpa Population in Nepal." Social Science and Medicine 16:141-148.

_____. 1982b. "Biological function activity and dependency among elderly Sherpa in the Nepal Himalayas." Social Science and Medicine 16:135-140.

Bergner, M. and B. S. Gilson. 1981. "The Sickness Impact Profile: The Relevance of Social Science of Medicine." In The Relevance of Social Science for Medicine, ed. L. Eisenberg and A. Kleinman. Dordrecht, Holland: Reidel, pp. 135-50.

Bergner, M., et al. 1976a. "The Sickness Impact Profile: Validation of a Health Status Measure." Medical Care 14:57.

_____. 1976b. "The Sickness Impact Profile: Conceptual Formulation and Methodology for the Development of a Health Status Measure." International Journal of Health Service, 6:393-415.

Borkan, G. A. and H. A. Norris. 1980a. "Assessment of Biological Age Using a Profile of Physical Parameters." Journal of Gerontology 55:177-185.

_____. 1980b. "Biological Age in Adulthood: Comparison of Active and Inactive U.S. Males." Human Biology 52(4):787-802.

Bourliere, F. 1970. The Assessment of Biological Age in Man. Public Health Papers, No. 37. Geneva: WHO.

Buckley, E. C. and J. R. Roseman. 1976. "Immunity and Survival." Journal of the American Geriatric Society 24:241-48.

Butler, R. N. and M. I. Lewis. 1982. Aging and Mental Health: Positive Psychosocial and Biomedical Approaches. St. Louis: C. V. Mosby.

Cain, M. 1977. Household Time Budgets. VFS Methodology Report No. 1. Dacca: Bangladesh Institute of Development Studies.

Cain, M., S. R. Khanam, and S. Nahar. 1979. "Class, Patriarchy and Women's Work in Bangladesh." Population and Development Review 5:405-38.

Chambers, L. W., et al. 1976. "Development and Application of an Index of Social Function." Health Services Research, Winter, 430-41.

Clark, M., and B. G. Anderson. 1967. Culture and Aging. Springfield, Ill.: Charles C. Thomas.

Cole, T. M. 1971. "Goniometry: The Measurement of Joint Motion." In Handbook of Physical Medicine and Rehabilitation (2n ed.), ed. F. H. Krusen. Philadelphia: W. B. Saunders.

Commission on Chronic Illness. 1957. "Chronic Illness in a Large City." Chronic Illness in the United States, vol. 4. Cambridge, Mass.: Harvard University Press.

Costa, P. T., and R. R. McCrae. 1980. "Functional Age: A Conceptual and Empirical Critique." In Second Conference on the Epidemiology of Aging, ed. S. G. Haynes and M. Feinleib. U.S. DHHS NIH Publication No. 80-969.

Cunningham, D. A. et al. 1969. "Active Leisure Time Activities Related to Age among Males in a Total Population." Journal of Gerontology 23:551.

Damon, A., et al. 1972. "Age and Physique in Healthy White Veterans at Boston." Aging and Human Development 3:202.

Duke University Center for the Study of Aging and Human Development. 1978. Multi-dimensional Functional Assessment: The OARS Methodology. Durham, N.C.: Duke University.

Durnin, J. V. G. A. 1966. "Age, Physical Activity and Energy Expenditure." Proceedings of the Nutrition Society 25:107-13.

_____. 1967. "Activity Patterns in the Community." Canadian Medical Association Journal 96:883-86.

Durnin, J. V. G. A., et al. 1961a. "Food Intake and Energy Expenditure of Elderly Women with Varying Sized Families." Journal of Nutrition 75:73.

_____. 1961b. "The Food Intake and Energy Expenditure of Some Elderly Men Working in Heavy and Light Engineering." British Journal of Nutrition 15:587.

Durnin, J. V. G. A., E. C. Blake, and J. M. Brockway. 1957. "The Energy Expenditure and Food Intake of Middle Aged Glasgow Housewives and Their Adult Daughters." British Journal of Nutrition 11:85-94.

_____. 1961. "The Food Intake and Energy Expenditure of Elderly Women Living Alone." British Journal of Nutrition 15:499.

Durnin, J. V. G. A., and R. Passmore. 1967. Energy, Work and Leisure. London: Heinemann Educational Books.

Edgertown, V. R., et al. 1979. "Iron-Deficiency Anaemia and Its Effect on Worker Productivity and Activity Patterns." British Medical Journal 2:1546:49.

Edholm, O. B. 1966. "The Assessment of Habitual Activity.: In Physical Activity in Health and Disease. ed. K. Evang and K. L. Anderson. Proceedings of the Beitostolen Symposium. Baltimore: Williams & Wilkins.

Eisdorfer, C., and D. Cohen. 1980. "Diagnostic Criteria for Primary Neuronal Degeneration of the Alzheimer's Type." Journal of Family Practice 11:553-57.

Erasmus, C. 1955. "Work Patterns in a Mayo Village." American Anthropologist 57:332-34.

Exton-Smith, A. M. 1982. "Epidemiological Studies in the Elderly: Methodological Considerations." American Journal of Clinical Nutrition 35:1273-79.

Finch, C. E., and L. Hayflick, eds. 1977. Handbook of the Biology of Aging. New York: Van Nostrand Reinhold.

Fink, M., M. Green, and M. B. Bender. 1952. "The Face-Hand Test as a Diagnostic Sign of Organic Mental Syndrome." Neurology 2:46-59.

Fishback, D. B. 1977. "Mental Status Questionnaire for Organic Brain Syndrome with a New Visual Counting Test." Journal of the American Geriatric Society 25:167-70.

Folstein, M. F., S. Folstein, and P. R. McHugh. 1975. "Mini-Mental State: A Practical Method for Grading the Cognitive State of Patients for the Clinician." Journal of Psychiatric Research 12:189-98.

Foster, G., and B. G. Anderson. 1978. Medical Anthropology. New York: John Wiley & Sons.

Garn, S. M. 1980. "Human Growth." Annual Review of Anthropology 9:275-291.

Gilson, B. S., et al. 1975. "The Sickness Impact Profile: Development of an Outcome Measure of Health Care." American Journal of Public Health 65:1304-10.

Goldman, R. 1979. "Decline in Organ Function with Aging." In Clincial Geriatrics (2d ed.), ed. I. Rossman. Philadelphia: J. B. Lippincott, pp. 23-59.

Goldsmith, S. B. 1972. "The Status of Health Status Indicators." Health Services Report 87:212-20.

Goldstein, M. C., and C. M. Beall. 1981. "Modernization and Aging in the Third and Fourth World: Views from the Rural Hinterland in Nepal." Human Organization 40:48-55.

Granger, C. G., C. C. Sherwood, and D. S. Green. 1977. "Functional Status Measures in a Comprehensive Stroke Care Program." Archives of Physical Medicine and Rehabilitation 48:558-61.

Grgic, A., et al. 1976. "Joint Contracture--Common Manifestation of Childhood Diabetes Mellitus." Journal of Pediatrics 88:584-88.

Gurland, B., et al. 1977-78. "The Comprehensive Assessment and Referral Evaluation (CARE): Rationale, Development, and Reliability." International Journal of Aging and Human Development 8:9-42.

Haberman, P. 1969. "The Reliability and Validity of the Data." In Poverty and Health, ed. J. Kosa. Cambridge: Harvard University Press.

Hauser, P. M. 1976. "Aging and World Wide Population Change." In Handbook of Aging and the Social Sciences, ed. R. H. Binstock and E. Shanas. New York: Van Nostrand and Reinhold pp. 58-116.

Heron, A., and S. Chown. 1967. Age and Function. Boston: Little Brown.

Hickey, T. 1980. Health and Aging. Monterey, Calif.: Brooks/Cole.

Howell, T. J. 1949. "Senile Deterioration of the Central Nervous System." British Medical Journal 1:56.

Isaacs, B., and A. T. Kennie. 1973. "The Set Test as an Aid to the Detection of Dementia in Old People." British Journal of Psychiatry 123:467-70.

Johnson, A. 1975. "Time Allocation in a Machiguenga Community." Ethnology 14:301-10.

Jones. E. W., B. H. McNitt, and E. M. McKnight. 1973. Patient Classification for Long-Term Care: User's Manual. DHEW Publication No. HRA 7403017. Washington, D.C.: U.S. Govt. Printing Office.

Kahn, R. L., et al. 1960. "Brief Objective Measures for the Determination of Mental Status in the Aged." American Journal of Psychiatry 117:326-38.

Kane, R. A. and R. L. Kane. 1981. Assessing the Elderly: A Practical Guide to Measurement. Lexington, Mass.: Lexington Books.

Kastenbaum, R. and S. Sherwood. 1972. "NIRO: A Scale for Assessing the Interview Behavior of Elderly People." In Research, Planning and Action for the Elderly, ed. D. P. Kent, R. Kastenbaum, and S. Sherwood. New York: Behavioral Publications.

Katz, S., and C. A. Akpom. 1976. "A Measure of Primary Socio-biological Functions." International Journal of Health Sciences 6:493-508.

Katz, S., S. C. Hedrick, and N. S. Henderson. 1979. "The Measurement of Long-Term Care Needs and Impact." Health and Medical Care Services Review 2(1).

_____. 1970. "Progress in Development in the Index of ADL." Gerontologist 10:20-30.

_____. 1966. "Prognosis after Stroke. II. Long-Term Course of 159 Patients." Medicine 45:236-45.

Katz, S., et al. 1963. "Studies of Illness in the Aged. The Index of ADL: A Standardized Measure of Biological and Psycho-social Function." Journal of American Medical Association 185:914-41.

Kaufert, J. M., et al. 1979. "Assessing Functional Status among Elderly Patients." Medical Care 17:807-17.

Lawton, M. P., M, Ward, and S. Yaffee. 1967. "Indices of Health in an Aging Population." Journal of Gerontology 22:344-42.

Lichstein, E., et al. 1974. "Diagonal Ear-Lobe Crease: Prevalence and Implication as a Coronary Risk Factor." New England Journal of Medicine 290:615-16.

McGandy, R. B., et al. 1966. "Nutrient Intakes and Energy Expenditure in Men of Different Ages." Journal of Gerontology 21:581-87.

Maddox, G. L. 1962. "Some Correlates of Difference in Self-Assessment of Health Status among the Elderly." Journal of Gerontology 17:180-85.

_____. 1964. "Self Assessment of Health Status: A Longitudinal Study of Selected Elderly Subjects." Journal of Chronic Diseases 17:449-60.

Maddox, G. L., and E. B. Douglas. 1973. "Self-Assessment of Health: A Longitudinal Study of Elderly Subjects." Journal of Health and Social Behavior 14:87-93.

Mazess, R. B., ed. 1974. International Conference on Bone Mineral Measurements. DHEW Publication No. 74-863. Washington, D.C.

Montgomery, E., and A. Johnson. 1978. "Machiguenga Energy Expenditure." Ecology of Food Nutrition 6(2):97-106.

Montoye, J., P. W. Willis III, and D. A. Cunningham. 1968. "Heart Rate Responses to Sub-Maximal Exercise: Relation to Age and Sex." Journal of Gerontology 23:127.

Mortimer, J. A., L. M. Schuman, and L. R. French. 1981. "Epidemiology of Dementing Illness." ed. J. A. Mortimer and L. M. Schuman. In The Epidemiology of Dementia, Monographs in Epidemiology and Biostatistics. New York: Oxford University Press, pp. 3-23.

Moss, M. S. and M. P. Lawton. 1982. "Time Budgets of Older People: A Window on Four Lifestyles." Journal of Gerontology 37:115-23.

Nag, N., B. White, R. Pect. 1978. "An Anthropological Approach to the Study of the Economic Value of Children in Java and Nepal." Current Anthropology 19:293-306.

Nagi, S. Z. 1976. "An Epidemiology of Disability among Adults in the U.S." Milbank Memorial Fund Quarterly 54:439-67.

National Center for Health Statistics. 1974. Health Survey Procedure: Concepts, Questionnaire Development, and Definitions in the Health Interview Survey. PHS Publication No. 1000, Vital Health Statistics Series 12, No. 24, DHEW Publication No. HRA 74-1709. Rockville, Md: DHEW.

_____. 1977. Current Estimates from U.S. Health Interview Survey. Vital Statistics, Series No. 10, Rockville, Md.: DHEW.

Newman, S. J., et al. 1976. "Housing Adjustments of Older People: A Report of Findings from the Second Phase." Mimeo. Ann Arbor, Mich.: Institute for Social Research, University of Michigan.

Norgan, N. G., A. Ferro-Luzzi, and J.V.G.A. Durnin. 1974. "The Energy and Nutrient Intake and the Energy Expenditure of 204 New Guinea Adults." Philosophical Transaction Royal Society of London 268:309-48.

Pfeiffer, E. 1975. "A Short Portable Mental Status Questionnaire for the Assessment of Organic Brain Deficit in Elderly Patients." Journal of the American Geriatrics Society 23:433-41.

Pfeiffer, E., ed. 1975. Multidimensional Functional Assessment: The OARS Methodology. A Manual. Durham, NC: Center for the Study of Aging and Human Development, Duke University.

Rivlin, R. S. 1981. "Nutrition and Aging: Some Unanswered Questions." American Journal of Medicine 71:337-40.

Rose, G. A. and H. Blackburn. 1968. Cardiovascular Survey Methods. Geneva: World Health Organization.

Rossman, I. 1977. "Anatomic and Body Composition Changes with Aging." In Handbook of the Biology of Aging, ed. C. E. Finch and L. Hayflick, New York: Van Nostrand Reinhold, pp. 189-221.

Rossman, I. 1979. "The Anatomy of Aging." In Clinical Geriatrics (2d ed.), ed. I. Rossman. Philadelphia: J. B. Lippincott, pp. 3-22.

Rothe, M. 1981. "The Diagnosis of Dementia in Late and Middle Life." In The Epidemiology of Dementia, Monographs in Epidemiology and Biostatistics. ed. J. A. Mortimer and L. M. Schumann. New York: Oxford University Press, pp. 24-61.

Salvosa, C. B., P. R. Payne, and E. F. Wheeler. 1971. "Energy Expenditure of Elderly People Alone or in Local Authority Homes." American Journal of Clinical Nutrition 24:1467:70.

Saris, W. H. M., and R. A. Binkhorst. 1977a. "The Use of Pedometer and Actometer in Studing Daily Physical Activity in Man. II: Reliability of Pedometer and Actometer." European Journal of Applied Physiology 37:219-28.

_____. 1977b. "The Use of Pedometer and Actometer in Studying Daily Physical Activity in Man. II: Validity of Pedometer and Actometer Measuring the Daily Physical Activity. European Journal of Applied Physiology 37:229-35.

Schoenberg, D. S. 1981. "Methodological Approaches to the Epidemiological Study of Dementia." In The Epidemiology of Dementia, Monographs in Epidemiology and Biostatistics. ed. J. A. Mortimer and L. M. Schuman. New York: Oxford University Press, pp. 117-31.

Shanas, E., et al. 1968. Old People in Three Industrial Societies. New York: Atherton Press.

Shephard, R. J. 1978. Physical Activity and Aging. Chicago: Yearbook Medical Publishers.

Sherwood, S., et al. 1977. "The Needs of Elderly Community Residents of Massachusetts." Mimeo. Dept. of Social Gerontological Research, Hebrew Rehabilitation Center for the Aged, 1200 Centre St., Boston, MA 02131.

Sidney, K. H., and R. J. Shephard. 1977. "Activity Patterns of Elderly Men and Women." Journal of Gerontology 32:25-32.

Snider, T. H., et al. 1959. "Simple Bedside Test of Respiratory Function." Journal of American Medical Association 170:1631.

Spradley, J. 1979. The Ethnographic Interview. New York: Holt, Rinehart & Winston.

_____. 1980. Participant Observation. New York; Holt, Rinehart & Winston.

Steward, A., J. E. Ware, and R. H. Brook. 1977. "The Meaning of Health: Understanding Functional Limitations." Medical Care 15:939-52.

Stone, J. L. and A. H. Norris. 1966. "Activities and Attitudes of Participants in the Baltimore Longitudinal Study." Journal of Gerontology 21:575-80.

Stuart-Harris, C. H., et al. 1965. "Definition and Classification of Chronic Bronchitis for Clinical and Epidemiological Purposes. A Report of the MRC by Their Committee on Aetiology of Chronic Bronchitis." Lancet 775-79.

Tissue, T. 1972. "Another Look at Self-Rated Health among the Elderly." Journal of Gerontology 27: 334-42.

Townsend, P. 1963. "Measuring Incapacity for Self-Care." In Processes of Aging (Pt. II), ed. R. H. Williams, C. Tibbits, and W. Donahue. New York: Atherton Press.

Trussel, R. D. and J. Elinson. 1959. "Chronic Illness in a Rural Area." In Chronic Illness in the U.S., vol. III. Cambridge, Mass.: Harvard University Press.

United Nations. 1980. Selected Demographic Indicators by Country, 1950-2000: Demographic Estimates and Projections as Assessed in 1978. SER R/38. United Nations.

U.S. Department of Health, Education, and Welfare. 1972. Limitations of Activity due to Chronic Conditions. Public Health Services, Series 10. Washington, D.C.: U.S. Govt. Printing Office.

Weiner, J. S., and J. A. Lourie. 1969. Human Biology: A Guide to Field Methods. IBP Handbook No. 9. Oxford: Blackwell Scientific Publications.

WHO. See World Health Organization.

World Health Organization. 1968. Exercise Tests in Relation to Cardiovascular Function: Report of a WHO Meeting. Geneva: WHO.

3
Age Estimates and Their Evaluation in Research

NANCY HOWELL
Center for Advanced Studies in Behavioral Sciences
Stanford, California

To study old age, we have to know how old the people are. Finding out how old they are is a homely task that may be trivial in some situations, and really very difficult and challenging in others. There are only a few places in the world and times in history when essentially everyone can provide accurate information on his or her own current age and/or year of birth. Since these are the places and the times when most social science research has been done, we are inclined to forget that the opposite is the usual case for humankind. And even in a society in which most people are aware of their birthdays and lots of written records are kept, there may still be special groups like the elderly that present special problems in finding out how old they really are.

In parts of the world that lack written and numerical records, and a cultural definition of the importance of numbers and dates, the people may have no idea of what is meant when an age is asked for, or the name of the year in which one was born. Instead, many cultures have a set of concepts describing the stages of life through which people pass. Other cultures may have a concept of age which is subjective and changeable over the life course, reflecting status and prestige as much as the duration of time. Under such circumstances of study, it is tempting to use time and age loosely, simply learning about attitudes toward age without attempting to pin down the actual age of individuals at a point in time. Indeed, that decision may be the only possible one if resources for study are limited and time pressures are great.

However, the cost of the decision to ignore age will be substantial. Accurate description of the study population is not possible when age is unknown, nor are comparative studies so that one can identify what is special or unusual about the study group. In addition, age cannot be used as a variable in cross-tabulation, or in hypothesis formulation, when age is a relevant variable for explanation or control--and it usually is.

It this chapter we will review techniques of data collection and data analysis designed to cover the whole range of research situations that analysts may encounter. We will consider good and poor (or nonexistent) records, clear or vague social concepts of age and aging, large and small populations, and situations in which the analyst has much or little time and energy and resources to devote to the task of estimating age and evaluating others' age estimates. In all these contexts, we will be trying to suggest ways of making useful age estimates, with some known probability of accuracy. The alternative of giving up, it will be argued, may be essential as an alternative, but it is to be avoided wherever possible.

So many kinds of problems may arise in these kinds of study that solutions may often have to be tailor-made to the situation. This chapter suggests guidelines for the construction of tailor-made methods, but will almost surely overlook certain problems that will emerge in some research situations. The suggestion that a demographer be consulted is probably the most useful single piece of advice that can be offered here. In the interest of encouraging the spirit of "do it yourself" and of assisting researchers to understand and cooperate with the demographer who is asked to provide some specific help, this chapter consists of three sections.

In the first section, I will consider the evaluation of age estimates and the method by which they were obtained, and will offer some guidance on the correction of estimates, if necessary. The second section, The Process of Making Estimates, will present a range of available input information and the ways of getting informants to cooperate in the estimation procedure. In the third section, Summary and Applications to the Oldest Age Group, I will summarize the principles of age estimation, and will offer practical advice to researchers who need to make such estimates, especially when the focus of interest is in old age.

THE EVALUATION OF AGE ESTIMATES

All data on age, whether derived from birth and death registers, documents such as passports or family Bibles, or the undocumented assertion of the individual or close associates, will consist of some combination of truth and error, omissions and bias, overstatements, understatements, illegible entries, and confused and confusing informants.

Good advice is to forget about defending your data from the charge that it incorporates sources of error. Cheerfully admit that the data are not perfect, and get on with the job of evaluating the sources of error, random and biased, and the degree of accuracy, the task that Ken Wachter calls "pinning the fuzz on the data" (Wachter 1978).

If the errors are randomly distributed throughout the data, so that all items are equally likely to be in error, the conclusion of your evaluation may well be that it is not appropriate to make any corrections to the data, but merely to specify the level of precision permitted by the error rate.

If your evaluation indicates that biased error may be present, it will likely be necessary to investigate carefully the way the data was collected, recorded, and transcribed. At each stage, we have to test for the presence of bias. And when our tests confirm the presence of bias--systematic distortions of the pattern of the truth, errors that are concentrated in certain categories rather than scattered randomly through the population--we have to decide what measures to take to correct the bias. Under some circumstances, we might actually change our data records: to include what we believe to be more accurate information, for instance, or to add missing persons. Under other circumstances we might modify our interpretation of the raw data, systematically adding or correcting in the analysis what we believe to have been omitted or distorted in the data collection. And occasionally we might conclude as a rational step that the nature of the bias is such that the data are unusable, and cannot be relied upon to teach us anything about the population in question.

Our tools and tasks in this evaluation of the quality of data are similar to those of the detective in fiction. We use deduction, the study of consistency or contradiction within various sources of data on the same subject, the study of motive, means and opportunity for bias on the part of informants, record-keepers, and analysts. We do not, however, care "who done it." We want to figure out *what* was done, in order to make a rational analysis that will allow us (if possible) to eliminate the distortion, and keep the accuracy, in our analysis.

Techniques for Complete Data from Large Populations

Let us start with techniques appropriate to the situation in which we have data from all the members of a large population. An example of this kind of situation is a contemporary national census.

We start with the raw data brought in by the census-takers, and evaluate the data on age. Our first step is to construct an age pyramid by single years of age from the raw data, and look at the patterns of numbers from year to year of age.

Figure 3.1 shows the 1960 population of the Philippines, from the UN *Population Yearbook* of 1965. This information happens to be presented for the two sexes mixed, as it is plotted, although it is more common and generally more useful to see the data for the two sexes separately, in which case the graph takes the familiar form of a pyramid. In either case, you are very likely to observe at this stage of analysis one of the commonly observed patterns of age misstatement: age heaping, age rounding, and/or age vanity. The extent to which you observe these patterns will tell you something about the culture and the society you are studying, something about the way that the data was collected, and something about the rate and pattern of errors in the data.

"Age heaping" is the commonly observed pattern of finding more people at certain ages and fewer at others than expected. The most usual form of age heaping in advanced industrial countries, when the question asked is "What was your age at your last birthday?" is to find excess numbers in ages ending in zeros and fives (. . . 20, 25, 30, 35 . .) and fewer than expected in the intermediate years (. . . 21, 22, 23, 24..26, 27. . .) It is common to find that this pattern is more noticeable among the older cohorts than among younger people, perhaps as a result of the dual causes that young people tend to be more aware of every year of their age, and that young people tend to be more highly educated than older people in the same society, even controlling for social class. While heaping is typically more accentuated at older ages, the same years are most commonly chosen for heaping and avoiding at all age groups.

We interpret heaping as simply rounding, by informants who don't bother to update their perception of their age every year, so to speak. They may perceive themselves as being at 30 years, or 40 years or 50 years, for example, not for the exact 365 days between birthdays but for some longer period of time, until they perceive themselves as approaching another socially important birthday, such as 35, 45, or 55. Heaping tends to lead to some underestimation of ages in the population, as people err more after the crucial birthday than before it. But in general, heaping is so pervasive, and its effects are so nearly eliminated by the simple grouping of data by age into five-year categories (0-4, 5-9, 10-14 . . . at last birthday) that heaping is a phenomenon to be investigated but not corrected. The usual measure of age heaping is the

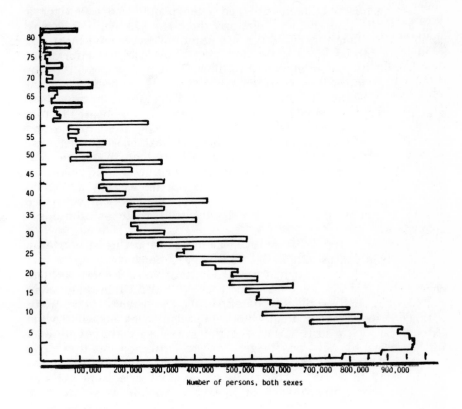

FIGURE 3.1.   Age heaping in a census, shown by single-year age
distribution, population of the Phillipines, 1960.
From Shryoke and Seigel, *Methods and Materials of
Demography*.

number of years individuals would have to be moved to smooth the age distribution, divided by the number of persons involved. A crude measure can be calculated by calculating the expected number at each age as a linear function. A better measure uses stable population models (Coale & Demeny 1967) or a logit-fit age distribution (Brass 1971). It is good practice to calculate the measure of heaping for the two sexes separately, and if they approximately match, to simply interprete the heaping measure as an average error of measurement of age.

Heaping has also been observed when people are asked for a year of birth rather than an age, and the same pattern of favoring numbers that end in zero and five is noted. Very precise measures of heaping can be made if the data collection asks the informants to provide both age and the year of birth.

Other methods than reported age or year of birth may produce different patterns of bias. It is a curiosity about heaping, for example, that the people who do it the least and who are, in this sense, most accurate about their age reporting are Chinese and Korean people, for whom the astrological calendar and the associated cycles of years are highly salient over the whole life cycle. These populations remind us that deviations from a smooth distribution of individuals over years is not necessarily a sign of age misreporting. Inauspicious years may genuinely have fewer events, as people modify their behavior to accomodate these expectations.

A second pattern of error and bias in age reporting by educated informants in census data is age rounding, or emphasis upon certain socially important ages. It is noticeable that you get more heaping on the youngest age at which people are allowed to do things they want to do, such as the age of eligibility for drivers' license, for voting, or for drinking, than would otherwise be expected. To the extent to which a jurisdiction uses the same age (say, twenty-one) for a series of new priviledges, an accentuation of the trend appears. When a jurisdiction changes from one socially important age to another (such as change in the drinking age from eighteen to twenty-one), the "bump" of age rounding moves to the new age.

It is curious that this phenomenon can be noted on the census, despite the fact that an untrue claim to legal age will have no effect on access to the desired behavior. Nevertheless, we see this effect also in old age, at the age of retirement and access to social insurance and old age assistance. Generally, this trend contributes to overestimation of age, as people who are not quite old enough to qualify for age-related privileges report themselves as older.

The third commonly observed pattern of age misstatement is age vanity, the tendency to report oneself somewhat older in youth, somewhat younger in middle age, and often considerably older than one is in old age. This tendency, an example of bias more than random error, is a troubling issue for people engaged in gerontological research. Old people, once they reach a point where extreme age is something to take pride in or obtain recognition for, tend to "age" more than one year per year in their subjective impressions. This subjective impression has been observed many times not only in the old people, who may be considered to have a failing memory, but also for their friends and relatives, who might be considered to be expressing surprise that the person has survived so long. By age eighty the tendency to report age as older than it really is is noticeable in North American society, and by age one hundred people tend to gain a year in their subjective impressions every few months.

After one is satisfied that all that can be learned by comparing the numbers from one single year of age to the next has been achieved, it is well to compare the number of individuals at each age for the two sexes. In general, we expect to see somewhat more males than females at each age in infancy and youth, because about 105 males are born for each 100 females. But since mortality for males tends to be somewhat higher than that for females at all ages in virtually all societies, we expect to see a crossover in the relative numbers at some age during middle childhood to early adulthood, increasing gradually over increased years of age. Stable population models can provide guidance on the size of the difference between the sexes at various ages, for varying levels of mortality and rates of population growth (Coale & Demeny 1967).

Deviations from this pattern can be due to differences between the sexes in migration behavior (either into or out of the group), differences between the sexes in any one of the three patterns of age misreporting, or an unusual age-sex pattern of mortality in the history of this population, especially deaths of adult men in wars. It is wise to investigate and evaluate the effects of the first two possible causes of deviations from the usual sex patterns of age before concluding that an unexpected sex ratio at certain ages is evidence of unusual mortality patterns in the past.

Another kind of further investigation of single-year age pyramids can be performed by subdividing the data by additional variables, such as regions of the country, urban and rural places, and characteristics of the population, such as income, occupation, education, residence in single-family dwellings, and so on. In general, we expect to find subpopulational differences in the extent to which the indicators of misreported ages turn up, and the analyst must draw upon his or her knowledge of the population to know whether these differences make sense. You are likely to find that much of the error is clustered in the segments of the population that are least educated, and least cooperative with the census, but the exact pattern cannot be predicted in advance. Keep in mind that this technique requires whole populations--men, women, and children--to be interpretable, and it requires a minimum of about five thousand persons to give valid indicators of the patterns of misreporting. The large numbers are required by the large number of subdivisions of the population--at least eighty-five for each sex--needed to analyze age data by single years of age.

Evaluation of Data from Smaller Populations

If you do not have such large numbers to work with, it will be essential to group the data into larger and fewer age categories, and the techniques just discussed cannot be used. It may still be possible, however, to make a systematic evaluation of the accuracy of the data. Figure 3.2, for instance, shows comparisons of the proportion of the population in each five year age group as estimated in the census for several countries, compared with the proportion expected in the stable population model with the same vital rates of birth and death as those populations (Coale & Demeny 1977; UN 1978). This technique can be used with much smaller groups, provided that the data are based upon the whole population (Howell 1979).

Another approach to the problem is through the comparison of several (at least two) sources of data. These techniques of comparison are generally more laborious than single-year age pyramid analysis, but can be done independently of the size of the group and may not require the cooperation of the informants if the documents are publicly available. Data are evaluated by searching documents such as birth certificates, church baptismal records, newspaper notices, family Bibles or archival materials such as letters and diaries, for information on the dates of crucial events such as births. The dates sought do not have to be drawn from a population of highly related people (although the search will be more efficient if they are), and it is not necessary to check all of the dates if the number is large. It is more useful to check a randomly selected sample of the total than an opportunistically selected subgroup, because a random sample can provide information on the accuracy rate of data for the whole population, while a nonrandom sample cannot be generalized.

When errors are revealed by consulting two or more sources, they should not be corrected without careful thought of the ways in which the pattern of accuracy and error will be changed by making the corrections. Corrections may nullify the hard work of

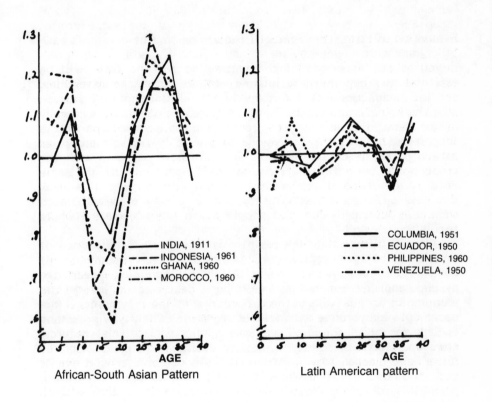

FIGURE 3.2   Patterns of age misreporting for five-year age groups in the female population. Ratio of reported to actual proportion in age group. From U.N., Manual IV.

evaluations, leaving you with a basically unevaluated data base. When corrections are made, careful records of the process of detection and correction should be kept and reported fully in any report of the research. Caution about making corrections to the data base is particularly important when the subgroup examined is not a random sample of the whole. Record comparisons are also "record linkage" (Willigan & Lynch 1972; Stephenson 1981) and literature on this topic should be consulted.

And finally, we can evaluate the quality of age data by a looser technique if we must. This technique involves comparing several independent methods of estimation of age of the same set of individuals, plotting the results of the various methods against each other, and calculating the mean and standard deviation (or other measures of the spread of the estimates) for the difference in estimated age by various techniques. Figure 3.3 shows an example of the comparisons of the ages of 142 !Kung San individuals, independently estimated by Edwin Wilmsen in 1974 and by me in 1968. Each point on the graph corresponds to a person, plotted as the intersection of the two age estimates. If Wilmsen and I had agreed perfectly on the year of birth of these people, all of the points would have fallen on the diagonal line. Instead, we see a pattern of general agreement within three years, a few disagreements as great as five years, and a pattern of disagreement such that Wilmsen estimated people to be several years younger than I did.

We will discuss the methods of estimation use by Wilmsen and myself in the next section of this chapter. Here we need only mention that one method might be an age calendar, plotted by asking people whether they were born before or after certain well-known and datable events. Another method might be guesses based upon appearance by a trained observer. Clearly this method is best for quite small populations, and is particularly useful in situations where there are no written records, although in principle there is no reason why written records could not provide one or both sources of information. In several studies of nonliterate peoples (Rose 1960; Howell 1979), rather laborious and indirect methods of estimating age from people who could provide no direct input turned out to be surprisingly robust and convincing, even though the method may involve a mean error of several years in either direction. Observations of illiterate societies over a period of time show that guesses of age are likely to be at least moderately accurate over most of the life span, and that aging is a fairly predictable and observable process. The most difficult period of time to guess ages is, of course, old age.

We will evaluate the plausibility of age estimates by unsystematic and opportunistic methods only if there are no alternatives.

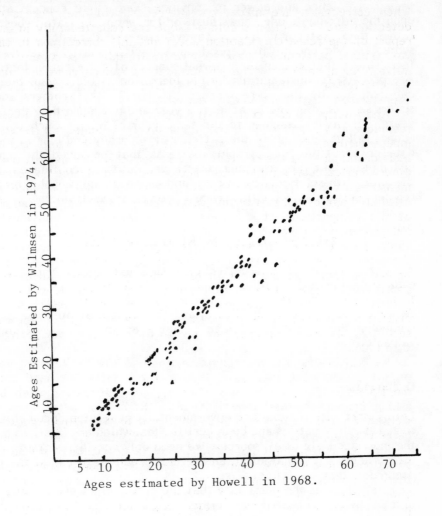

FIGURE 3.3   Comparison of Wilmsen's and Howell's estimates of the ages of 142 individuals at /ai/ai Botswana. Each point represents the intersection of independent estimates, made on the basis of appearance and place in the relative age order. The average difference is that Wilmsen puts them 2.19 years younger. The mean absolute difference is 2.29 years.

The reason for using such "quick and dirty" methods is, of course, their convenience and power to convince. One might concentrate upon the informants one knows best, or for whom the data is best, rather than systematically try to evaluate the data for all the subjects. And one might depend upon logical relations between facts rather than search for external support of the claimed facts. Are parents, for instance, uniformly identified as older than their children, and by the correct range of years? Are brothers and sisters separated in age by at least a year and not more than thirty years? Are twins assigned to the same year of birth? Such tests cannot tell us much about the patterns of accuracy and bias in the data or about the demographic patterns that produced the age distribution; but they can increase or decrease our confidence in the data, with relatively little cost, and hence should probably be a regular part of the evaluation process (Howell 1979:31-46).

THE PROCESS OF MAKING ESTIMATES

We are probably always better off using existing sources, and evaluating the bias in other people's methods of age estimation, than in depending entirely upon our own ability to guess ages. Hence documents, when available, and the opinion of other people (including the person whose age is being estimated) are always valuable.

Documents

Let us start with official and governmentally generated documents, such as birth registries and birth certificates, which are likely to be the most accurate of all sources. We need only note a few kinds of inaccuracies which may exist, and several problems of use of these documents that sometimes arise.

First, there is the possibility that the documents were produced in a sloppy or haphazard way, either consistently or from time to time. We can check upon this by starting with a relatively small number (say fifty) of well-known informants, and looking up the documentation on them, to see if they and the facts of their cases are identifiable in the records. If you can't find the entries for the people you know best, you have a minimal indication of the difficulty you would encounter with a larger and more randomly selected group.

The "fault" may not be in the integrity of the clerks and record-keepers, contemporary or at the time of the birth, but in the culture itself. The informants may have been named formally in one way, but may have come to use a somewhat different name over the years, as their identity was formed. Middle names often shift to first names, long names may be shortened, and names that were originally fond jokes may come to be accepted as real names. In some parts of the world, it is even likely that the last name may have several variant spellings, which may be changed between recording at birth and the present time (Weiss et al. 1980:41-62). In addition, civil records are usually recorded on a geographical basis, and it is often very difficult to scan a number of locales to find an informant. Between births and deaths and migrations, it is very common to find a turnover of population of one-third in ten years (Wylie 1960), even in extremely traditional and apparently stable communities.

It is often difficult to allocate the difficulties in finding the records of particular individuals to the categories such as (1) original problems of recording, (2) failure to identify the correct geographical jurisdiction, (3) name change, or (4) other sources of failure to recognize the correct certificate. Even in the case of living individuals who cannot be found in the records, however, it may be possible to place their births by identifying them as close in age to someone else in the population who can be found in the records.

A special problem arises in the interpretation of birth certificates for the very old, and that is the problem of positive identification of the individual with the correct certificate, as opposed to that of someone else in the family who may have the same name. Some of the apparently well documented cases of extreme old age have eventually been resolved by the discovery that a person who is genuinely old nevertheless has the documents of a parent or grandparent with the same name. This mistake is more likely to occur with the oldest members of the population, for whom there are no living contemporaries or elders who might notice and correct discrepancies (such as names of parents, or place in the birth order).

A second type of available documents is produced by churches, through baptismal records, marriages, burials, and so forth. Baptismal certificates are like birth certificates issued by civil authorities in that they provide a standard form for information on name, parents' names, place and date of birth, and so on. In a number of communities, they have proven wonderfully useful in producing a detailed picture of whole communities (Willigan & Lynch 1982). In general, church records are subject to the same kinds of potential sources of bias and error as governmental records, plus a couple more.

For one thing, church records tend to be kept by only one person at a time, and hence they are subject to greater variability than governmental records. When the priest or deacon charged with the responsibility is interested in the task and a methodical person, the records are likely to be very good, but if he is replaced by someone who cares little about it, the quality may deteriorate quickly and may make even the earlier records useless.

Church records also have the problem that it is not entirely clear how one becomes eligible or ineligible to be recorded. While all the residents of an area are supposed to be included in civil records, it is not so clear who is or is not a member of a church. This is particularly a problem if something about a birth or something about a family (like nonmarriage of the parents) violates church rules of conduct.

In both civil and church records, the period of delay between birth and registration may generate problems. In general, the shorter that delay typically is, the fewer problems of omission and error we expect to be creeping into the records. Where there are delays, we have to look carefully to assess whether infants who die at birth or prior to registration are being included. If they are not, our data base provides evidence on the age of those who survive to adulthood, but does not provide information that can be used on infant mortality rates, and hence also underestimates the fertility of the group.

Information from Informants

Another, and perhaps more convenient, form of data collection on age involves asking the subject or informant directly how old he/she is or when he/she was born. Where this is done in the form of a census, collected quickly by people who have no previous knowledge of the population, the quality of the data may be discouragingly low. Indeed, even where individuals are literate and have access to their own documents, this context is the source of the commonly observed patterns of age misreporting, discussed earlier. But where more time can be spent, where the data collectors know something about the population, and where they are willing to learn about the cultural concepts of numbers, perceptions of age, and the perception of the data collection process, the results may be far better (Caldwell & Caldwell 1976).

Naturally, one is suspicious about the quality of the data when the information is collected under military or authoritarian government auspices. The subjects of the study may have their own reasons for noncooperation with the survey. And one is naturally even more suspicious when there are rewards and punishments attached to certain kinds of responses, such as food ration cards, access to pensions, tax deductions, or the possibility of conscription to the military.

One is convinced of the accuracy of the data when one gets to know population members, when there is internal consistency between answers given by the same person at different times, or by different persons in answer to the same question. In addition, as discussed in the section on evaluation, you can compare the results of a survey of informants with documents, historical records, or earlier censuses or surveys.

Information from Physical Evidence

Finally, we should mention at least in passing the methods of age estimation that are appropriate when we can count upon neither documents nor the opinion of informants and observers. Physical anthropologists estimate ages of both living and deceased persons by examination of their teeth, the growing ends of bone, or by cellular examination of bone or teeth. These methods are a more rigorous version of the use we make of hair color, skin texture and wrinkles, and posture when we make guesses about people's age from their appearance.

Age estimation of skeletons is a fascinating problem (Meindl et al. 1981), and it offers the possibility of eventually being based upon sound understanding of the biological changes of tissues over the life span. But the estimates produced in this way will always and necessarily fail to allow for individual variance based upon different experiences, environments, diet, and genetic constitution that we can readily see in living populations of people who are known to be the same age. Skeletal estimates for which there are no additional sources of data will necessarily lose information on the variance as opposed to the central tendency of the aging process.

For living populations, of course, the same techniques of examination of bone and teeth can be used to supplement other information, when the methods are not too difficult or harmful to the subject. I cannot personally imagine the research project which would convince me that it was reasonable to X-ray living people, or to take samples of their bone or teeth, to estimate their age, as there are more accurate ways to obtain the same information by questionning.

SUMMARY AND APPLICATIONS TO THE OLDEST AGE GROUP

The methods that have been discussed in this chapter are based upon the applicaton of stable population theory for whole populations, in which any deviations from the assumptions of stable population theory--that the birth and death rates have been un-changing over the life span of living people, and that the population is closed to migration--are small and random in direction. An example of this approach can be seen in my study of the Dobe !Kung (Howell 1979), in which the ages of nonliterate peoples are estimated by age ranking and fitting stable-population-model curves to the living population. It must be admitted that this approach to age estimation tends to incorporate increasing sources of error as it is applied to older members of the population, for whom random sources of error can cancel out, but for whom systematic deviations from the assumptions of stable population theory accumulate. Old people present special problems of age estimation and evaluation.

One problem in gerontological studies is that the group of subjects may not be related to one another in a way that learning the age of one will help very much in learning the ages of others. If they only met in old age, they will not know which one is older, and they (and the analysts) are likely to mistake poor health and infirmity for older age. In such a case, all you can really do is increase the effort made to document ages by reference to certificates, family bibles, or other papers, on the one hand, or to substitute detailed knowledge of the events in individual's lives for the systematic information derived from a whole population.

In a literate society, you can probably always come quite close to an exact age even if the person in question is not literate, if you are willing to devote the time to the detective task. The method is simply talking about the events of the whole life, and the stage of life that the target person had reached at the time of those events. Since some of those events can be dated (even if not by your informant), you will soon have a framework of stated events and undated events that will tell you when your informant married, when his or her children were born, when various moves and migrations were made, and so on.

Frustratingly enough, the most difficult event to date in this way is precisely the one we want most, the date of birth. The reason it is so difficult, of course, is that no one remembers his or her own birth, and among old people you are not going to find observers of the events, such as the mother or older relatives, who remember and can provide datable details.

Even where there are surviving witnesses to the birth, some studies have found that dating births by reference to other events, the so-called event calendar method, may not be very reliable for births. Blacker (1967) reported for a Kenyan population, for instance, that witnesses may remember the datable event clearly (the example was a visit by Queen Victoria to the colonies) and may remember the birth, but since the two events have no relation to one another, they may not be able to report reliably on which happened first.

The date of birth may have to be estimated, finally, after much interviewing of the informant about the events of his or her life and the datable events that occurred around that time, by moving backward a set number of years to the earliest datable event in the subject's life that one can establish. The test of this kind of data collection, naturally, is the internal consistency of the results of the interviews, carried out over several visits and asking about a number of different topics. The positive aspect of this kind of data collection is that it is usually interesting and rewarding for both the informant and the investigator. An enormous amount of additional information about the life and ideas and attitudes of the informants will necessarily be revealed in the process. It is, in effect, old-fashioned fieldwork, and anthropologists don't need to be taught to do it, but only to remember to keep pressing for the externally datable events along the way. The negative side of this kind of data collection is that it is enormously time consuming, and there is no guarantee that the informant will eventually produce an internally consistent and plausible event outline and schedule.

Probably no investigator has the patience to collect this kind of data from more than a hundred or so informants, and thirty or forty would probably be a more reasonable goal if the investigator cannot count upon documents to supplement the investigation. The age data produced for such a small number of informants would not be useful for complicated statistical analyses, but may be invaluable for case studies.

I hope that this review of techniques has convinced investigators that age determinations frequently deserve a considerable investment of time and energy from the investigator, and that the method of age determination should always be questioned by the reader before accepting an otherwise surprising result. On the other hand, I hope that the listing of problems that may be encountered is not so formidable that investigators decide to give up before starting on this complex task. There are almost always some resources--documents, opinions, or assertions--that can be used as raw materials for constructing age estimates, and investigators who have put their mind to it have frequently found that different resources can be found to serve as a basis for an independent evaluation of those age estimates.

BIBLIOGRAPHY

Biesele, M., and N. Howell. 1981. "The Old People Give You Life": Aging among !Kung Hunter-Gatherers." In Other Ways of Growing Old, eds. P. Amoss and S. Harrell. Stanford, Calif: Stanford University Press.

Blacker, J.G.C. 1967. "Use of Sample Surveys to Obtain Data on Age Structure of the Population Where Respondents Cannot Give Accurate Data: Some Kenyan Experiments." In World Population Conference, 1965, 3:126-30.

_____. 1971. "Some Unsolved Problems of Census and Demographic Survey Work in Africa." In International Population Conference, London, 1969, 1:277-85. Liege: International Union for the Scientific Study of Population.

Brass, W. 1971. "On the Scale of Mortality." In Biological Aspects of Demography, ed. W. Brass. New York: Barnes & Noble.

Caldwell, J., and A. A. Igun. 1971. "An Experiment with Census-Type Age Enumeration in Nigeria." Population Studies 25:287-302.

Caldwell, J. C. 1976. Toward an Understanding of Contemporary Demographic Change: A Report on Semi-structured Interviews. Australian Family Formation Project, Monograph No. 4. Canberra: Australian National University.

Cho, L. J. 1971. "Korea: Estimating Current Fertility from the 1966 Census." Studies in Family Planning 2:74-78.

Coale, A. J., and P. Demeny. 1967. Regional Model Life Tables and Stable Populations. Princeton, N. J.: Princeton University Press.

Dyke, B., and W. T. Morrill. 1979. Genealogical Demography. New York: Academic Press.

Hill, K., H. Zlotnik, and J. Durch. 1982. Procedures for Reducing the Effects of Age Errors on Indirect Demographic Estimation Techniques. Laboratory for Population Statistics, Scientific Report Series No. 35. Chapel Hill: University of North Carolina.

Howell, N. 1979. The Demography of the Dobe !Kung. New York: Academic Press.

Lee, R. D. 1979. "Methods and Models for Analyzing Historical Series of Births, Deaths and Marriages." In Population Patterns in the Past, ed. R. D. Lee. New York: Academic Press.

Meindl, R. S., C. O. Lovejoy, and R. P. Mensforth. 1981. "Skeletal Age at Death: Accuracy of Determination and Implications for Human Demography." Paper presented at the meetings of the American Association of Physical Anthropology, Detroit.

Murphy, E. A. 1978. "Genetics of Longevity in Man." In The Genetics of Aging, ed. E. Schneider. New York: Plenum.

Pfeiffer, S. 1980. "Age Changes in the External Dimensions of Adult Bone." American Journal of Physical Anthropology 52:529-32.

Pollard, A. H., and G. W. Pollard. 1981. "The Demography of Aging in Australia." In Toward Older Australia: Readings in Social Gerontology, ed. A. L. Howell. Queensland, Australia: University of Queensland Press, pp. 13-43.

Rose, F. G. G. 1960. Classification of Kin, Age Structure, and Marriage among the Groote Eylandt Aborigines. New York: Akademie-Verlag and Pergamon.

Saw, Swee-Hock. 1967. "Errors in Chinese Age Statistics." Demography 4:859-75.

Scott, C., and G. Sabagh. 1970. "The Historical Calendar as a Method of Estimating Age: The Experience of the Moroccan Multi-Purpose Sample Survey of 1961-63." Population Studies 24:93-109.

Seltzer, W. 1973. Demographic Data Collection: A Summary of Experience. Occasional Paper. New York: Population Council.

Shryoke, H. S., Jr., and J. Seigel. 1971. Methods and Materials of Demography. Washington, D.C.: U.S. Bureau of the Census.

Skolnick, M., et al. 1979. "A Computerized Family History Data Base System." Sociology and Social Research: 63:506-523.

Stephenson, C. 1981. "The Methodology of Historical Census Record Linkage." Journal of Family History 5:112-15.

Stockwell, E. G. 1966. "Patterns of Digit Preference and Avoidance in the Age Statistics of Some Recent National Censuses: A Test of the Turner Hypothesis." Eugenics Quarterly 13:205-8.

Thatcher, A. R. 1981. "Centenarians." Population Trends (London) 25:11-14.

United Nations. 1967. Manual IV: Methods of Estimating Basic Demographics Measures from Incomplete Data. Department of Economics and Social Affairs, Population Studies No. 42. New York: UN.

van de Walle, E. 1968. "Characteristics of African Demographic Data." In The Demography of Tropical Africa, ed. W. Brass et al. Princeton, N. J.: Princeton University Press.

Voros, A. W., and D. Metselaar. 1958. "The Reliability of Dental Age as a Yardstick to Assess the Unknown Calendar Age." Tropical and Geographical Medicine 10:175-80.

Wachter, K. W. 1978. Studies of Historical Social Structure. New York: Academic Press.

Weiss, K. M., et al. 1980. "Wherefore Art Thou, Romio?": Name Frequency and Their Use in Automated Genealogy Assembly." In Genealogical Demography, ed. B. Dyke and W. T. Morrill. New York: Academic Press.

Wiligan, J. D., and K. A. Lynch. 1982. Sources and Methods of Historical Demography. New York: Academic Press.

Wilmsen, E. N. 1979. Diet and Fertility among Kalahari Bushmen. African Studies Center Working Papers, 14. Boston: Boston University.

Wylie, L. 1960. Village in the Vaucluse. New York: Harper.

You Pok Seng. 1959. "Errors in Age Reporting in Statistically Underdeveloped Countries." Population Studies 13:164-82.

4
Historical Demographic Methods of Life-Course Study

DAVID I. KERTZER
Department of Sociology &
Anthropology
Bowdoin College

ANDREA SCHIAFFINO
Department of Sociology
University of Bologna

Among the new frontiers in the study of age are the systematic use of a life-course approach and the use of demographic sources to place aging in historical perspective. Both of these developments are notable for their unusually interdisciplinary nature; they are the product of converging strands of work conducted by a wide variety of social scientists, ranging from demographers and sociologists to historians and anthropologists. This chapter deals with the methodological intersection of these two frontiers, the application of a life-course perspective to historical demographic materials, and the use of historical demography for life-course research. We argue that the methods that have been developing in this sector will greatly enrich anthropological research on age. Moreover, it is our belief that anthropologists have much to offer in the development of historical demographic methods of life-course study, and we would like to provide some indication of the nature of this contribution.

LIFE-COURSE PERSPECTIVES

Over the past two decades, a growing number of sociologists and psychologists interested in the study of age have embraced what has come to be known as a life-course or life-span perspective (Riley, Johnson & Foner 1972; Elder 1975; Baltes, Reese & Lipset 1980). Instead of compartmentalizing analyses of various age groupings (e.g., adolescents, the elderly), these scholars have attempted to place the entire life course in a common analytical framework, studying age-related norms and behaviors as a system of interrelated parts. Only very recently have anthropologists begun to explore the analytical possibilities afforded by this approach, though there is reason to believe that its use will increase sharply in the next few years (Keith & Kertzer 1984).

In the life-course view, aging is a life long process conditioned by biological, psychological, social and cultural factors. Patterns of aging change over time as the society changes, and different patterns of aging are found within the same society at the same time as a result of social differentiation. Of special importance in operationalizing life-course research are "life events," which may be defined as noteworthy occurrences in an individual's life, such as marriage, entering the labor force, and/or having children, going to war, and death (Hultsch & Plemons 1979). Life events and their temporal relationships are among the primary objects of examination in life course study. The study of life events also has a cultural dimension, for each society has norms regarding age-appropriate transitions and behavior, which provide social sanctions for those who do not follow the proper cultural life script (Neugarten, Moore & Lowe 1965). Closely tied to this, of course, is the behavioral dimension, involving the actual sequence and timing of events in an individual's life.

The cohort is a central tool of life-course analysis. A cohort refers to a set of people who are either born in the same specified period (e.g., one year or one decade) or who experience a life event in such a period (e.g., all those who married in a specific five-year period). The more the society is changing, the greater we would expect the differences to be in the life-course patterns followed by different cohorts. The effect of particular historical changes (e.g., industrialization, or a war) on the lives of people in a society can be studied by comparing cohorts in this way. People at different stages of their life course at the time such events occur may be hypothesized to be affected differently by these events. Life-course cohort analysis permits us to determine just what these effects may be and how they come about.

HISTORICAL DEMOGRAPHY, ANTHROPOLOGY, AND THE STUDY OF AGE

One of the most important developments in the social study of age and aging in recent years has been the increasing sensitivity to the historical dimension. This parallels a growing recognition among anthropologists and sociologists that societal processes can only be understood if the historical time dimension is taken into account. Analysis of why social patterns and cultural norms are the way they are cannot be complete without an appreciation of the range of societal differences, both historically and cross-culturally. Needless to say, the mechanisms of social change can only be elucidated through historical study.

There are a variety of sources of historical data related to age and the life course, including diaries, court records, wills, letters, governmental surveys, and the records of various institutions (from orphanages to poor houses). In addition, for recent history, oral historical accounts may be employed. Historical demographic sources complement these other sources and offer a number of advantages not found elsewhere. For the anthropologist, especially, the fact that demographic sources refer to the entire population rather than to merely one portion of it is a great advantage. Diaries and most other written records provide us only with the view of the literate elite, but vital registers, censuses, and population registers give us access to the lives of the illiterate masses. The information commonly recorded in such documents includes many of the most important life events: birth, marriage, motherhood/fatherhood, migration, death. Moreover, some of these sources allow us to see the changing domestic context in which people lived: when did the individual leave the parental household? In what circumstances did newlyweds go to live with the parents of the bride or the groom? Did men and women take up residence with a married child when their own spouse died? If so, which child? And which individuals were most likely to remarry?

Not all historical demographic sources permit us to address such life-course questions directly, for we must be able to follow individuals through time in order to do so. Methods for such life-course study through the use of historical demographic sources are still in early development. In the remainder of this chapter we examine the most commonly used sources in historical demography and discuss some methodological issues involved in employing them for life-course study. Specific techniques developed by the authors in an Italian historical demographic study are briefly described as an example of the operationalization of a life-course perpective and the kinds of contributions anthopologists can make.

MAJOR SOURCES FOR HISTORICAL DEMOGRAPHIC
LIFE COURSE STUDY

Studies of the nature of the life course of individuals in the past and the impact of historical change on these life-course paths can make use of a variety of sources. Some of these are classic archival documents, the only ones used by most historical demographers, while others may be especially valuable where documentary materials are lacking, or where longitudinal study is impossible with available archival sources. Here we have in mind oral historical methods. Of course, insofar as the oral historical approach is used--here in the form of retrospective life histories--only the most proximate historical past is accessible. Moreover, people's memories are selective, incomplete, and often biased. Thus, where there is a possibility of using archival sources, these offer the great advantage of providing a longer historical period, allowing us to better understand social change and the life course.

The major sources of historical demographic data are population enumerations (censuses), vital registrations, and population registers. In addition, a wide variety of other documentary sources have been employed, from wills to tax lists. However, these are generally of ancillary use. Thus we begin by looking briefly at three primary data sources and their uses for life course study.

CENSUSES

Censuses, perhaps the best-known source of demographic data, have a number of advantages in research. Indeed, the census has been a standard part of anthropological fieldwork since fieldwork began. It enumerates all individuals living in a delimited area at a particular time; it indicates the household groupings in which they live; and it provides a variety of demographic and social information about each person. However, while such censuses are important, they do not directly permit life-course study. This is not to say that many social scientists have not attempted to generalize about life-course experiences in a society on the basis of a single census. Indeed, this has often been done by dividing the population into age groups (cohorts) and assuming that all cohorts experience events in a given age range in the same way that those currently in that age range do.

As an illustration of this method and its fallacies, let us look at the data in Table 4.1 from a hypothetical census, taken in 1900. What can we say about the life course from such census-based data? The temptation is to interpret these cross-sectional age-related differences as life-course differences. For example, we might claim that the experience of any of the cohorts represented here--let us say that of those born in the late 1840s and aged 50-54 in 1900--is pictured by the age-group percentages represented in the table. Thus, by the time these people were in their early twenties (in the 1870s), 80 percent were living with at least one parent and only 20 percent were married. Ten years later, when they were in their early thirties, 20 percent were living with at least one parent and 75 percent were married. But, in fact, there is no basis for making such life-course generalizations on the basis of cross-sectional data. The experience of any given cohort is the product of the interaction of a variety of factors--not only cultural, but also economic, demographic, and political--and these factors change over time. Since different cohorts pass through this historical time at a different point in their life course, we may expect them to show life-course differences. While 50 percent of the 25 to 29-year-olds in 1900 were living with at least one parent, we cannot know whether 0 percent or 100 percent of the 50 to 54-year-olds had been living with a parent back in the 1870s, when they were that age. It should be stressed that this problem does not simply pertain to historical materials, but to censuses conducted by anthropologists in the course of their own contemporary research. Life-course material cannot be extrapolated from single cross-sectional distributions.

Attempts have been made to circumvent this problem by using a series of censuses, and following actual cohorts through time. Thus, for example, if censuses are taken every ten years, we can examine the life-course pattern of those born in the 1850s by comparing those aged 0-9 in 1860 with those aged 10-19 in 1870, 20-29 in 1880, etc. Table 4.2 may be produced through this method. Here we see the dimension added to the single, 1900 census data by use of a series of censuses. The cross-sectional data for 1900 are represented by the indicated column, which shows a fairly high proportion of married males among those under 20, with a gradual increase in proportion married leading up to 100 percent of the male population married by age 40. Yet this was not the experience of any of the cohorts actually living in 1900. Those in the oldest cohort shown, aged 10-19 in 1870, had experienced no marriages before age 20. Moreover, 90 percent of them had been married in 1890 when in their thirties, compared to just 60 percent of those in that age range in 1900. As for the youngest cohort represented in 1900, while they had a high rate of marriage under age 20, a large proportion of them (20 percent) were still unmarried in 1930, when they were in their forties

The use of successive censuses is far preferable to use of a single census in drawing conclusions about the life course and changes in life course patterns over time. However, it has some serious limits. First of all, it enables us only to look at aggregate changes in cohorts, and not at the relationship between events in the lives of individuals. For example, we could determine the proportion of those aged 15-19 who had left the parental home and the proportion of this age group who were employed, but we could not determine the temporal relationship between these events. A related problem is that, when we compare cohorts, similar aggregate life-course patterns may obscure important individual differences. To illustrate this point, let us take the question of income changes through the life course. If we found that income level was unchanged between ages 30 and 40 for two different cohorts, could we say that they had the same life-course experience as far as income is concerned? The answer is no. This is because, for example, everyone in one cohort might have maintained the same income over the ten-year period of the life course, while in the other cohort all individuals experienced major changes in income, but these evened out in the aggregate (Riley, Johnson & Foner 1972:47).

An additional problem in using successive censuses is known as the "compositional fallacy," and is found where "changes in the kinds of people composing the cohorts are erroneously attributed to processes of individual aging or of cohort flow" (Riley 1973:44). If we trace the experience of a cohort over time, using the method of successive censuses (or surveys), the aggregate changes found cannot be simply attributed to changes in people's lives at all. It may be that the people found in the cohort at a later point in time are not representative of the people in that same cohort at any earlier point in time. There are two primary forces responsible for these compositional changes: mortality and migration. If mortality or migration operates selectively for a given variable, changes in the value of that variable across time may simply be a function of the changed composition of the population under study. For example, if those with greater formal education tend to live longer, we might find that cohorts show significant increases in formal schooling as they age from 60 to 70 and from 70 to 80 years. Such changes would not necessarily reflect any additional schooling for any member of the cohort.

In short, if our interest is in tracing life course processes, a single census is of very little use and a succession of censuses, while of some utility, has substantial limits. Where the possibility of gathering longitudinal data exists, following individuals through time offers a great many analytical advantages.

VITAL REGISTRATION RECORDS

Over the past quarter century, scholars have hailed a revolution in historical demography, a revolution occasioned by the development of studies based on the nominal linkage of vital registration records. The "family-reconstitution" method, as it came to be called, was pioneered in France, and most of the studies resulting from it have been conducted there. However, the method has been picked up by historians throughout much of Western Europe, and these scholars have now produced a large body of findings (Flinn 1981).

In essence, the family-reconstitution method focuses on a particular parish or group of adjacent parishes in which a lengthy series of birth, marriage, and death records is found. It has been used primarily as a means of studying the history of marriage and fertility. For each marriage record, for example, the names of the people being wed are checked against the birth records of an earlier period to determine the ages of the man and woman at marriage. By then checking all subsequent birth records (which give parental information), the fertility history of the marriage is documented. The death records are checked through time to determine the date of dissolution of marriage. The period of widowhood following such a death, and the nature and extent of remarriage, can then also be studied by linking the records of the new widow or widower against subsequent marriage, birth, and death records.

The French family-reconstitution method brought nominal linkage into the mainstream of historical demography, a field that had previously relied almost entirely on aggregate data (e.g., number of deaths in a locality per year). As such, it offered the possibility of a life-course approach in historical demographic study, with individuals being followed from birth to death. Though thus far largely employed in studies of fertility, the reconstitution method is suited for studies of aspects of life more commonly associated with old age as well. The fate of widows and widowers, and how their position changed through time and differed across space, for example, can be approached through the reconstitution method. The relationship between people's marital experience and fertility history on the one hand and their mortality on the other can also be investigated, though thus far this has rarely if ever been studied.

The techniques that have been invented for doing family reconstitution--usable in any society which has running birth, marriage, and death registers--have been described in detail by Fleury and Henry (1965) and, in English, by Wrigley (1966). We will not go into them here, but we would like to point out a few limitations of this approach.

Many of the problems with the reconstitution approach affect all life-course research in historical demography.[1] First of all, in order to follow individuals through time, records must be of excellent quality and be complete, criteria that are generally met less and less often the further back in history one goes. Following the lives of individuals is also much more expensive and time-consuming than employing aggregate data. Scores of communities can be studied using aggregate data for everyone studied using nominal linkage. Problems of alternative spelling from record to record, particularly in societies having a high rate of illiteracy, often make linkage a frustrating and difficult task.

Another problem common to such historical life-course studies is occasioned by geographical mobility. The crux of the problem is that while vital registration records are based on locality, people's lives are not. People move from place to place through their lives with little regard for the difficulties they inflict on historical demographers by moving from one registration jurisdiction to another. In the classic French case, where a single parish's records are studied, this means that we can follow the marital history of only those individuals who remained in the same parish throughout their marriage. Indeed, the situation is even worse, for since marriages take place in the parish of the bride, the man who marries a woman of another parish will not have his marriage recorded in the records of his own parish, even though he lives in that parish continuously from birth to death. For these reasons, in reconstitution studies only a minority of the population has their entire life course, or even their marital life course, recorded. More important, there is no reason to believe that this minority is representative of the whole population. Generally speaking, the larger the geographical area examined, the higher the proportion of lives the researcher is able to follow, for people can be traced as they pass from one parish to the next. For this reason, a number of such geographically broader reconstitution studies have been initiated in recent years.

The anthropologist interested in tracing the changes that have occurred in the life-course patterns of a population should consider the possibility of using vital registration records for a reconstitution study. However, before this is attempted, the following points must be investigated:

1. Complete birth, marriage, and death records are needed for the entire historical period of interest. The gap of even a year can create some difficulties, and several gaps would make the research virtually impossible.

2. The records must be of sufficient quality to allow for nominal

linkage. Of related importance are cultural norms regarding naming. Where many people have the same name, or where parent and child commonly have the same name, determining unambiguously who is being referred to in each record entry may be difficult.

3. The geographical area covered by the registration must be compared with the social geography of the people to determine the extent to which people moved into and out of the registration area. Where the lives of only a minority of the population can be followed, the representativeness of that minority must be weighed. It may not be worth the expenditure of time and funds to detail life-course patterns of a small and unrepresentative minority of the population of the past.

POPULATION REGISTERS

In a number of European countries, there has been a registration system going back over a hundred years that has followed the population continually through time. Known as population registers, this documentation is based at the commune level and keeps track of all local residents as they move from house to house and from commune to commune, and as they experience birth, marriage, fertility, and death. Countries that had such systems by the mid-nineteenth century include Belgium, Holland, Italy, and parts of Germany. A similar but religiously based system is found in Sweden and Finland, going back to 1686 (Kalvemark 1979). Japanese household registers, extending from 1665 to 1868, provide somewhat comparable data (Smith 1978).

Although these registers provide a massive amount of information about the lives of people in the past, they have to date been used rather infrequently for social historical studies. We believe that they are potentially outstanding sources for life-course patterns in the societies in which they are found. A well-kept population register obviates most of the painstaking work needed in family reconstitution, as demographic information on the same individual--for the length of the individual's residence in a locality--is already linked together in the individual's population register entry. Moreover, as the European population registers commonly exchanged information among communes in the case of individuals living in one commune who experienced an event in another, one of the major sources of incomplete information in family-reconstitution studies is minimized. Thus, when a woman of commune A went to have her baby in commune B, where her mother lived, commune B sent a copy of the birth registration to commune A. Similarly, when a man of commune C married a woman of commune D in that commune, commune D sent a copy of the wedding registration to commune C. Death and migration were also commonly dealt with in this way. Of particular importance also is the fact that the population registers trace not only people's demographic behavior, but also their coresidential behavior, that is, whom they lived with continuously through their lives. For anthropologists, this makes these records much richer than vital registration material, for they permit direct inquiry into domestic group processes.

Each country's population register is organized differently; however, for illustrative purposes we briefly describe the population register found in Italy.[2] The Italian population register was begun, particularly in the north, in 1865, upon the founding of the Italian nation, and it continues today. Every individual must register with the commune into which he or she moves, and a copy of this registration is sent by the commune of destination to the person's commune of emigration. For each individual, then, we have date of entry into the commune and an indication of the commune from which the individual came; similarly, we have date of exit from the commune and the commune of destination. All births, deaths, and marriages involving commune residents also must be registered with the communal officials. If such an event takes place outside the commune of residence, a copy of the communal registry is sent by the commune in which the event occurred to the commune of residence.

The communal population register is composed of two primary parts, a household booklet and an individual form. Each administratively identified household has a sheet listing household members at the time the household first appears in the commune, and this list is continuously updated as new individuals enter and as household residents depart. The name of the household head is indicated, with dated changes, and a variety of genealogical, demographic, and occupational information on each resident is included.[3] In addition, each resident of the commune has an individual form found in the population register, containing all personal information found in the household registers, and containing dated cross-references to the local households in the registry in which the individual is found. Each commune also has birth, marriage, and death registers, but these entries are routinely transcribed into the population register forms of the commune's residents, and thus for most purposes the task of "reconstitution" has already been done by the communal officials.

One limitation that studies based on population registers share with family-reconstitution studies is that, where migration rates are high, only an unrepresentative minority of the population may be followed from birth to death. However, unlike research based on vital records, population registers point the researcher to the location of successive portions of the life course of emigrants. For each emigrant the commune of destination is listed, and the researcher may go to that communal archive to pick up the course of the individual's life; if necessary, the individual may then be followed through successive moves. Since the individual portion of the population register is indexed or arranged alphabetically, such checking is feasible. Needless to say, however, the more scattered the migration among different communes, the more time-consuming the research becomes. Moreover, not all communes have kept their nineteenth-century records in an orderly fashion, and in some cases portions of the documentation have been destroyed. Thus, the practicability of such tracing of the life course of migrants must be evaluated according to the local archival circumstances.

DEVISING A RECORD SYSTEM FOR HISTORICAL LIFE COURSE DATA

In order to conduct true life-course study, it is necessary to have data sources that record the exact dates of life events, whether these sources be vital registrations, population registers, or retrospective oral histories. Moreover, as people are born at different times, live different lengths of time, and experience different events in different orders and at different points in their lives, the convenient formats for data input used in cross-sectional studies cannot be employed. We think it would be useful here to describe the system of record organization and data management that we have devised in our study of the impact of industrialization on the life course in the area of Casalecchio, near the city of Bologna (1865-1921).[4]   While this study is based on the Italian population register, it utilizes data from a variety of sources, and, in general, the approach is adaptable for use with other sources of historical life course data.

Where different data sources are employed, covering the same population, one of the fundamental methodological challenges is to make sure we know when two references refer to the same individual and when they refer to different individuals. We will not go here into this problem, other than to note that there is now a substantial literature on the use of computer linkage for this purpose (Dyke & Morrill 1980). Such nominal linkage, whether done electronically or manually, involves not only comparing the names of individuals, but also other identifying information, such as names of father and mother, birthdate, and birthplace. Thus, identifying data consist of those items that do not change through the individual's life. Insofar as two individuals have the same name, or, conversely, the same individual is listed under different spellings of the same name in different records, the problem of determining which records refer to which individuals can become difficult.

We assign each individual a unique identification number. All input records relating to that individual are provided with that number, which is the basis on which different records pertaining to the same individual may later be linked. Identification numbers, for anthropological purposes, should also be assigned to both father and mother of each individual in the study, whether or not these parents ever fall directly into the study population. If, for example, a single commune is under study, it may be that the individual's parents never lived in that commune. However, by identifying parents and providing them with unique identification numbers, we are later able to trace genealogical relations through the population. For instance, if we know that two men, living in different households, had the same parents, we know that they are brothers. In our record-keeping system, all individual records pertain to a resident individual, whose identification number is always found in columns 3-8 of that record. Every individual who ever lived in the commune during the period under study thus has a series of such records. Other individuals, who never lived in the commune during the period, may be assigned identification numbers insofar as we need to enter them on one of the data records of a commune resident (as in the case of the nonresident mother or father described above). Such individuals, dubbed "phantoms," do not have any of their own record forms, and thus their identification number never appears in columns 3-8 of a data record form.

In the Casalecchio study, a number of data input forms are used. Five of these--the basic identifying record, the coresidential record, the household address record, and the household head record--are derived primarily from data found in the population register. The marriage record form is based on two sources: the civil marriage register and parish marriage registers. A separate form is used for each manuscript census existing for the period of study. Separate forms are also used for a variety of different annual tax records, for annual school attendance records, and for annual conscription lists. Each individual who ever lived in Casalecchio during the study period has to have at least three records: the basic identification record (01), a migration record (02), and a coresidential record (04). If the person was never present in the commune during a census, no manuscript census record would be compiled. Similarly, if the individual never married while a resident, no marriage form would be compiled.

For all forms referring to individual records, a similar format is followed, in which the first two columns of the record specify the kind of record in question (01, 02, etc.), and the following six columns provide the individual's identification number.

It is worth stressing that this system has been devised to be *independent* of any single locality. The residence of any individual at any point in his or her life course is not assumed by the system, but is indicated in form 02, which provides dates of entry to and exit from the specified commune. Insofar as a study is simply based on data from a single locality, this means that we may only be following a portion of the life course of any individual, a portion specified in form 02, used in conjunction with data on dates of birth and death (if occurring while the individual is a resident) found in form 01. In the case of individuals who leave that locality and later return, we would have two forms 02 for the same individual, each specifying a period of residence.

It is one of the basic characteristics of this system that, insofar as the record forms deal with life-course events that are repeatable, the forms themselves are repeatable for the same individual. Other than form 01, which provides the basic identifying information on the individual, the same individual may have more than one record form for most of the other records. An individual who reimmigrates, for example, will have at least two migration forms (02) compiled. An individual who marries more than once has at least two marriage forms (03) compiled. An individual who changes household, similarly, has at least two coresidence forms (04) compiled. Being censused may itself be conceived as an event that is repeatable from an individual's point of view. The repeatability of records is crucial to life-course study, for life-course events are themselves repeatable, and different individuals experience different numbers of recurrences of various events.

The repetition of marriage in Italy in this period is a widespread phenomenon linked to the fact that there was a lack of reciprocal recognition between the church and the state regarding marriages. Thus, it was common practice for individuals to be first married in church and later to have the marriage civilly legitimated by marrying in town hall. A code indicates for each form 03 which type of marriage is involved.

As is especially evident in forms 02 (migration) and 04 (coresidence), in recording a *variable* number of repetitions of the same event for each individual, depending on the "eventfulness" of the individual's life during the period of study, it is crucial that a date be provided for each such event. Some individuals' records, such as those stillborn, will be very limited, while others will have scores of variables entered.

Coresidence

One of the major goals of the Casalecchio project is to place people's coresidential experience in life-course perspective. This involves tracing their changes in household arrangements from their birth to their death, or through the lesser portion of the life course in which they come under study. In doing this, we are interested in the influence that various life events and changing historical circumstances have on coresidential choices and the impact that coresidential circumstances have on behavior, especially on fertility, marriage, and migration.

The system of record organization just described permits us to follow the coresidential life course, rather than being bound to larger household units, which often obscure the life-course experiences of individuals (Schiaffino 1981a; Kertzer & Schiaffino 1983). The system we have created for this purpose can be used by anyone with access to sources providing dated changes in household of residence for all individuals in a given population. The population register is one such source, but retrospective life-history data could be used in some cases, if the defects of memory and the problem of differential survivorship are taken into account.

For purposes of population register recording, the authorities divided the population into household units, each with an indicated head. The household form kept by the commune was designed to list dates of entry and exit of every person who ever lived in that household. Using these forms, we created record input form 04, which, for each individual, gives date of entry into each household in which he or she lived, along with the identifying number of the household in question. For each household in which the individual lived during the period of his or her life under observation, one 04 form is compiled. By later comparing these household entry dates with the dates of residence in each commune under observation (form 02), the full dated succession of households in which the individual lived is created.

Of course, this information by itself is of little use. We want to know changes in the coresidential situation of each individual through the life course, and this can only be known by identifying the others with whom an individual lived at any point in time and how this changed in relation to various events. The household identification numbers used in form 04 permit us to do this, for used together with the dates of residence in each household, these allow us to determine who else was living with any individual at the time that person came under observation (e.g., at birth), and changes in the individual's coresidents (even within the same numbered household) through the life course until the end of observation (e.g., at death). This is simply a matter of determining all those having the same household identification number (form 04) through time.

Thus far we have been discussing only record forms based on individuals, but we use two input forms based on the administratively defined households referred to earlier. These are compiled by using the household forms of the population register. One input form (90) simply provides a dated series of addresses within the commune at which the household was found, thus providing data on intracommunal movements and enabling us to pinpoint exactly where any individual lived at any point in time. Another input form (91) gives the dated succession of household heads. Using genealogical and marriage data from the individual records, we have written a genealogical tracing program that enables us to follow changes in the relationship of any individual to his or her household head through the individual's life course.[6]

The key to creating an anthropologically informed method of kinship and coresidential analysis is to retain all possible genealogical detail in entering data into the file. For example, the use of such coding categories as aunt, uncle, or grandfather--found commonly enough in historical research--should be avoided wherever the sources permit greater detail. The distinction between paternal or maternal grandparents, for example, may be crucial to understanding postmarital residence patterns. Where names of the father, mother, and spouse of every individual can be found, these must all be utilized in the data file (and these kinsmen should be provided with identification numbers). With such information for all individuals in the file, it is a relatively simple matter to trace kinship relations between any two individuals in the population, or to trace the kin relations of all people living in the same household. It is also possible in this way to identify all individuals who fall in a specified category of kin relationship with any specified individual. We can thus ask such questions as the extent to which people had kinsmen living in the same community and what kinds of kinsmen they were.

ANALYZING LIFE COURSE DATA

Although the overwhelming use of cross-sectional data in social-scientific research is in part due to the greater availability of such data compared to longitudinal sources, part of the reason for this one-sidedness is the scarcity of methods for longitudinal data analysis. Methods for analysis of cross-sectional data have been highly developed, and such data are easily used in conjunction with canned statistical programs. But discussions of how to analyze continuous life-course data are rare indeed, and only a few anthropologists, sociologists, and demographers have attempted such work. Yet if life-course research is to make progress, such methods must be devised and developed. In this section we discuss some ways in which this may be done.

The first problem with life-course data is finding a method for storing it in computer files, a method that allows efficiency of access to the parts of the data that are needed for any subsequent analysis. This raises some rather technical issues which are beyond the scope of this chapter, but one or two points should be made here.[7] In cross-sectional studies, data can be organized in a file by individual, with each individual entry having a specified series of variables, and with each variable occupying a particular column (or columns). In the most common case, the length of all individuals' data records is the same (though certain variables may be left blank), and access to data is simply accomplished by specifying the columns in which the variables in question are to be found.

This storage system is not useful for life-course data because some lives have more events than others, and many events may be repeatable. Moreover, unlike cross-sectional data bases, in longitudinal research there is the additional factor that different, limited portions of an individual's life may come under observation, with people entering and exiting from observation continuously over time. To create a fixed format computer file comparable to that described for cross-sectional data, one would have to determine the maximum number of occurrences of each event that happened to any individual in the study, allowing that many columns for the repetition of the event in every individual's record. This would make the size of the data file staggeringly large, with the great bulk of the file blank.

One solution to this problem is to have a record input format, such as the one developed for Casalecchio, that provides a separate form for each repeatable event (e.g., migration), with the form itself repeatable. The records for each individual in the data base are variable in number, ranging from 0 entries for some (e.g., a census in which the individual was not found, or no 03 form if the individual never married while a resident), to many entries for others (e.g., an individual who married three times, or who re-immigrated several times). For each individual, a directory file entry is provided, indicating for that individual how many records of each type are in the data base. Using this directory, any variable for that individual can be retrieved.

Longitudinal analysis is greatly facilitated if the data can be transformed into a format suitable for use with standard statistical programs. This means transforming the variable length, variable record material in the data file into fixed format output for analysis. This is the primary responsibility of the retrieval system. The retrieval system is used to look for individual cases that satisfy the designated criteria; it then reads the relevant variables into a fixed format output file. This means that to create any file the analyst must specify the variable of interest, the date or dates to be used in identifying the value of that variable, and the characteristics of the individuals for whom such data are sought. For example, we could set up an output file by selecting all women who were ever widowed and, for each such individual, reading into the output file her date of birth, date of widowhood, date of remarriage (if any), and date of death or emigration. This would, for example, enable us to study remarriage patterns among women.

One of the key dimensions of life-course study is duration, the time spent in a given state between two specified events. The retrieval system must be able to compute durations based on such indicated events, and to place these as single variables in fixed format output files for analysis. The computation of duration is facilitated by first converting all calendar dates in the basic file into integer dates, based on days or months. The first number, 00001, represents the first day or month which could possibly occur anywhere in the data set (e.g., the birth date of the oldest individual living at the beginning of the study period). If we were using days as our unit and 00001 were used for January 1, 1750, then January 2, 1750 would be transformed to 00002, and so on.

Once this dating system is adopted, the computation of durations is simply a matter of subtracting the value of one variable from the value of another. For example, if we want to create a variable for duration of marriages, we can identify which of each pair of spouses died first and subtract the integer date of the wedding from the integer date of the death. In studying migration we could create a fixed format file that contains a variable specifying duration of residence in the commune for each emigrant. This variable is computed by subtracting date of entrance into the commune from date of exit. As emigration and immigration are repeatable, a single individual may have more than one such duration of residence.

Given this method of life-course data storage and retrieval, a wide variety of simple statistical procedures may be used for analysis. It should be noted that the data management system is used not only to retrieve values of variables that are in the original data files, but also to create new variables by relating the variables found in the file. One example of this, of course, is duration. Another is the creation of fertility histories for women by using the mother's identification number found in every individual's basic identification record (form 01).

In addition to the standard analytical techniques found in packaged programs such as SPSS, one other method for analyzing these longitudinal data deserves mention, the life-table approach. This has already been employed by Van de Walle and associates (Watkins & McCarthy 1980), using data from the Belgian population register, and by Schiaffino (1981b), using the Italian population register. The life-table method, of course, has been developed for modeling mortality data, based on age-specific death rates, and showing life expectancy for each age. The method is also useful, however, for life-course applications, for it provides a means of analyzing transition rates between two states.

The life-table approach to the analysis of life-course data allows us to aggregate individual-level data on the timing and duration of events, and to compute the probability of a transition occurring to an identified population "at risk." To construct such a life table, we need first to identify just what this population at risk is and how time point 0 is computed. In the traditional life table, of course, the zero point is birth and the end point is death. In adapting this method to life-course study, however, any life event can be used as the zero point, with any specified subsequent life event used as the end point.

To illustrate how the life-table method can be used in life-course research, we examine a hypothetical case concerning remarriage. We can identify all those in our population of study who were widowed in a given period of time. These can then be divided into those who subsequently remarry, those who remain in the population but do not remarry, and those who depart from observation (through death or emigration) without remarrying. For purposes of this example, we assume that everyone remarries before death or emigration, with the distribution pattern shown in Table 4.3.

The first column (x) indicates the number of years that have passed since widowhood. The second column (sx) gives the number of individuals (standardized to begin at 1,000) who remain in the population at risk (of remarriage in this case) at the beginning of year x. The third column (r_x) reports the number of individuals (also standardized to an initial population size of 1,000) who remarry during year x. The fourth column (q_x) shows the probability that an individual who was not yet remarried by the beginning of year x will be remarried before the end of that year. Thus, q_x is computed simply by dividing r_x by s_x.[8]

Columns 5 and 6 refer to total number of person-years lived by the cohort before remarriage. Column 5 (L_x) shows the total number of person-years lived by those still in the population (i.e., not yet remarried) during year x (between x and x + 1). For the purposes of simplicity this is computed in table 4.3 by adding to the full year lived by all the "survivors" through that year an estimated mean of one-half year lived by those who remarry during the year. In other words, we want to know, How many person-years were lived by widow(er)s during year x? Taking the first row, referring to the first year after widowhood, we see that eight hundred people survived the year without remarrying and hence accounted for eight hundred person-years of widowhood. However, the two hundred who remarried during the year also spent portions of that year as widow(ers). We estimate that on average they spent one-half year each as widow(ers), though the exact data would be available in our life-course data file.

Column 6 provides a summation of widowhood-years lived by the cohort at year x and for all subsequent years (Tx). This is computed simply once all values for x in the table have been computed. Tx simply equals the sum of all values of x for year x and all subsequent years. Finally, we would like to know the "life expectancy" of the widowhood of members of the cohort at any given year of widowhood. For example, for all those who will eventually remarry, how many years on the average will they continue to live as widow(ers) after having been widowed two years? This figure is easily computed by dividing Tx by sx. Performing this computation for an x of two years, we see that the mean number of years left before remarriage for these individuals is 1.20.[9]

CONCLUSIONS

To date, most historical work on aging in anthropology has utilized a life-history method, with demographic study in social anthropology being confined largely to censuses and synchronic analyses. However, recent life-course research by anthropologists employing historical demographic materials has implications both for more adequate anthropological study of life histories and for cross-cultural research on the life course in general.

One of the principal criticisms of life-history study in anthropology is that it tends to be idiosyncratic, rather than generalizing. Needless to say, the qualitative dimension of the life-history method is one of its greatest strengths, but the quantitative methods described in this chapter for use with life-course data may be adapted for the analysis of life-history material to give the life-history approach more generalizability and firmer empirical foundation. We recognize that there are problems with this use of life-history data, for those who did not survive to be interviewed are not represented in the sample. This biases any resulting description of the population at a past point in time, for survival is socially selective. Moreover, researchers must confront the problems created by inaccurate and incomplete memories. Nevertheless, the quantitative life-course study of life-history data remains a worthy challenge for anthropologists.

More important, the anthropological use of historical demographic materials promises to make its own distinctive contribution to historical life-course study. Perhaps the major anthropological contribution may be found in the study of kinship and domestic group processes, where anthropologists bring their analytical expertise to bear on historical materials. Historians, demographers, and others have been looking to anthropology for guidance in this area, with many casting about, either employing ad hoc typological schemes or uncritically borrowing the schemes others have used. The anthropologically informed analysis of such life-course data as have been described in this chapter promises to shed considerable light on processes of coresidence by relating these to kinship systems, and by relating coresidence and kinship to such crucial life events as marriage, bearing children, migration, and death. In short, while distinctively anthropological methods are being adapted to aid in the life-course analysis of historical demographic materials, new methods jointly pioneered by anthropologists and other social scientists promise to extend the scope of anthropological research on age.

NOTES

The research on which this chapter is based has been supported by a grant (HD13415) from the National Institute of Child Health and Human Development.

1. From a demographic perspective, life-course events consist principally of birth, marriage, fertility, migration, and death.

2. Description of the Belgian population register may be found in Gutmann and Van de Walle (1978).

3. Needless to say, not all completed forms follow the ideal.

4. For further details, see Schiaffino and Kertzer (1982) and Schiaffino (1982).

5. Schiaffino is largely responsible for the creation of the data record system described here.

6. This program was written by Joel Richardson and is described in Karweit and Kertzer (1986).

7. See Karweit and Kertzer (1986) for a detailed discussion of longitudinal data storage and retrieval systems. The storage and retrieval systems described in this section were designed under the direction of Nancy Karweit.

8. The life-table example provided in table 4.3 makes the simplifying assumption that the only exit from the population of widowed individuals is remarriage. This allows us to compute q_x by dividing r_x by s_x. However, where emigration and death are also factors that deplete the widowed population under study, these must be entered into the life table and used in computing q_x. In such cases, the probability of remarriage during year x of all individuals who had yet to remarry at the beginning of that year would be computed as follows:

$$q_x = \frac{r_x}{s_x - 1/2\, m_x - 1/2\, d_x}$$

where m_x is the number of widows emigrating during the year x and d_x is the number of widows dying in year x. The simplifying assumption is made here that people leave through migration and death, on the average, half-way through the year. However, the exact rate could be computed by using the actual data on timing of emigration and death.

9.   Schiaffino (1981c) has applied this life-table approach to the analysis of remarraige in a recent study of Bologna and Reggio Emilia.   Further details on the construction of life tables may be found in most demographic method texts (e.g., Matras 1973).

TABLE 4.1

Cross-Sectional, Age-Grouped Data

Ages	Percentage of males who reside with one or both parents	Percentage of males who are unmarried
10-14	95	100
15-19	90	95
20-24	80	80
25-29	50	50
30-34	20	25
35-39	15	12
40-44	10	10
45-49	5	10
50-54	0	10

TABLE 4.2

Cross-Sectional vs. Aggregate Cohort Data

| | | | Percent of Males Ever Married | | | | |
Ages	1870	1880	1890	1900	1910	1920	1930
40-49	90	100	100	100	90	85	80
30-39	90	95	90	60	70	75	70
20-29	60	50	50	40	50	45	40
10-19	0	5	10	20	10	10	5

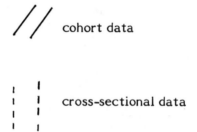

//   cohort data

cross-sectional data

TABLE 4.3

Life–Table Method Applied to Duration of Widowhood for Those
Who Eventually Remarry

x	sx	rx	Qx	Lx	Tx	ex
Years lived since death of spouse (x)	Survivors to year x	Number re–marrying at year x	Probability of remarry-ing at year x	Widowhood-years lived by cohort — At year x	At year x and all subsequent years	Mean widow-hood years remaining
0	1000	200	.200	900	2150	2.15
1	800	300	.375	650	1250	1.56
2	500	250	.500	375	600	1.20
3	250	150	.600	175	225	0.90
4	100	100	1.000	50	50	0.50
5	0					

BIBLIOGRAPHY

Baltes, Paul B., Wayne W. Reese, and Lewis P. Lipsitt. 1980. "Life-Span Developmental Psychology." Annual Review of Psychology 31:65-110.

Dyke, Bennet, and Warren T. Morrill. 1980. Genealogical Demography. New York: Academic Press.

Elder, Glen H., Jr. 1975. "Age Differentiation and the Life Course." Annual Review of Sociology 1:165-90.

Fleury, Michel, and Louis Henry. 1965. Nouveau Manuel de Depouillement et d'Exploitation de l'Etat Civil Ancien. Paris: Institut National d'Etudes Demographiques.

Flinn, Michael W. 1981. The European Demographic System, 1500-1820. Baltimore: Johns Hopkins University Press.

Gutmann, Myron P., and Etienne van de Walle. 1978. "New Sources for Social and Demographic History: The Belgian Population Registers." Social Science History 2:121-43.

Hultsch, David F., and Judy K. Plemons. 1979. "Life Events and Life-Span Development." In Life-Span Development and Human Behavior vol. 2, ed. Paul B. Baltes and Orville G. Brim, Jr. New York: Academic Press.

Kalvemark, Ann-Sofie. 1979. "The Country that Kept Track of Its Population." In Time, Space and Man, ed. Jan Sundin and Erik Soderlund. Atlantic Highlands, N. J.: Humanities.

Karweit, Nancy, and David I. Kertzer. 1986. "Data Base Management for Life Course Family Data." In Family Relations in Life Course Perspective, ed. David I. Kertzer. Greenwich: JAI Press.

Keith, Jennie, and David I. Kertzer. 1984. "Introduction." In Age and Anthropological Theory, ed. David I. Kertzer and Jennie Keith. Ithaca: Cornell University Press.

Kertzer, David I., and Andrea Schiaffino. 1983. "Industrialization and Coresidence: A Life Course Approach." In Life-Span Development and Human Behavior, vol. 5, ed. Paul B. Baltes and Orville G. Brim, Jr. New York: Academic Press.

Matras, Judah. 1973. Populations and Societies. Englewood Cliffs, N. J.: Prentice-Hall.

Neugarten, Bernice L., Joan W. Moore, and John Lowe. 1965. "Age Norms, Age Constraints and Adult Socialization." American Journal of Sociology 70:710-17.

Riley, Matilda. 1973. "Aging and Cohort Succession: Interpretations and Misinterpretations." Public Opinion Quarterly 37:35-49.

Riley, Matilda White, Marilyn Johnson, and Anne Foner. 1972. Aging and Society, vol 3: A Sociology of Age Stratification. New York: Russell Sage Foundation.

Schiaffino, Andrea. 1981a. "Analysis of Life Strategies in the Household Context: Methodological Perspectives." Paper presented to the General Conference of the International Union for the Scientific Study of Population, Manila.

_____. 1981b. "Un Aspect Malconnu de la Demographie Desvilles: L'Emigration." Paper presented to the Colloquio Italo-Francese sulla Demografia Storica delle Citta, Aix-La-Baume, France.

_____. 1981c. "Quelques Donnees sur le Remariage dans un Milieu Urbain: Bologne aux Dix-Neuvieme et Vingtieme Siecles. In Marriage and Remarriage in Populations of the Past, ed. Jacques Dupaquier et al. New York: Academic Press.

Schiaffino, Andrea, and David I. Kertzer. 1982. "General Guide and Codebook." Casalecchio Project Handbook, part 1. Mimeo.

Smith, Robert J. 1978. "The Domestic Cycle in Japan." Journal of Family History 3:219-35.

Watkins, Susan C., and James McCarthy. 1980. "The Female Life Cycle in Belgian Commune: La Hulpe, 1847-1866." Journal of Family History 5:167-79.

Wrigley, Edward A. 1966. "Family Reconstitution." In An Introduction to English Historical Demography, ed. David E. C. Eversley, Peter Laslett, and Edward A. Wrigley. London: Weidenfeld and Nicolson.

5
Emics and Age: Age Differentiation and Cognitive Anthropological Strategies

CHRISTINE L. FRY
Department of Sociology & Anthropology
Loyola University, Chicago

In gerontological research, especially that of a psychological nature, the terms "cognitive" and "cognition" are frequently encountered. The effect of age on mental abilities is a pervasive question in old-age research. In anthropological research, "cognitive" refers to considerably different issues. It is the mentalistic, ideational aspect of humans, which anthropologists identify as culture, that is the concern of cognitive anthropology or ethnoscience. This perspective within anthropology takes a very specialized view of culture in utilizing language to explore assumptions about reality in a specific culture. In this chapter we shall briefly examine the position of ethnoscience in anthropology and the assumptions about culture made by cognitive anthropologists. We then turn to the substance of this chapter: how cognitive anthropological techniques are applied to age and the organization of age differences.

ANTHROPOLOGY AND COGNITIVE ANTHROPOLOGY

Ethnoscience or cognitive anthropology is an established component of the anthropological tradition. At one time, in the late

1950s and during the florescence of the 1960s, ethnoscience bordered upon being a revolutionary and charismatic movement in anthropology, generally known as the "new ethnography." As routinization occurred, the ethnoscientific elicitation procedures and the modes of analysis became part of the anthopological tool kit and subsequently have enriched the research strategies available to anthropologists in investigating broader questions on culture and social organization.

These strategies are of great significance in that they enable us to resolve a basic dilemma in cross-cultural research: that of ethnocentrism. This kind of ethnocentrism is not the rather crude bigotry or prejudice and feelings of cultural superiority we generally associate with the term "ethnocentrism." Instead, the ethnocentric biases are the subtle ones inherent in language conceptualization, and thought patterns, all of which are products of enculturation. When John Fischer and Ward Goodenough, in their study of postmarital residence patterns on the island of Truck, discovered that they did not always agree on the statistical pattern (see Goodenough 1956), they also pointed to an interesting paradox in anthropological research. Although we study other cultures through long-term fieldwork aimed at understanding the culture and its people on their own terms, in building a science of culture we have simultaneously created a culture of anthropology. The culture of anthropology and the native cultures we study are two different things. For the purposes of cross-cultural comparisons, where comparability and standardization are among the paramount issues, a procrustean merger of the native with the scientific culture is often accomplished with all the resultant problems. These problems have been discussed in the extensive literature associated with the use of the Human Relations Area Files (HRAF) and with the problems of comparability in cross-cultural research.

Procrustean beds are not a hallmark of anthropology. In resolving this paradox, anthropologists enriched their scientific culture by making a distinction between the "emic" and the "etic," which parallels a distinction in linguistics between the "phon*emic*" and the "phon*etic*" (Pike 1967). "Emic" refers to the native culture and to research that attempts to transcend the biases which are inherent in the subtle ethnocentrism of the observer's culture and the categories implicit in that culture. To reveal the native view or the inside view, rigorous elicitation procedures are used to obtain the salient distinctions (in terms of contrasts and distinctive features) of the categories and the organization of the semantic domains (described later). Most significantly, it is the informant's judgment as to the correctness and appropriateness that is critical as the anthropologist charts the native culture and builds models of that culture. "Etic," on the other hand, refers to the culture of anthropology and the type of research that incorporates the results of research in a native culture into the framework of anthropology and generally agreed-upon variables within the respective anthropological specializations. Emphasis is not on the native view, nor are the informant's judgments as crucial to the respective anthropologist's description and analysis. The two kinds of research entail considerably different research goals and assumptions about the phenomena we study.

ETHNOSCIENCE AND ASSUMPTIONS ABOUT CULTURE

How culture is conceived, of course, depends on the questions asked and the theory behind the questions. Ethnoscience views culture as an ideational, cognitive phenomenon. Culture is best seen as a model or models by which humans organize and simplify the world. Culture is the code through which we perceive order in the universe. Although most ethnoscientists will point to nonlinguistic information as important, the general agreement is that language is the key to the cultural code. Cognitive anthropology emphasizes this linguistic nature of culture primarily because (1) culture is acquired from others and (2) humans use culture to negotiate and to communicate with each other in a predictable manner. For both to occur, a flexible and infinitely productive code is necessary. Language is that code.

With this linguistic view of culture, the broadest theoretical goal is to link up lanuage with decision making and ultimately behavior. Although drawing from linguistics, ethnoscience takes a somewhat different strategy in that the semantic organization encoded by language is the target of investigation. Hence, ethnoscience is often referred to as "ethnosemantics." Ethnosemantics, as a research strategy, contains a relatively small number of fairly well-understood notions. These include such concepts as lexemes (Conklin 1962), semantic domains (Lounsbury 1964a), componential analysis (Goodenough 1965), feature of meaning, dimension of meaning, paradigms, taxonomies, indexes, and trees. Obviously we cannot discuss these or other basic concepts of ethnoscience in detail in this context, nor is it necessary to do so. (For a more comprehensive survey of ethoscience, see Colby 1966 and 1975; Kay 1966; Tyler 1969; Romney & D'Andrade 1964: and Hammel 1965).

For our purposes, humans name things. The names are labels, words, or morphemes, which in analytic terms are lexical units or *lexemes*. Names or lexemes are not disconnected or singular, but are associated with and grouped with other lexemes into named classes (sometimes they lack markers), which in turn are organized into larger groupings. Thus, a *semantic domain* consists of a class of objects, all of which share at least one *feature* of meaning differentiating them from other semantic domains (i.e., in our culture, tables, chairs, sofas, and desks are representatives of the domain of furniture, as contrasted with ice cream, sandwiches, salads, and steaks, which are representatives of the domain of food). The immediate task of ethnosemantics is to discover something about the formal pattern of meanings underlying the domain (Kay 1966). This is accomplished through a *componential analysis,* in which the *dimensions* of meaning are discovered and the *features* of meaning (values of the dimensions) are mapped onto a set of lexemes. These mappings display a limited number of patterns outlined as follows:

1. *Index:* An arrangement of lexemes along the values of one dimension (e.g., money is organized according to an increase in dollar value or fractions thereof; chronological age involves an increase in number of years; or dictionaries and telephone directories are organized by position in alphabetical order). An index is the only arrangement between lexemes that is unidimensional.
2. *Taxonomy:* An arrangment of lexemes hierarchically organized according to a principle of inclusion. Because a taxonomy is hierarchically organized, it is (1) multidimensional and (2) characterized by levels of contrast (e.g., the Linnaean taxonomy with the levels of contrast ranging from the most inclusive of kingdom to the levels of lesser inclusion of phylum, class, family, genera, and species), involving contrasts at each level with things at the lower levels being kinds of things at the higher levels.
3. *Paradigms:* An arrangement of lexemes (1) whose underlying dimensions are multiple and (2) whose dimensions intersect. Because the dimensions intersect, paradigms are usually presented in matrix form with the features (values) being demarcated by the cells of the matrix.
4. *Trees:* An arrangement of lexemes by the sequential contrast of one feature at a time. This is usually represented in a branching diagram appropriately called a tree. The branches in such diagrams indicate the successive choices between two alternatives (+ or -) and imply no hierarchical arrangement. Also, the tree is used when the features of meaning do not intersect except with one or two features of meaning.

Ethnosemantic analysis has been applied to a wide range of semantic domains, including kinship terms (Lounsbury 1964a, 1964b; Goodenough 1956), ordering drinks (Frake 1964), driving automobiles (Wallace 1965), riding the subway (Fry 1972), locating a flop

(Spradley 1972), and even to age (Fry 1976, 1980; Kirk & Burton 1978). The primary strategy for determining the arrangements of these semantic domains is for the anthropologist to try to become the equivalent of the newly linguistic child who is rapidly building models of these domains by asking questions: "What is it?" "Is it the same as X?" "Why is it not an X?" etc. In essence the ethnographer is asking, "What do I need to know to be able to generate the culturally correct behavior (and hence to understand it) of an Australian --a Bushman? --a Yanomamo?" or any other culture in the world. One such important domain, which, with the above exceptions, has not been systematically explored on a cross-cultural basis, is age. Age is an important domain because (1) it is a universal feature of human life based on differential maturity and time, and (2) by being primary, age, along with sex, becomes a component of the statuses in the basic institutional structure of any society.

THE SEMANTIC DOMAIN OF AGE

If we are to take the ethnosemantic approach to age, we must be prepared to divest ourselves of *a priori* notions about this semantic domain. For instance, is age an index? If it is an index, what is it indexing? Time? Maturity? Our question is curious since large scaled, bureaucratized cultures, such as our own, are noted for their reliance on chronological age, which, as an index of time, is a proxy for lots of other things. Even in the tradition of anthropology, age is viewed as a graded series of life stages. As early as 1929, Radcliffe-Brown had coined the term "age grade" to refer to the "recognized divisions of the life of an individual as he passes from infancy to old age." On the surface age does appear to be an index. In all likelihood this is universal, since age does mirror a regularity in physical phenomena: that of differential biological maturation. In spite of our contention that culture is arbitrary, we find that folk classifications do conform to physical or ecological patterns. (For example, see Berlin & Kay's [1969] classic cross-cultural study of color terms.)

Yet, at a deeper level, age may not be an index. Other dimensions mey be present, which are organized according to one or any combination of the principles of taxonomies, paradigms, or trees. Indeed, those who have investigated aging in complex, Western societies lament the use of chronology as being too simple and as masking variability (Butler 1968). Even the distinctions between life time, historical time, and social time (Neugarten & Datan 1973) underscore the dimensionality of age. If age is dimensional, then how can we elicit the deeper structure and the semantic

organization of an indexed series of age grades? In the remainder
of this section, general strategies suitable for adaptation to specific cultural contexts are discussed. The issues include discovery procedures and strategies for more focused research on the domain of
age.

Ethnosemantic elicitation involves a sequence of procedures. It
begins with exploration of cognitive maps with a few informants
and moves toward more extensive investigation of cognitive maps,
using standardized instruments with a larger number of informants.
Exploratory elicitation strategies involve considerable and lengthy
contact   with   informants,   so   practicality   alone   limits   us   to
comparatively few informants (i.e., less than twenty). These key
informants   are   not   selected   on   a   probability   basis,   but   are
intentionally selected to include major social divisions and to be
more   accessible,   knowledgeable,   and   articulate   than   others.   In
strategies where the questions are targeted and the instruments are
designed to elicit adequate data from a comparatively brief
encounter with an informant, we are not limited to a handful of key
informants.   Since   the   concerns   are   representativeness   and
variability, attention should be given to probability sampling of a
larger number of informants (see Keith, chap. 1).

ELICITING THE SEMANTIC DOMAIN AND LEXEMES OF AGE

The   initial   question   is,   What   is   there?   How   is   the   world
differentiated and grouped by similarities? Since age is an ascribed
characteristic of people, a reasonable strategy is to explore the
larger domain of "people." What kinds of people are there? Of
course, there are lots of kinds of people differentiated by criteria
other than age. At this point the intent is to discover if age is a
semantic domain with a lexical marker (i.e., "age") for the entire
domain and then to discover the lexical markers delineating the
divisions within the domain (i.e., "young," "middle," "old"). This
domain is distinct from other domains and their subdivisions (e.g.
gender: male and female). In very few cultures do we find age an
explicit or singular domain organizing social life. Even in age-set
or generation-set societies, age is not singular.   Although age
explicitly organizes the male, public domain (Kertzer & Madison
1984), age is intertwined with and indicative of work/productive
status and marital/reproductive status (Fry 1985). In effect, *the
domain we are seeking is not age, but the life course and its
stages*. Age calculated either chronologically (20-30 years) or
categorically ("young adult") is a gloss for age norms, statuses, and
expectations that people use to organize their progression through
the life course.

In answering the question, What is there? our first task is to collect the lexemes or names informants use to talk about different kinds of people. We have a choice of elicitation frames contingent upon how much prior knowledge we have of the ethnographic setting. If very little is known, it is wise to explore the domain of "people." Ask key informants for the different kinds of people that live around here. These informants, in all probability, will talk about one domain at a time, although they may not volunteer all the subdivisions or distinctions they make in that domain. Note-taking is focused on recording the lexemes marking the domain and those subdividing it, along with information indicative of their meaning. Questions are directed toward the informant's expanding on each domain (Are there any more kinds of this class of person?) and on the discovery of other domains (Are there any other kinds of people?).

If the ethnographer is already familiar with the culture, this thorough examination of the domain of "people" could be abbreviated. One can focus on age and elicit the lexical markers within the domain because of the theoretical priority of age. The advantage is that it is time effective, but it runs the risk that the ethnographer is assuming *a priori* that age or the life course is a semantic domain.

It may take considerable patience or probing to get informants to articulate their thoughts using this eliciting frame. Age and gender are givens of the actors in the social arena. Givens do not receive the kind of cognitive priority that is accorded the issues people are most conscious of, issues that are used to make decisions or that are controversial. This does not mean, however, that these ascriptive qualities are any less subject to cultural elaboration. It is this cultural elaboration we are trying to examine. The intent of collecting these lexemes is not to create a thesaurus of age, but to set the stage by having the names or phrases with which to elicit the attributes of age.

COMPONENTIAL ANALYSIS AND AGE:
THE DISCOVERY OF THE STRUCTURE OF MEANING

Lexemes or the phrases an informant uses to divide the life course are the glosses for the deeper levels of meaning. It is the task of the ethnographer to discover this meaning. In the language of ethnosemantics, the ethnographer undertakes a componential analysis of the lexemes. Componential analysis, a "buzzword" of the 1950s and 1960s, refers to the examination and discovery of the structure of meaning. Every lexeme marks a category which is differentiated from contrasting categories within that domain. Objects, actions, and feeling states meeting the necessary conditions of class membership are its "denotatum" (that which is being denoted or included in the class). The defining features of a class--i.e., the necessary and sufficient conditions for membership in it--are its "significatum" (Morris 1946). A componential definition is an expression of its significatum (Lounsbury 1964a).

In spite of a rather esoteric vocabulary, the discovery of the necessary and sufficient conditions for membership in a class is by no means mysterious. However, the researcher has to make a choice on the units which will be the target of data collection and analysis. These units may emphasize the significata or the denotata and the overall strategy may involve a combination of both. If the significata are our emphasis, then the researcher begins by looking at categories in an attempt to discover the significata. If the denotata are the emphasis, the researcher begins by looking at things or objects and their similarities and differences to learn how informants arrive at larger groupings or categories. In the end, we are trying to understand the significatum, we just go about it differently. The decision of which strategy to employ rests on a combination of theoretical and practical considerations.

Categories and their significata should be selected as the unit under circumstances where the theoretical priority is set on the categories and where the ethnographer is confident that there is a high degree of agreement across informants--i.e., there is little intracultural variance, or if there is, it is highly patterned. It is unclear if this second condition can be met in most ethnographic settings. We do know that age categories display high variability in urbanized and bureaucratized societies in the number of groupings differentiated (Fry 1976). A remaining empirical question is the intracultural variability of age categories in smaller scaled and more homogeneous societies. At this point we just do not know, but we suspect that agreement is higher in these smaller scaled settings and that variance is probably patterned. With high variability we are left with the nagging question of comparability of units and creative attempts to merge the heterogeneous groupings of several informants into composite models.

If agreement in age categories is known to be low and the variability is difficult to attribute to specific factors, then the alternative is to use the denotata. The advantage here is that the ethnographer can present similar stimuli to any number of informants and by analyzing their groupings, it is possible to abstract the significata. The disadvantage is that the significata may not demarcate a discrete set of categories with neat defining features. This is a goal of ethnosemantics. However, where intracultural variability is high, we may not be able to achieve this goal because these categories collectively do not exist. Still, by using the denotata and the ordering of denotata, we can discover the structuring of a domain and the significata in the absence of sharply defined categories. If this strategy is used, the researcher should be prepared to use computer modeling of the domain of age, especially if large numbers of informants are used.

Once a decision is made concerning overall strategy, there are two steps in our discovery procedures. The first is the discovery of attributes informants use in differentiating within a domain. The second is the discovery of how these attributes combine in differentiating either categories or the denotata.

ELICITING THE ATTRIBUTES OF AGE

General strategies to elicit the attributes of any domain are contingent upon decisions about the priority of categories or the denotata. If the categories are the unit, then a fairly direct interview with several informants through multiple sessions focusing on these categories is appropriate. Here the stance of the ethnographer approximates that of a three- to four-year-old child, who is rapidly becoming a linguistic and enculturated being. If the denotata become our unit, quite heterogeneous strategies may be used, which present informants with problems to resolve using their requisite knowledge--e.g., the structuring of their categories and the domain in which we are interested. Both work equally well depending upon the cultural context; practical and theoretical decisions about eliciting frames; and the proclivities and expectations of informants. In effect, these strategies can be seen as complementary and an ethnographer may well decide to use both, once more is known about the domain of age.

In strategies where categories are the focus, the ethnographer, after eliciting the lexemes of age, proceeds by asking informants to talk more about these age categories or life stages. Interviewing becomes more focused following a "grand tour" or overview from informants. The focused questions shift to differences and similarities. In understanding the componential meaning of the divisions in a life course, a necessary question is on the differences between "X" and "Y." Also, the ethnographer wants to know in what way(s) people classed as X are similar to each other. The results in field notes amplify the initial lexemes into accompanying descriptions containing attributes and notes on the differences between and possibly the transition points expected as people move through the life course. Since a life course mirrors age, attempts should be made to link up life stages with age either relatively (younger/older) or absolutely (years) in societies where chronological age is more the norm.

After interviews with several key informants, the next task is to begin to build a preliminary componential model through analysis of interview notes. First major discrepancies between informants must be addressed. Some may be "splitters," making eight or as many as fifteen life stages, while others may be "lumpers," differentiating as few as three or even two stages. The task is to abstract from the key informants' models a working model, by examining the attributes they use; the range of variation in attributes; and the consistency with which they are used across informants in responding to the questions on similarities and differences. This working model should be taken back to key informants for their reactions, revisions and for judgments regarding the "grammaticality" or cultural appropriateness of the provisional model. A real test of a model is to try to use it to place people of known characteristics into an age grouping. If the model is "not correct" or the novice ethnographer needs to know more, key informants will exercise their veto.

This general strategy has a distinct advantage: with the kind of questions asked, informants become trained. In responding, they must think about the semantic organization of the domains being probed, and along with the ethnographer they learn about their culture. Some of these informants become "super informants," sometimes becoming more of a colleague than a native. This also may have its disadvantages. In thinking about a semantic domain and elevating it to conscious levels, informants have a tendency to reify their classifications and to systematize them. Their folk classifications become contrived classifications, which are more akin to our scientific classifications in that they are logically consistent (Kempton 1981). Folk classifications tolerate more fuzziness and internal inconsistencies. For some purposes and some domains this is ideal. For others it is problematic. The main danger in employing this strategy to investigate age or the life course is that informants and the researcher may reify an index. In all probability, however, informants will present a researcher with multiple criteria for inclusion in a life stage. Indexes are not usually built on multiple criteria.

If categories prove to be too variable across informants, alternative strategies should be considered. During the past two decades researchers using ethnosemantic strategies have incorporated a wide range of eliciting frames into our tool kit. Most of these mimic real life tasks, involve problem solving, and entail a sorting procedure or a principle of inclusion and exclusion. This can involve anything from the sorting of old shoes to the circling of different shapes of pottery on a grid (see Kempton 1981). Given the skills of informants, the culturally appropriate strategies for solving problems, and the ethnographer's imagination in adapting and devising a frame in which to elicit attributes within the domain, the possibilities are nearly infinite.

One very useful technique is to make the eliciting frame into a game for informants to demonstrate their skills. Guessing games are rather basic with multiple variants cross-culturally. Spradley (1979:169-70), in his discussion of asking contrast questions, suggests the old parlor game of twenty questions. The strategy in this game is the elimination of inappropriate significata and the retention of the correct significata until an informant feels ready to venture a guess on either the category or a denotata (object) in the mind of the ethnographer. If we use a variant of this guessing game as an eliciting frame for age, we can eliminate some of the preliminaries (e.g., the animal, vegetable, mineral question) and zero in on age.

For instance, our initial question could begin, "I know a man/ woman who is from around here and I know his/her age. I want you to guess his/her age and I am going to give you twenty questions to figure out his/her age. Once you think you know his/her age feel free to guess." The informant is challenged and sets out to demonstrate ability; the ethnographer patiently records the questions seeing what attributes the informant needs to know (significata) before venturing a guess. In this game roles are temporarily reversed, since it is the ethnographer who must answer questions. This means, if the game is to be a successful eliciting frame, that the ethnographer must know enough to provide reasonable answers. Otherwise the game is an exercise in frustration. If the direct interviewing technique is used prior to the game technique, the ethnographer should have enough information to provide reasonable answers and this ability will improve the more the game is played.

The puzzle-solving strategy is quite variable depending on theoretical priorities and cultural context. For instance, the unit can be something other than a person (denotata). If the researcher feels there is sufficient evidence that agreement on categories is high, the categories themselves can be used. The eliciting frame here could be, "I have here a number of age categories [presenting them to the informant]. "I'd like you to ask me questions to see if you can guess which of these terms I am thinking of." Restrictions can be placed on the game disallowing yes-and-no answers and the selection of a term with the question, Is this it? It is not the ability to guess, but the pattern in the retention and elimination of characteristics and priority given to kinds of questions, that is the important information for the ethnographer.

DISCOVERING HOW THE ATTRIBUTES OF AGE COMBINE

Once the attributes (or potential significata) are discovered, the next task is to arrive at the necessary and sufficient conditions for class membership, by understanding (1) the minimal attributes needed and (2) the way in which attributes intersect or co-vary to form a class. If age is an index and is unidimensional, the ethnographer's task is to discover the thresholds of category membership using chronological, functional, or social attributes. If age is more complicated than an index (e.g., a paradigm, tree, or taxonomy) or is an index based on multiple criteria, then the task of the ethnographer is also more complicated. The investigator at this point begins to ask questions on the grammaticality of combinations in an effort to discover the rules of age.

An "old standby" in the ethnosemantic tool kit to discover the attributes that are most similar or most different is the strategy of triad tests. Using pencil and paper, three attributes are placed together and informants are asked to indicate which two go together (are most alike) and which of the three is least like the other two. For age, we would ask the informant to select the two that are the closest in age (e.g., widowhood, grandchildren, first job). Triad tests are elegant elicitation procedures, in that informants seem to like doing them and they provide direct indicators of the organization of attributes. However, triad testing is limited by the number of attributes involved. The larger the number of attributes, the more triad items are needed to exhaust all logical combinations.[1] Informants may be patient, but their patience may wear thin with excessive numbers of questions. If we are using terms (lexemes) or a small number of attributes, then triads will work fine. Otherwise, alternative strategies should be explored.

Although the specific strategy is limited only by the ethnographic context and what the ethnographer hopes to accomplish, we will suggest two somewhat different informant-oriented tasks. Both of these involve using combinations of attributes, thereby asking informants either to describe people or to make judgments about people using trial combinations. Another consideration must be made. In addition to differing by age, people also differ by gender. The way in which the attributes of age combine may be sex specific, sexually neutral; or certain attributes may be more salient for one sex than the other. To discover sex differentiation as well as the culturally meaningful configurations of age attributes, we must become more concrete by asking informants to look at men and women of differing ages. The tasks suggested involve either informant manipulation of attributes to

configure people or computerized configurations of possible people
to ask informants to evaluate.

Informant Manipulation of the Attributes

Just as game strategies work in eliciting the attributes of age,
games combining the intent of triad tests with sorting tasks will
work in obtaining informant's judgments about similarities/dif-
ferences. Informants can be given the attributes and asked to do
something with them. One task is to ask informants to use the
attributes to describe people; first themselves and then people of
different ages who are known to the informant. By asking about
important attributes and attributes which tell them very little and
if they need more attributes to describe thet person, we test the
completeness and the priority given to the attributes we have
previously elicited. By asking about age and life stage of this
"created" person, we collect age profiles. These profiles can be
used to create age-norm tables for each sex. These tables are best
organized by domain (e.g, marital status, status of children), with
the attributes on one axis and age on the other. This enables the
ethnographer to calculate the age saliency of specific domains and
the norms for the thresholds and exits within that domain.

Other tasks are more abstract in that the context of a person is
not used. Informants can be asked to sort the attributes by age and
then to indicate why they sorted into the respective groupings.
This may prove to be a difficult task in that the attributes alone
may tell informants very little about age. Another task is to have
them sort by kind of attribute. Although age is our focus, the life
course is our unit. This more inclusive unit encompasses several
domains (e.g., marriage, children, education, work). By having
informants sort by domain, we discover (1) if the domains the
ethnographer is using to organize the attributes are also the ones
used by informants and (2) if these domains are logically complete
from informants' perspectives.

Computerized Manipulaton of Attributes

In this high-technology age it is possible to instruct a computer to
combine the attributes even when the logical and "ungrammatical"
combinations exceed two hundred thousand possible combinations.
The main problem is to find a program or programmer. Programs
have been designed to combine attributes into descriptions of
people.[2] These descriptions can be taken to informants, who can
then be asked about the plausibility of this combination of

attributes, the attributes that tell them the most about age, and those that provide the least information; and if they would like more information.

An advantage of this technique is that computers do not know the norms and will "create" unusual people. Informants may laugh, but usually they will also think about why these odd people are implausible and about the age norms involved. Also, when a large number of attributes and domains are involved and the number of descriptions generated would be impossible to present a pool of informants, the computer can randomly sample and present a smaller number of possible people. The results of informants' reactions can be analyzed through age-norm tables, as suggested earlier.

These strategies are not exhaustive, but are intended to be suggestive of other possibilities. Once attributes have been elicited, we need to know the way they are used: as significata to define age cetegories, or as significant features of denotata (people) to assign them to an age category or life stage. Informants' judgments about how the attributes can be or are combined to define an age or life stage are the necessary data. These data provide us with a definition of the life course in the setting involved and the age norms of that setting.

DEVELOPING INSTRUMENTS FOR LARGER SAMPLES

Ethnosemantic eliciting frames and very large samples are two things that usually do not go together. Eliciting data from large samples requires standardization in questions and preferably in responses which are also limited in variability. Also, survey instruments must be time effective to administer. Ethnosemantic strategies, in the search for the emic, are the antithesis of *a priori* standardization. In the search for meaning, it is necessary to use open-ended responses to our eliciting frames. These are the kinds of questions that are counter-productive on large samples. In spite of this, ethnosemantic procedures have been used on larger samples. Notably these involve standardization in eliciting frame and in responses, such as triad tests; or standardization in the stimuli presented to respondents, such as in sorting tasks. Other alternatives are standardization in eliciting frame to elicit open-ended responses.

The reasons for developing an instrument appropriate for a larger sample must be thought through carefully. The costs of obtaining data from larger samples are quite high, considering the time needed to construct samples and instruments; to contact respondents; to administer instruments; and to reduce and analyze quantities of data. Obvious reasons to use large samples include examination of intracultural variance and the evaluation of hypotheses. For some purposes, a smaller, not larger sample is more appropriate.

Instruments used to investigate age, using an ethnosemantic elicitation strategy, use a sorting task. Examples include my earlier work in Indiana to investigate the life course in Midwestern America (Fry 1976, 1980). More recently, Project A.G.E. has employed an "age game" to investigate the meaning of age in different kinds of communities and cultures (Fry 1984; Keith 1984; Ikels 1984). The essence of these instruments is the presentation of a common set of stimuli to respondents with a common set of instructions on what to do with the stimuli, and agreement among interviewers on procedures to elicit and record responses. The stimuli are called "social persona" or "persona." These are descriptions of people presented using attributes that are age salient. These are the very same attributes that have been elicited and for which age norms have been established using a small number of key informants. Respondents are instructed to sort these persona, the only restrictions being that they sort according to age and that they group the persona by similarity in age or life stage. At the conclusion of the sorting, the respondents are asked a number of questions about the groupings they have made, including such basics as age range and name.

Sorting tasks have a lot to offer in flexibility and adaptability, and they can provide a framework for other questions about the life course. Since people have little difficulty sorting one kind of thing from another, sorting is a technique transportable from one culture to another. Also, what is being sorted can be adapted to a local context in both form and content. Once a respondent has completed sorting, the interviewer can proceed by asking further questions about the groupings the respondent has seen as important. Potentially these groupings or life stages are useful units through which to investigate a variety of issues defined as salient by the theory of the investigator.

In contemplating creating an instrument using a sorting task to investigate the life course, several issues should be carefully considered. These include the definition and content of what is being sorted (persona); the form in which the items to be sorted is presented to respondents; and considerations to be made in the development of the protocol.

Defining the Persona

The first and most critical problem is deciding upon the features to define the content of the persona to be sorted. This problem can be resolved using the lessons learned in eliciting the attributes of age and in discovering how they combine. Questions remain in deciding the number of attributes to use to describe the persona; defining a range of persona to adequately represent the desired age ranges or life stages; defining persona who are plausible; and deciding upon the number of persona to use in the sorting task. Again, informants, should be consulted. Trial persona should be defined and informants' judgments ascertained as to their plausibility and their age; informants' comments about the most important and least important attributes are invaluable in deciding upon the selection and definition of appropriate persona. In the final selection, persona should be distributed across the age range desired and should contain persona who are typical or normative as well as persona who are less typical but still plausible. Unless only men or only women are of theoretical interest, the persona will be divided between males and females, with additional decisions to be made about sorting them together or separately. The number of persona to be used is a combination of what respondents will tolerate (e.g., how long it takes them to sort) and the number needed to represent different ages.

Presentation Formats

In presenting the persona the requisite skills of the population must be considered. What is needed is something that is sortable, something that conveys the age attributes of a persona and allows the respondent to examine and to place that persona with respect to other persona. An impossible ideal would be to miniaturize people and to have them, when called upon, step forward and announce their age attributes. Since we can't do that, compromises are in order.

Among literate populations, sorting tasks using the life course as a framework have been undertaken. Presentation formats have used 3 x 5 cards and English words or Chinese characters to represent the attributes of age (Fry 1981; Keith 1984; Ikels 1984). Writing has distinct advantages, in that the attributes can be presented as lexemes and can be presented in a variety of list-like or descriptive formats. Also, writing on cards is portable. Respondents can pick up the cards, ponder them while reading, and arrange and re- arrange them with little or no interference from the interviewer. Writing also brings its disadvantages, in that we assume that respondents have comparable reading skills and that all respondents read the description of each persona in its entirety. These assumptions are probably not justified in most populations.

Among nonliterate populations, our strategies should not be narrowed to those assuming literacy. In literate societies, when an illiterate or a vision-impaired respondent is interviewed, the solution is to read the descriptions to respondents. This may work well for literate populations. However, where literacy is not the norm, ethnographers should examine the graphic representations people use in daily discourse and/or the recreational games they play. Just as people in industrialized societies are familiar with office supplies, 3 x 5 cards, and card decks and games, people elsewhere have a material culture, graphics, and games. These should provide potential avenues to explore in devising an appropriate presentation format. One suggestion is the development of icons or ideographic symbols to represent the age attributes and their combination in defining persona. Such symbols should be easy to teach and should convey a lot of information. For instance, anthropologists convey a lot about different kinship systems using circles, triangles, vertical lines, horizontal lines, equals, slashes, and so on, and with very few problems they communicate their meanings even to introductory students.

Another method of presenting persona, one that can be used in both literate and nonliterate societies, is through photographs of people of differing ages. If this alternative is selected, decisions have to be made concerning the selection of people--i.e., their ages and whether or not they are known to respondents. An advantage of photographs is they are sortable and portable and do convey a lot of information. The disadvantages, however, may outweigh the advantages. Photographs, by definition, emphasize physical characteristics. Physical characteristics may, indeed, be important attributes of age, but nonphysical attributes may be equally or more important. Nonphysical attributes will be more difficult to adequately represent in photographs. Also, if the photographed people are known to respondents, the ethnographer may find that they are sorting on the basis of additional information not always known to the ethnographer. On the other hand, if the people in the photographs are not known to the respondents, the basis for sorting rests on physical and material clues.

Development of a Protocol

Once we have persona to be sorted, we need a protocol to instruct respondents and to elicit the desired data from the completed sorting. A set of instructions to respondents is one of the most important components of the protocol. Sorting is easily grasped by respondents; it is more difficult to communicate what they are sorting on and the parameters of their sorting. Considerable thought should be given to instructing respondents and to prompts interviewers can use in responding to questions and blank looks. Along this line, the protocol should give the interviewer an opportunity to note difficulties with the sorting task and, to give respondents an oppportunity to explain what they did either in a global form or on a group-by-group basis. Beyond such basic issues as names and ages of age groups and a standard way to record the results of the sorting, the content and specific items of the protocol are dictated by the theory directing the research.

CODIFICATION AND ANALYSIS OF THE RESULTS

Methodology does not stop with data collection, but extends to the management and processing of that data through to analysis. Space requirements make it impossible to probe here the complex issues of data management and analysis. However, two issues are especially critical for the type of data elicited through the strategies we have discussed: codification and the most productive analytic frameworks.

Codification

As should be apparent, codification of the results can be complicated, since we have a labyrinth of information. Not only do we have variables that will require a content analysis in order to determine the range of variation and the emic coding categories, but we have an even more basic issue regarding the units to be analyzed. Unless all informants divide up the life course in the same way, use the same number of divisions, use the same criteria to differentiate life stages, and use the same lexemes, we must come to grips with intra-cultural variation and the problem of informant relativity. This problem becomes more acute as the responses of larger numbers of informants constitute our data. For instance, if a persona sort is used, we should ask, Is our unit the category or the cards/persona within the category? Our initial response is that the category is our unit. They are what we want to understand. Pragmatically, however, we encounter this problem of standardization unless we empirically know there is very little or no variance. There is nothing to guarantee that the categories of one informant will be identical with those of another. It could well be that in ethnographic contexts where age sets or age grades are explicit organizers of the social field, more standardization and less variance would be encountered. At this point we have no evidence one way of the other. We do know that in large-scaled societies where chronological age is the common denominator, we do have considerable variance. Research in the United States has documented a wide range of variation in age grades with informants making from two to fifteen divisions and using over two hundred lexemes (terms/phrases) to identify those divisions (Fry 1976). Similar variance is also apparent in our current reseach in two U.S. communities and Hong Kong (Fry 1984; Keith 1984; Ikels 1984). Thus, we have a very real problem of what are the units to be coded. In resolving this issue two principles serve as guidelines.

1. *Code Primary Data.* Secondary data (data which is more interpreted) can be obtained through data-modification procedures that collapse the primary data. This means that as much information as possible should be coded on the most primary unit of analysis. If a persona sort is a portion of our data set, then coding of theoretically salient variables should be done on a per/persona basis, since these are the only units that are standard from one informant to another. This, of course, involves tremendous redundancy, as the same information is scored for each persona in any one group. Data-modification options in such statistical packages as SPSS may reduce redundancy in coding by enabling us to transform the variables coded on a per/category basis to a per/persona basis. However, before becoming committed to this type of coding format, careful thought should be given to the limitations of the data-modification options and the feasibility of using such transformations.

2. *Coding Can Be Either Emic, Etic, or Both.* All coding, however, should be informed by the theory and the hypothesis being evaluated. For some purposes, we may want to impose an etic variable rather than to code exclusively emic, primary data. For example, in partially resolving the problem of informant relativity, we can define "young," "middle," and "old" divisions of the life course and can superimpose them on all informants' categories who divided the life course into more than three divisions. If this is done after the data have been collected, explicit criteria should be used (e.g., on the basis of the lexemes "young," "middle," and "old," or their equivalents used to name the categories. If this decision has been made prior to data collection, informants who make more than three divisions can be asked to group them into these more standard categories. Although we gain in standardization and comparability, we still have not completely resolved the problem of informant relativity, since even these groupings are not necessarily identical across informants.

Analysis

Analysis of cognitive data requires fairly specialized statistical packages. Conventional parametric and nonparametric statistics that demonstrate co-variation in the data often lead to inconclusive results. Most of the variables are of a categorical level of measurement. Even those expressed in terms of age (i.e., age ranges of a category or even the category number) are not productive interval-level variables, since they tell us something about the persona or the grouping: namely, its relative position with respect to other such units. The only real variable suitable for correlational or regression analysis is the number of groupings, which is ordinal at best. Ethnoscientific data is more amenable to analysis geared toward examining the empirical relationships in data and displaying those relationships in a visual form (graphic or geometric) rather than in a metric form. Such modes of analysis as multidimensional scaling (Romney, Shepard & Nerlove 1972; Kruskel & Wish 1977); cluster analysis, including hierarchical clustering (Johnson 1967): and monothetic subdivisive classification analysis (Whallon 1972) are examples of this class of approaches.

Since a number of statistical packages are available with differing capabilities, it is unwise to comment upon specific procedures. Generally, these modes of analysis assume that objects (in our case, persona) are being judged according to similarity or difference. Data read into these programs are scores of proximity or distance between each persona. Each program will tell us something different about the empirical relationships between the data. Multidimensional scaling will plot the points along coordinates in building geometric representations in N-dimensional space. We usually select the representation with the fewest dimensions: one that is interpretable and that has a satisfactory "stress" or "goodness of fit" measure provided by the program. A multidimensional goaling solution best approximates a paradigm in the underlying pattern of arrangement between the objects scaled if two or more dimensions are used in the representation. If only one dimension is used, then the representation is an index. Cluster programs work through the data, selecting the objects that are the most closely related, clustering them and then proceeding to looser and looser clusters until all of the objects are grouped. The resulting image is a dendrogram, with a metric statistic to indicate the "tightness" of the cluster. Although it is not necessarily the case, if a hierarchical cluster program is used a hierarchy is assumed, these dendrograms may approximate a taxonomy. Monothetic subdivisive classification programs proceed in a somewhat different fashion, by first dividing the objects into two groups and then further dividing each of these groups into half until the individual objects are reached. The result is again a dendrogram, which in organization parallels the tree structure discussed earlier.

INTERCULTURAL AND INTRACULTURAL VARIATION

For purposes of cross-cultural comparisons, ethnoscience has assumed intracultural uniformity. In spite of recognized variation and disagreement about the standards among informants in any one culture, ethnographic descriptions have been concerned with an "authoritative" view that masks variance (see Goodenough 1970:98-103). Ethnographers are not to be faulted for ignoring variation, since when dealing with macrocultural differences in unfamiliar settings, the variance within the setting is not as great as the variance between settings. This is especially clear when we realize that ethnographers are building models of these settings informed by people living in those settings. It is very difficult to argue that these models have psychological reality for any one or all of the informants in that culture. By using elicitation procedures and analytic procedures such as those discussed in this chapter, we can learn how Americans organize age in comparison with how the Chinese do it and contrast them with Bushman or Yanomamo people. Using aggregated data, our points of contrast are the salient attributes and their structuring (indexes, paradigms, taxonomies, trees, or any combination of the above).

Intracultural variation should come as no surprise: culture is a code, but a code that is individually generated as people interact with others and become enculturated. We recognize the potentials for considerable variation. Cultural codes need only be sufficiently standardized for communication to occur. Wallace identifies these as equivalence structures (Wallace 1970:27-36). The models and especially the deeper structure of these models can tolerate considerable variance and still be compatible enough for communication to occur. In all likelihood, the range of variation is not infinite; thus, with an adequate sample of cognitive structures, it should be possible to isolate some of the major situational factors fostering certain variants.

CONCLUSIONS

Ethnoscience or cognitive anthropology--what can this approach tell us about age and cross-cultural research on age? The elicitation procedures, by being explicit and standardized in format, give researchers comparability without making *a priori* assumptions. If we use these procedures to create instruments to elicit data from larger samples, we have very powerful tools to explore those normative, evaluative, and potentially nonverbal symbolic aspects of a culture which are intersected and shaped by age. Finally, these elicitation frames permit us to determine ethnographically and empirically the deeper organization of age. The analytic procedures reveal how an ascribed, primary feature of humans is interlocked with other ascribed and achieved aspects of social structure and organization. At this stage of our research, all we can say is that we are casting seeds on fertile fields and our harvest is bound to be plentiful.

NOTES

The intellectual history of this chapter is longer than most. The original basis stems from my own dissertation research in Indiana in the early 1970s. By the time the earlier version of this chapter was written and published in 1980, the research design for Project A.G.E. was being developed by Jennie Keith and myself, and many of those ideas were incorporated into that chapter. This revised version of that chapter has the benefit of a new wave of data collection in two U.S. sites and in Hong Kong and the lessons of a year of analysis. The influences here are difficult to disentangle, and I acknowledge that many contributions of Jennie Keith and Charlotte Ikels. As another wave of data collection is in the offing, the input of still others who will try to use these strategies in even more diverse locations has had its impact. I thank Patricia Draper, Anthony Glascock, Jeanette Dickerson-Putman, and Henry Harpending for their comments on these strategies. Michael Burton read and constructively commented on many of the elicitation and analytic procedures in the earlier version of this chapter. Finally, I acknowledge two grants from the National Institute on Aging, which supported the work upon which this chapter is based (R13 AG2268-01 and P01 AG03110-01,02,03).

1. For example, with only 9 attributes set in triads, we need only 28 items for logical completeness. When we increase the number of attributes to 50, we need 1,128 items.

2. Jennie Keith, of Swarthmore College, has a student, Ian Aurebach, who designed a program that will construct and print out all combinations of attributes organized in domains to "create" people. This program is also capable of randomly sampling a selected percentage of all possible combinations.

BIBLIOGRAPHY

Berlin, Brent, and Paul Kay. 1969. Basic Color Terms: Their Universality and Evolution. Berkeley: University of California Press.

Burton, Michael L., and A. Kimball Romney. 1975. "A Multidimensional Representation of Role Terms." American Ethnologist 2:397-408.

Butler, Robert N. 1968. "The Facade of Chronological Age." In Middle Age and Aging, ed. B. L. Neugarten. Chicago: University of Chicago Press.

Cancian, Francesca. 1975. What Are Norms: A Study of Beliefs and Actions in a Maya Community. New York: Cambridge University Press.

Colby, B. N. 1966. "Ethnographic Semantics: A Preliminary Survey." Current Anthropology 7:1-20.

_____. 1975. "Cultural Grammars." Science 187:913-19.

Conklin, Harold. 1962. "Lexicographical Treatment of Folk Taxonomies." In Problems in Lexicography, ed. F. W. Householder and S. Saporta. Bloomington: Indiana University Research in Anthropology.

Frake, Charles O. 1964. "How to Ask for a Drink In Subanun." In The Ethnography of Communication, ed. J. Gumperz and D. Hymes. Washington: Special Publication of the American Anthropologist 66: Part 2.

Fry, C. L. 1972. "Rules from the Underground; A Cognitive Ethnography of the New York Subway System." Western Canadian Journal of Anthropology 3:199-27.

_____. 1976. "The Ages of Adulthood: A Question of Numbers." Journal of Gerontology 31:170-77.

_____. 1979. "The Artifacts of Age." Paper presented at the 39th Annual Meeting of the Society for Applied Anthropology, Philadelphia.

_____. 1980. "Cultural Dimensions of Age: A Multidimensional Scaling Analysis." In Aging in Culture and Society, ed. C. L. Fry. New York: Praeger (a J. F. Bergin Book).

____. 1984. "Age in Old Bordertown." Report from Project AGB: A Cross-Cultural Comparison of Aging in Communities Around the World. Synp., 83rd Annual Meeting of Am. Anthropological Association.

____. 1985. "Culture, Behavior, and Aging in the Comparative in Perspective." In Handbook on the Psychology of Aging (2nd ed.). V. E. Birren, V. W. Schaie (eds.). New York: Van Nostrand Reinhold.

Goodenough, Ward. 1956. "Residence Rules." Southwestern Journal of Anthropology 12:22-37.

____. 1965. "Yankee Kinship Terminology: A Problem in Componential Analysis." In Formal Semantic Analysis, ed. E. A. Hammel. Washington, D.C.: Special Publication of the American Anthropologist.

____. 1970. Description and Comparison in Cultural Anthropology. Chicago: Aldine.

Hammel, E. A. 1965. Formal Semantic Analysis. Washington, D.C.: Special Publication of the American Anthropologist.

Ikels, C. 1984. "Methodological Issues in Cross-Cultural Research on Aging." In Report from Project AGE. Symp., 83rd Annual Meeting of the Am. Anthropological Association.

Johnson, S. C. 1967. "Hierarchical Clustering Schemes." Psychometrika 32:241-54.

Kay, Paul. 1966. "Comments on Colby." Current Anthopology 7:20-23.

Keith, J. 1984. "Age in an American Suburb." In Report from Project AGE. Symp., 83rd Annual Meeting of the Am. Anthropological Association.

Kempton, Willett. 1981. The Folk Classification of Ceramics: A Study of Cognitive Prototypes. New York: Academic Press.

Kertzer, D. and O. B. B. Madison. 1984. "Women's Age-Set Systems in Africa." In Dimensions: Aging, Culture & Health, C. L. Fry (ed.). S. Hadley, Mass.: Bergin & Garvey Publishers.

Kirk, Lorraine, and Michael Burton. 1978. "Meaning and Context: A Study on Contextual Shifts in Meaning of Maasai Personality Descriptors." American Ethnologist 4:734-61.

Kruskal, J. B., and M. Wish. 1977. Multidimensional Scaling. Beverly Hills, Calif.: Sage.

Lounsbury, Floyd G. 1964a. "The Strucural Analysis of Kinship Semantics." In Proceedings of the Ninth International Congress of Linguistics, ed. H. G. Lunt. The Hague: Mouton.

_____. 1964b. "A Formal Account of Crow- and Omaha-Type Kinship Terminologies." In Exploration in Cultural Anthopology, ed. W. Goodenough. New York: McGraw-Hill.

Morris, C. W. 1946. Signs, Language and Behavior, New York: Prentice Hall.

Neugarten, Bernice L., and Nancy Datan. 1973. "Sociological Perspectives on the Life Cycle." In Life-Span Developmental Psychology, ed. P. B. Baltes and K. W. Schaie. New York: Academic Press.

Pike, Kenneth L. 1967. Language in Relation to a Unified Theory of the Structure of Human Behavior (2d ed.). The Hague: Mouton.

Radcliffe-Brown, A. F. 1929. "Age Organization Terminology." Man 1929:21.

Romney, A. Kimball, and Roy G. D'Andrade, eds. 1964. Transcultural Studies in Cognition. Washington, D.C.: Special Publication of the American Anthropologist.

Romney, A., Rodger Shepard, and Sara B. Nerlove, eds. 1972. Multidimensional Scaling: Theory and Application in the Behavioral Sciences (2 vol.). New York: Seminar Press.

Spradley, James P. 1972. "Adaptive Strategies of Urban Nomads: The Ethnoscience of a Tramp Culture" In The Anthropology of Urban Environments, ed. T. Weaver and D. White. Washington: Society for Applied Anthropology Monograph No. 11.

_____. 1979. The Ethnographic Interview. New York: Holt, Reinhart & Winston.

Tyler, Steven, ed. 1969. Cognitive Anthropology. New York: Holt, Reinhart & Winston.

Wallace, Anthony F. C. 1965. "Driving to Work." In Context and Meaning in Cultural Anthropology, ed. M. Spiro. New York: Free Press.

____. 1970. Culture and Personality. New York: Random House.

Whallon, Robert, Jr. 1972. "A New Approach to Pottery Typology." American Antiquity 37:13-33.

6
Age and Life-Course Transitions

CORINNE N. NYDEGGER
Medical Anthropology Program
University of California, San Francisco

Anthropology has been a major contributor to the literature on transitions in the life course. First, the earliest specific linkages between age and social transition were established by studies of age-grading (dealt with elsewhere in this volume). Second, ethnographers have traditionally provided an overview of the modal life course of their populations, usually in terms of typical life stages. These accounts had a strong influence on early formulations by theorists of the life course, such as Jung and Erikson, and they continue to be used in cross-cultural comparisons. Third, ritualized transitions between life stages are customarily given detailed treatment and have been a focus of interest in themselves, especially since van Gennep's classic study (1908).

However, in the final analysis, the value of life-course constructs lies in the degree to which they can help us clarify those complex linkages among biological, psychological, social, and historic factors which account for *patterning* of life trajectories, both intra- and interculturally. The modal or typical life course is inadequate for this task, having all the faults of the similar "family life cycle" construct (Elder 1978; Spanier & Sauer 1979). Necessarily, both ignore the diversity of lives characteristic of complex, highly individualized societies--and more common in "simple" societies than once thought. The constructs describe only the most common results of interactions among many factors.   Thus, by excluding variation, they provide no analytic purchase.

The need is evident to clarify concepts that tap critical dimensions of the life course and devise new methods of handling the complexities of lives through time, and these problems are now receiving unprecedented attention from scholars representing many disciplines (e.g., Estes & Wilensky 1978; Modell & Hareven 1978; Tuma, Hannan & Groeneveld 1979; Baltes, Reese & Lipsitt 1980; Brim & Ryff 1980; Myerhoff 1980; Reese & Smyer 1983; Johnson 1983; Hagestad & Neugarten 1985). As a result of such recent work the topic of this chapter--the old issue of the linkage of age to life-course changes--which once seemed simple, is proving to be complex and recalcitrant. This is due in large part to three over-lapping, persistently problematic conceptual areas and their difficult methodological sequelae: age-role transitions, the multi-dimensional life course, and normative social timetables.

AGE TRANSITIONS

To begin with: what do we mean by age transitions in the life course? In the purest sense, they are changes in social status due solely to attainment of particular chronological ages. Such age transitions result from dependable biological changes that exhibit relatively narrow ranges of variation; the classic examples are the end of infancy and the onset of puberty. But one is hard put to find other examples of transitions reflecting age alone, though our popular press is doing its best to create them by means of articles about "the forties," "the fifties," and the like. Nevertheless, even in our calendar-conscious society, the bulk of what are thought of as age transitions generally are also role transitions. A wealth of anthropological evidence indicates that this is typical of traditional cultures as well.

A basic question in relation to any particular transition, then, is whether (1) we are dealing with *age qua age*; or (2) the change is primarily a *role transition* and age is simply a concomitant due to customary role sequencing; or (3) age, though not primary, exerts an independent influence to *modify* the role transition in some significant way. These distinctions, which may seem merely pedantic, make a difference to research design and interpretation. For example, if age is merely in adventitious association with a role change, to focus on age itself leads to neglect of the important variables and to serious errors in interpretation.

Gerontologists were initially beguiled by simple chronological age and relied heavily on it as an independent, explanatory variable. However, as Birren long ago noted (1959), age explains nothing and is a thoroughly unsatisfactory variable; Wohlwill (1970) even suggested that age be treated as a *dependent* variable. We have been spared the full consequences of this misplaced emphasis by the strong age orientation of our society's role sequencing, which ensures that age indexes a great deal more than age alone: it has been a rough, but effective, index of role stages in the life course. But it therefore ensured continued confusion among factors which must be disentangled if we are to understand their effects. However, in this we are being aided by processes of social change, which are reducing many of these age-role stage correlations (e.g., student = young) and forcing their reconceptualization.

The problem of age in life-course transitions, then, can be clarified initially by approaching it in terms of role transitions, these linked to age by empirical evidence rather than by a priori assumption. Brim and Ryff, for example, utilize this perspective in their "life events typology," in which they postulate three dimensions: probability of occurrence, generality, and age-relatedness of various events (1980: table 1). Although they do not distinguish explicitly between role events and non-role events, it is evident that the "high probability of occurrence" events are restricted to biological and role events and that these are most strongly correlated with age. It is predominantly the fortuitous or nonnormative events, with low probabilities of occurrence, that are weakly related to age. Though we cannot deal with nonnormative events in this chapter, it should be emphasized that this apparently simple concept raises complex issues in actual use. The reader is referred to the excellent critique by Reese and Smyer (1983) of various taxonomies of life events recently developed by psychologists.

ROLE TRANSITIONS

Since Linton's initial formulation of status and role (1936), these concepts have been elaborated by researchers working from many different perspectives (e.g., Merton 1957, Goffman 1958: Goodenough 1965, Biddle & Thomas 1966, Sarbin & Allen 1968; Rosow 1976). The terms early entered the common vocabulary of social science and thence spread to everyday speech, losing precision with each stage. A similar history can be traced for "transitions," from van Gennep (1908) to Glaser and Strauss (1971) and the *Ladies' Home Journal*. Despite distortions of meaning (both popular and academic), the basic concepts remain viable. However. their ubiquity gives notice not to take meaning for granted, but to define our own usage unambiguously.

Traditional Perspectives

Because role transitions are examined from radically different points of view, the questions addressed necessarily differ. For example, from one macrosocial perspective, the emphasis is on roles as organizers of social participation. In gerontology, the concerns of this research are appropriately focused on studies of age allocation of roles, cohort flow and its effects on major roles, and social stratification by age (e.g., Waring 1975; Riley 1976, Streib 1976; Goody 1976). Another point of view highlights the formal properties of roles and role interactions, and has encouraged studies of interrole conflict, status inconsistency, and so on. This perspective is not prominent in gerontology, though research on retirement (Streib 1976) and some family and intergenerational studies (Bengtson & Cutler 1976; Neugarten & Hagestad 1976) address problems consonant with these concerns.

Moving from the broad, macrosocial perspectives to the microsocial, the focus shifts to the individual: the dramaturgical framework, models of role constraints, role sequencing, and so on. In gerontology, this has been the dominant perspective, but it has overwhelmingly been linked to psychological outcomes: for example, assessing the psychological effects of role events or correlates of role involvement. A major focus has been results of "role loss," that is, exit from long-term roles (widowhood, retirement, the "empty nest").

With few exceptions (such as Dowd [1975], working in an exchange framework), gerontologists have neglected the array of role issues raised by formal analysts. For example, studies of reciprocal role relations among the elderly have been limited to family contexts; role entry in old age is virtually ignored; changes within and between roles have seldom been included in studies of developmental psychological processes (Gordon 1972; Lowenthal, Thurnher & Chiriboga 1975).

Anthropological Perspectives

There is a clear need in gerontology for research based on a wider range of perspectives. Anthropologists, steeped in a tradition of role research, are especially well equipped to take advantage of this opportunity. To give just a few examples, models to investigate questions of long-term reciprocity and exchange among role alters abound in anthropological work on client-patron relations, the maintenance of poitical power, and the like. These can provide valuable suggestions for a new look at old issues in gerontology, as has been demonstrated in studies of support systems in single-room-occupancy settings by Sokolovsky and Cohen (1981), Eckert (1979), and others. Goodenough's (1965) "grammatical" techniques to scale the rights and duties associated with various roles may provide the rigorous model needed to estimate the effects of age on expectations among role alters. Tracing contextual and historical determinants of role change is the central focus of many acculturation and migration studies; techniques developed in this research could be fruitfully turned to the study of normative role transitions and their alteration over time.

A major emphasis in anthropology, of course, has been that of explicating the emic (this is often called cultural phenomenology). In terms of roles, the emphasis has been on formal and ritualized transitions, but this perspective could be applied more broadly. For despite all the work on roles, we still know least about the most common changes: the slowly transforming roles of family member, friend, worker. We recognize such changes most often after the fact, or when they are ceremonially confirmed. But the reality of continual changes, their determinants, and their meanings remain to be examined. Anthropologist are uniquely advantaged in dealing with these complex developments in that they are trained to integrate structual with phenomenal perspectives, are sensitized to the interweaving of roles and lives in distinctive historical contexts (Plath 1980), and are accustomed to handling the qualitatively rich data these problems demand.

The Role Course

Links are being forged between role and life-course theories and thoughtful critiques of problems in this work are provided by Clausen (1972) and Hagestad and Neugarten (1985). However, the emphasis has been on roles in relation to the lives of individuals or cohort groupings of individuals (of which George, [1980] gives an excellent summary). In recent years, only Rosow's work has focused on roles qua roles over the life span (1976). This perspective, which I will call the "role course," is a very promising one and should be particulary useful for anthropologists, as it facilitates comparative study.

Rosow (1976) devised a framework wherein status and role are viewed as independent rather than inherently linked. This yields a new typology of roles: institutional (status and role both present), tenuous (status without clear role), and informal (no status but recognized role). When traced across the life span, these role types exhibit distinctively different curves. This typology clarifies the nature of roles, suggests hypotheses about transitions in each type of role, and is particularly well suited to traditional field studies, wherein the total status-role structure can be examined.

Focusing on the nature of role changes in adulthood, I have used a role-classification scheme based on the nature of transitions: (1) Stable--no normative transitions (e.g., ward boss, lawyer in private practice, friend); (2) Sequencing--normative role transitions in an ordered sequence of segments (e.g., typical career ladders); and (3) Transforming--normative role changes (in response to changes in self or role alters) having no inherent ladder relationship (e.g. change in a parent's role when a child leaves home). This dimension can be combined with others, such as status equality/inequality, to yield useful typologies.   Though simple, such schemes begin to specify role-course dimensions, while remaining close to the data and their meaning.

There are any number of potential taxonomies, and we can expect the development of sophisticated, multidimensional models. But the point is that even the simple typologies described here begin to clarify gerontological disputes. For example, I have found that the problematic notion of role loss is appropriate for stable roles, is irrelevant for transforming roles, and is variable in sequencing roles, depending on exit expectations. Most important, this perspective provokes new issues and questions: socialization to the unmarked changes over time that are typical of transforming and informal roles, cross-cultural distribution of types of roles, synchrony among the various kinds of roles. Thus, a priori attention is not directed toward individual or psychological consequences of transitions, but remains focused on the role itself and the issues raised by changes during the role course.

MEASURING THE LIFE COURSE

Perhaps influenced by the segmental nature of our society and our lives, social scientists have come tardily to serious study of the multidimensional life course. It is probably fair to say that operationalizing strategies to deal systematically with life-course materials--that is, to measure them--is the least well developed aspect of the behavioral and social sciences, regardless of discipline. It is problematic for all. Reasons are not hard to find; I will briefly discuss only a few.

Analytic Problems

First, the list of potentially significant variables involved in an entire life, or even a segment of a life, is seemingly endless. This imposes the necessary, but agonizing, a priori task of winnowing and selecting out those particular ones we predict will prove to be critical--in other words, picking the winners.

Second, unfortunately there is a dearth of theory of the life course beyond childhood to assist us in targeting these promising variables (Clausen 1972). The life-course researcher faces the same problem as a five-year-old in a candy shop: limited means confronting unlimited choice. The result is often the same: paralysis of decision, finally resolved by a wild grab for the nearest, or the prettiest, candies. You may have noticed, for example, that the notion of "stress" has terrific consumer appeal under these conditions. However, consumer appeal and sales records are seldom the soundest bases of choice.

Third, lives are complex interweavings of factors, which are all too faithfully mirrored in the multiple confounding of the variables in our analyses. And age is notoriously problematic: it is normatively confounded with career stage, family stage--with all life stages. Age is further confounded with time and place, the "sociohistoric situation" (Gergen 1980) of lives, to which attention has been drawn largely in terms of the cohort (Ryder 1965), a kind of age grouping produced by ongoing social change. Through these linkages, age is then secondarily confounded with any variables linked to life stages or cohort; and so on and so on. Disentangling even a few key variables requires considerable ingenuity and is likely to demand unique, and difficult to obtain, samples (Nydegger 1981b).

Fourth, life-course research has primarily used variables that are intrinsically a-temporal, and examined them across time. This poses awkward questions of validity, of the comparability of the meaning of measures from one age to another or from one time to another. Does an instrument measure the same construct in adolescence that it does in old age? Does it measure the same construct in historic periods of affluence and growth that it did during the Depression? If not, it must be translated into age-appropriate or historically appropriate terms for valid comparisons. But not only is this difficult, it poses its own hazard: for some of these age changes are the very stuff of maturing, and the essence of the life course, just as changes in meaning may be the distillation of history. Overzealous elimination of differences in meaning in the search for age-free and history-free measures can blot out the life from the life course, and yield rather sterile variables of limited value.

Strategic Polarities

Currently there is a strong thrust to develop life-course measures in many disciplines, but most such efforts are in the formative stages. Therefore, rather than listing measures that may be out of date tomorrow, it seems more useful to organize this topic in terms of two strategic polarities, which are implicit in various approaches and which necessarily influence measurement. In this way, I also hope to highlight the unique contribution anthropologists can make to this effort.

Nomothetic vs. Contextualist Strategies. First, we can distinguish between *nomothetic* and *contextualist* strategies. The search for nomothetic ontogeny (an elegant mouthful meaning lawful regularities in development) is usually associated with developmental psychology, but anthropologists will recognize it in their own evolutionist tradition. This approach has been pronounced in child development from Freud to Piaget and has been extended into adult development by Erikson and others. For such researchers, intent on uncovering universal processes, any local perturbation (that is, contextually determined variation) is an extraneous source of error and confusion, which must be eliminated or controlled.

In gerontology, social change (i.e., history) has been the most widely discussed contextual source of error. Hence the extensive literature on cohort control by Schaie (1965), Baltes (1968), and others. However, from this point of view, class, ethnicity, sex, etc. are all contextual sources of error--a perspective unlikely to appeal to anthropologists. Nevertheless, this strategy does have the merit of keeping attention fixed on life-course *change*, clearly defined, as in the many studies arising from the longitudinal database at Berkeley's Institute of Human Development (e.g., Block (1971; Jones et al. 1971; Maas & Kuypers 1974; Eichorn et al. 1981).

An opposing strategy reverses the focus by targeting the social context itself and attempts to ascertain the way in which social context patterns lives. Historians such as Hareven (1978) and sociologists such as Elder (1974, 1979) have spearheaded the study of lives in relation to history, largely through studies of whole birth cohorts or part cohorts. Such research gives promise of a solid database for future comparative research. Indeed, comparative demograph is flourishing now in the field of family and history (e.g., Hareven 1978; Demos & Boocock 1978).

Parenthetically, intracohort variaton is marked, since demo-graphic and other factors cause differential exposure to cohort--defining experiences. Aside from Elder's work (1974), this critical issue has received too little attention conceptually and methodologically; nor are the principles of establishing cohort boundaries at all clear (Rosow 1978). These problems will have to be addressed in order to progress in the study of lives in historical time.

The relativism implied by *attending to*, rather than getting rid of, social contexts has caused a great deal of controversy, among psychologists in particular (Gergen 1980). Nevertheless, calls to integrate contextualism with developmental paradigms are being made, under the rubrics of dialectical psychology (Riegel 1979), ecology of human development (Bronfenbrenner 1977), and environmental psychology (Proshansky 1976). But no one knows how to go about establishing life-span developmental regularities in a cross-historical framework. or how to obtain what Thomae has called "change profiles" (1979), or how to solve the tricky question of external validity (Hultsch & Hickey 1978). Needless to say, this is also true for a cross-cultural framework. Surely anthropology, the relativistic and context-sensitive social science, could contribute to this integrative process.

Unidimensional vs. Holistic Strategies. Second, an emphasis on discrete, unidimensional variables is at one end of a continuum, holism at the other end. This is an age-old tension between fields such as experimental psychology and anthropology, between sociology and history. In life-course terms, it pits the "scientific" psychologist or sociologist against the "humanist" biographer, and is often the basis for misunderstanding and unproductive argument about the relative merits of research that is quantitative versus qualitative (an ambiguous dichotomy at best).

Presently, here too there is a slight, but very welcome, trend toward a midground accommodation. On the one hand, sophisticated analytic techniques now allow simultaneous examination of a large number of variables, as well as their interactions. Runyan (1980), for example, has developed a probability-based mode of analysis to investigate alternative routes and sequential stages of life courses--a more dynamic alternative to the familiar path analysis. However, such techniques require more highly quantified data than anthropologists generally obtain, although the new qualitative analysis techniques may prove helpful (Haberman 1978, 1979; Hollander & Wolfe 1973). On the other hand, some anthropologists are devoting attention to the problems of life-history methods (Langness & Frank 1981), and the multi-mini-biography strategy employed by others (e.g., Myerhoff & Simic 1978) points up commonality as well as uniqueness among lives.

Measures of the Life Course

Longitudinal study is, of course, the most elegant and certain design for investigating change, and such study has provided important data and an entire subfield of statistical analysis. (An excellent overview of methods is available in Nesselroade & Baltes

[1979]; and of data bases in Migdal, Abeles & Sherrod [1981]). Although few of us anticipate mounting truly longitudinal investigations, short-term follow-up studies are sometimes possible and should be pursued whenever practicable. However, typically we must settle for retrospective accounts, buttressed by whatever other evidence is available.

The basic data needed for life (or role) course studies are life histories, that is, the important events in respondents' lives (or roles) and their meaning. Depending on the requirements of the research, these may range from detailed biographies (discussed by Frank and Vandenburgh, chap 8. in this volume) to schematic life profiles. Recently, two gerontologists have developed methods that fall somewhere between these extremes: they avoid the profusion of idiosyncratic data typical of open-ended biography without losing the meaningful connectedness in individual lives (Matthews 1983; Johnson 1982). Matthews used a traditional biographical approach but with a specific and relatively narrow topical focus. In her case, this was friendship, but the method is adaptable to virtually any topic.

Johnson developed a method of obtaining two levels of data simultaneously: interviewers collected full life histories in a traditional open-ended format, but also coded sets of summary and predetermined variables. This facilitated immediate analysis of coded data while retaining the full life history for interpretive suggestions and subsequent intensive analysis. It is to be hoped that these and similar methods of streamlining biographical techniques will encourage a more general interest in and respect for life-course methods than is now the case among research funders.

At the schematic end of the continuum of life-course methods, the most popular technique to obtain a life profile is the life graph. In its initial use, the technique consisted of a two-dimensional grid, the baseline marked off in time intervals. Respondents themselves drew a line representing their life, showing its ups and downs. "No further definition is given, in order to allow the subject to give his own definition of what is important in producing the ups and downs" (Back & Morris 1974:218).

The life graph can be a useful and extremely flexible tool: the focus can be broad or narrow as we desire. For example, parenting histories and career graphs can readily be obtained; or the graph can be used as an aid to intensive life histories. I have found that it organizes interviews well and helps respondents to recall their lives' events in context. It is a particularly useful technique in profiling limited aspects of the life course: goals over time, the role course, and so forth.

Variants of this technique have been used by many gerontologists, and reliabilities for events are reassuring. Estimates indicate that, while present circumstances do affect perception of the past, reliability is good for events themselves and satisfactory for their relative ups and downs; distortion is primarily in amplitude of recalled reaction. For this reason, as well as to neutralize individual tendencies to large versus small responses, it is wise to express amplitudes as standardized scores rather than comparing respondents on raw scores.

Numerous scores can be derived from life graphs: range (eventful vs. uneventful lives), significant events (peaks or depressions), overall shape (upswing, downswing, fluctuating), evaluation of selected ages (old age, adolescence), and nature of role transitions (normative, nonnormative), to name just a few. The researcher can devise scores at whatever levels of quantification the study questions require. An additional asset is that life graphs link directly to historic time, and the impacts of major events such as wars can be assessed immediately by inspection. However, techniques to analyze these materials as whole lives are still primitive, consisting of little more than visual inspection and idiosyncratic categorization by pattern. Geometries of the life course have been recommended (Back 1980) but, to my knowledge, none have been developed.

A similar technique, but more researcher-determined, is the widely used life-event inventory. Best known through the work of Holmes and Rahe (1967; Gunderson & Rahe 1974) and the Dohrenwends (1974; Dohrenwend et al. 1978), life events have been examined in terms of their impact on specific outcomes, notably stress, health, psychological symptoms. However, as Hultsch and Plemons point out, the lists of events included vary widely, often combining "events which may be characterized as subjective and objective, voluntary and involuntary, positive and negative, and so forth (1979:18). Reese and Smyer further emphasize that the distinction between event as static product and event as process is blurred and confused (1983). The construct itself needs clarification; attempts at measurement refinement are premature.

Recently, major attempts have been made in dimensionalizing life events, so as to be more theoretically relevant. Reese and Smyer (1983) have expanded the Brim and Ryff (1980) taxonomy previously mentioned by intersecting the dimensions, yielding over thirty categories. Presumably still more could be identified: as Bandura (1982) has pointed out, even an adventitious, chance encounter can play a prominent role in shaping a life. Although controversy will arise over methods of life event analysis, all this concern is clearly rooted in the desire to capture at least some of the complexity of lives, and to move toward a welcome multivariate midground between unidimensional and holistic strategies.

However, whatever technique is used for obtaining life-history data, the potential for retrospective bias must be taken into consideration. The systematic biases thus far established are a tendency to judge the distant past more kindly as one moves farther from it (Field 1979) and to make sense out of the past, to bring it into line with current perceptions (Yarrow, Campbell & Burton 1970). Therefore, particular caution should be exercised in comparisons among respondents who are distributed across a wide age range.

Reports of emotions are especially likely to be untrustworthy. The major study in this area indicates that family folklore signi-ficantly determines recollections of childhood (Yarrow, Campbell & Burton 1970). Thus we must keep in mind that any life history is a reconstruction of the past: it may offer a better insight into current personal and even cultural organization than into real personal history (Myerhoff 1980). Life-history data cannot be simply accepted as accurate portrayal, especially of the emo-tional past, without additional supporting evidence (Brim & Ryff 1980).

AGE IN ROLE TRANSITIONS

What of the specific relationship of age to role transitions? Rosow has suggested that our institutional roles peak and then decline over the life span. tenuous roles eventually increase, and informal roles are relatively unaffected by age (1976). This analysis points to status as the critical element and leads us to examine structural, rather than psychological, factors governing transitions. Evidence pertaining to this issue is beginning to accumulate from comparative research in societies with different age allocations of responsible roles (Cowgill & Holmes 1972; Goody 1976; Fry 1980b, 1981; Mines 1981).

In terms of my classification of role transitions, although age may have limited relevance to stable roles, it is likely to play an important part within sequencing and especially transforming roles. In what way? This brings us back full circle to the initial questions about the relation of age to role transitions and to another set of problems: social timetables.

Social Timetables

It will come as no surprise to anthropologists to learn that the importance of social age far outweighs chronological age, at least in adulthood. And it is social age that determines, and is in part determined by, one's position on various role schedules: marriage, career rank, and the like. These normative schedules are collectively referred to as social timetables. Recent life-span research has begun to focus on these timetables as organizers of social life.

However, the issue is rather more complex than is generally understood. In essence, it is the old issue of levels of inclusion. Kluckhohn and Murray have probably stated this problem most succinctly: "Every man is in certain respects (a) like all other men, (b) like some other men, (c) like no other man" (1948:35). So with timetables: some are virtually universal, others specialized, and some idiosyncratic. For brevity's sake, I will ignore putative universal timetables of biological and cognitive development and will also bypass the question of cross-cultural variability to focus on the shared timetables we are most familiar with, those of our own society.

General Timetables. Thanks to the work of Neugarten (1968), Fry (1980a), and others, we know that there are broadly shared timetables for most major life transitions. We tend to agree about the approximate ages regarded as appropriate for most major transitions, at least within age cohorts, though it should be emphasized that there is a need for more empirical evidence on expectations and, especially, sanctions. (Good discussions of these issues and related research can be found in Elder 1975; Datan & Ginsberg 1975; Hultsch & Plemons 1979; Hagestad & Neugarten 1985). But it is important to distinguish among age norms, for, as we shall see, they refer to several different things.

In some cases, the consensus appears to be little more than a recognition of what is customarily the case--a kind of modal-age description. But, over time, what is customary tends to become what is right. As Cain (1964) pointed out, many age expectations about role stages and behaviors are truly normative. That is, they are preferred or ideal, and carry the diagnostic connotation of "ought" or "ought not." Some are even prescriptive and have been codified into law (as in the case of minimum age for marriage). I shall reserve the use of the term "normative" for those age expectations which are more than merely descriptive, which also carry some implication of rightness.

Furthermore, normative social timetables are not limited to age alone: the focus on age has led to the neglect of the more general kind of timetable, that of normative *ordering* among role stages. Although most discussions of timing since Roth's (1963) and Cain's (1964) seminal work have pointed out the need to examine synchrony among role stages, we have little data on normative expectations about synchrony to parallel the data on age norms; only Hogan (1978, 1981) has examined the extent to which role ordering varies in living cohorts. However, historians and an-thropologists document considerable variation over time (e.g., Uhlenberg 1974; Demos & Boocock 1978; Hareven 1978; Foner & Kertzer 1978.).

Norms of synchrony may prove to be more important than age norms. For example, in my study of fathers, respondents discussed appropriate ages for starting a family. The ages ranged over fifteen years, and many flatly rejected age as relevant; this is scarcely convincing evidence of strong age norms for this role stage. However, when starting a family was discussed in relation to marriage, a clear consensus emerged that a couple should wait two or three years after marriage before having children. It is evident that these men do share a normative timetable, but that age is less important than time since marriage. That is, the critical aspect for family timing is not age, but is a synchrony norm, involving the mesh with another family role.

It should be pointed out that age norms appear to be different in kind from synchrony norms, largely because I am focusing primarily on social *role* timetables. But no aspect of timing is as simple as it appears, and many age norms themselves are really another kind of synchrony norm, in this case an interlocking of social roles with a timetable predicated on folk developmental and aging theories. Note that we assume the existence of such theories, for there is little evidence on the matter. The topic begs for comparative ethnoscientific research.

Specialized Timetables. So far, I have been speaking about the most general timetables, involving those major life transitions which most of us undergo. But at a less general level we find specialized timetables, varying in the degree to which they are age or synchrony normative. Career schedules are the clearest examples, for each has its own well-established age and synchrony norms, but these differ so greatly from occupation to occupation that there is no general timetable of the worklife. Think for a moment of the different ages at which professional skills peak in football, in neurosurgery, in cabinetmaking, or, perhaps the most delayed, in philosophy.

At the other extreme are those sui generis schedules for which neither age nor synchrony are relevant, such as the patient-career trajectory described by Roth (1963). Many other timetables lie between these extremes, being more or less normative in respect to age or role synchrony. Because they are limited to subpopulations homogeneous in this regard, specialized timetables respond most readily to situational and ideological pressures and are capable of fairly rapid change. For example, since World War II, the historic norm that men marry after completion of their college education has been abandoned for graduate students; traditional age norms for women students are undergoing a similar fate.

Personal Timetables. Finally, we should acknowledge the most neglected form of temporal ordering, the personal timetable. Of course, such timetables are not shared, and not normative. But we have found a type of respondent whose own personal timetable has far more meaning than normative schedules. Ignoring the force of such self-imposed timetables increases errors of interpretation. Further, even when normative schedules are accepted, many individuals modify them in accordance with personal timetables.

Social, specialized, and personal timetables interact in various ways, from reinforcement to conflict. The scheduling of events is the resultant of all these forces, and to understand the meaning of any pattern, it is essential to take all life plans into account, as Mines' (1981) study makes clear. The effects of timing, then, arise from the meshing of timetables at all levels of inclusion. The complexity of timing research and the range of data required to do justice to the issues should be apparent.

Interdependent Timetables

To add to this complexity, current thinking about the life course emphasizes the interdependence of lives and the way in which individual transitions frequently are affected by, or even contingent upon, the life stages of others. Plath (1980) points this out for intimates ("consociates") and historians have described timetables for the family as a unit (e.g. Aldous 1978; Hareven 1981). Although family schedules may be less critical In modern societies than in the past, interdependent timetables remain another source of variation from the more general norms. (For a brief review of this topic, see Hagestad and Neugarten, 1985; for a discussion of methodological problems in studying interactive lives, see Klein, Jorgensen and Miller, 1979).

Measuring Social Timing

In the brief period since researchers have examined social timetables, a variety of measurable dimensions have been identified. For single roles: (1) *duration,* that is, the length of time a cohort requires to complete a transition, has been widely used for historical comparisons; (2) *order* and *spacing,* the sequencing of role changes and the time between sequenced transitions, also has been used for intercohort comparisons; (3) *timing,* when a transition occurs, is most closely associated with age norms and has received most attention in regard to both individual lives and cohorts. The much scantier empirical research on the meaning of roles has focused on (4) *synchronicity*, that is, the relative timing of transitions among two or more roles (studied particularly in regard to family and work roles); and (5) *compression* of transitions at a given time (studied in regard to stress).

It should be emphasized that the bulk of the work referred to has not analyzed these dimensions as they occur through actual lives, but has had to rely on aggregated data from various cohorts to construct typical patterns of change. (The outstanding exceptions are the few longitudinal studies of adults, such as Lowenthal et al. 1975; Eichorn et al. 1981). Such data on appropriate samples of real lives is sorely needed to assess the importance of these dimensions and to derive more refined measures. Moreover, the focus has been on clear, socially marked transitions such as graduation from high school, marriage, and so forth. This restricted view has precluded the investigation of the gradual changes associated with, but not limited to, transforming roles.

However, the most intractable problem in relating age to social roles is not the identification of dimensions, nor even their measurement. It is the difficulty of disentangling age and stage which are, by their very nature, usually confounded in normal populations. In research on the mesh between two or more roles, the same problem arises insofar as their synchrony is typical.

Pure age and pure role transitions present few problems. The difficulty lies in the common situation wherein age is normatively associated with role stage. No one strategy is uniformly successful, but examination of deviant cases (that is, off time, off age, or out of synchrony) can best disentangle age from role norms, to clarify which is primary or how age modifies particular role transitions (assuming the deviant cases are not also deviant in other ways and thus unsuitable for this purpose). In small groups, finding enough deviant cases to support conclusions may prove impossible; there will be only a handful of cases in the tails of a normal distribution of a small population. But hypothetical deviant cases, presented to informants for comment, can be an acceptable substitute if the research questions are about expectations and attitudes (the relative importance of age, the norms concerning age and other role stage prerequisites, etc.). What invention loses in authenticity, it makes up in clarity: variables can be manipulated at will and the red herrings of reality excluded. Although it is true that what is customary often takes on the moral tone of what is right, it seldom has the force of prescription, and deviance from the merely customary is seldom judged severely. Experienced field workers should be able to cope with this problem.

Another way to disentangle variables is the best or worst case, an obverse of Fry's variable clustering; this method is effective when variables are few in number and can be easily dichotomized or trichotomized (e.g., student/graduate, old/middle aged/young). The technique is simple: set up a matrix of all combinations of pairs, for example, in the simplest role-synchrony case: married/student versus married/worker; married/student versus unmarried/worker; unmarried/student versus married/worker; unmarried/student versus unmarried/worker. Respondents are asked to express a normative judgment about the most or least preferred case in each pair. Use of worst, rather than best, case has the advantage of working well with invidious variables.

This is merely a formal analogue of the intuitive two-variable question: "Would you rather marry someone old and rich, or young and poor?" And it is less cumbersome than it sounds, since some pairs generally can be eliminated as nonoccurring or simply silly (such as youg/rich versus young/poor). This technique ranks the importance of the variables and disentangles them to that extent, but it determines preferences only, offering no basis to discriminate between prescriptive and customary patterns. Degree of consensus shown by respondents often provides evidence of norms; if not, this judgment must be based on other data.

However, strategies of hypothetical cases will suffice only if our research questions concern attitudes and norms. The consequences of being off the norm can be obtained only from appropriately off-norm individuals. For example, in my studies of fatherhood, certain stereotypes about being late in this role were widely shared, but data from late fathers themselves refute these stereotypes. Thus questions about actual consequences of deviance demand sufficient deviant cases, a problem in small group research for which there is no solution. As Cattell warned his students: Life is not orthogonal.

LIVES IN HISTORY: THE COHORT

Even if we succeed in disentangling age and role stage in studying patterns of synchrony, age norms, consequences of off timing, and so forth, we can seldom determine whether our results are generalizable to other sociohistoric contexts. There is abundant evidence that change has occurred in such patterns over time, both in simple and complex societies. But how can we take history into account in realistic research designs? The most notable attempts to solve this problem, to assess the impact of social change on the life course and aging, have been centered around the cohort.

Cohort was originally a demographic and actuarial construct, grouping persons born during the same time span (usually ten-year intervals) to assist in the analysis of population, epidemiologic, and similar statistics. Ryder (1965) pointed out the important implications of this concept in relation to processes of social change and focused attention on the cohort as an index of shared experience of major events, such as wars.

Mannheim (1952) had earlier developed a similar notion in his concept of "generation"; this term still has currency, but "cohort" has been preferred, due largely to its apparent precision. In this tradition, political scientists and sociologists have been assiduous in searching out cohort effects, and the literature is voluminous (e.g., in gerontology, summaries in Riley, Johnson & Foner 1972; Hudson & Binstock 1976). The meaning of "cohort" in this sense is summed up succinctly by Bengtson and Cutler (1976:131): "Born during a given period of history, a particular age cohort experiences in similar ways the consequences of historical events." Thus cohort provides the conceptual link between history and individual lives.

Rosow identified the assumptions underlying the notion of cohort effects: "A social cohort: (1) consists of people who share a given life experience; (2) this experience is socially or historically structured; (3) it occurs in a common generational framework; (4) its effects distinguish one generation from another; and (5) these effects are relatively stable over the life course" (1978:67). It is clear that age-specific socialization is involved, but to date there has been no cross-fertilization between cohort and socialization theories.

Rosow (1978) also raised serious questions about the meaning of cohort, pointing out that the precision of definition is only apparent and that we really do not know how to establish meaningful cohort boundaries. Although definitions of cohort emphasize shared experiences, very little attention has been paid to this emic aspect: What is the meaning of a cohort experience to its members? what is shared? who shares it? which cohorts perceive themselves as such (viz., "our generation")? Only one study (Elder 1974) and a few papers (Nydegger 1977; Rosow 1978; Eckert 1978; Nydegger et al. 1983) have even raised such questions.

Anthropologists may be in the best position to contribute significantly to this area: they have been studying acculturation (under various rubrics) for years and much of this work, in essence, distinguished among cohorts. In fact, a few "cohort ethnographies" (Nydegger 1981a) exist in all but name (e.g.. Ross 1977; Myerhoff & Simic 1978). If we ally cohort sophistication with ethnographic technique, we can substantially expand and refine cohort theory.

While sociologists were preoccupied with the search for effects of specific historical cohort memberships, others have been equally determined to try to control these effects. For they pose the greatest problem for adult developmentalists and gerontologists, who must cope with those drastic social changes which confound cross-sectional age differences with the age changes they want to isolate. The most thoroughly investigated example is intelligence testing, which is strongly influenced by amount and kind of education, both of which have changed dramatically since the turn of the century (Botwinick 1977). How were true aging changes to be disentangled from the effects of cohort differences in experience?

Age Confounds

The logic of these confounds is simple, and the classic model is Schaie and Baltes's elegant analyses of age, cohort, and time of measurement (Schaie 1965; Baltes 1968; in sociology: Riley 1972, 1976). In brief, given this set of three time-defined variables, at any point when data are collected, there is a triple confound. This is logically inevitable, because "there is only one span of time involved, no matter how we measure it. It is as if we used a triangular ruler, each side in a different metric: the faces show different intervals but, since the length is the same, the correlation between faces is perfect. Any two sides yield the third" (Nydegger 1981b). This means that if a research design controls any one of these variables, the other two are inextricably confounded. For example, even if we carefully select the ages of our informants, their cohorts (their shared social history) will still be a function of their ages and any time (year) we "measure" them. The logic of the model suggests that comparisons among multiple analyses-- generally referred to as the cross-sequential design (Schaie 1965)--are required, for which both cross-sectional and short-term logitudinal data are necessary.

But this kind of confound is not limited to developmental studies, or to these three variables. Such confounds arise whenever we use multiple measures of time as variables in one analysis. For we are really projecting different meanings into what are merely different ways of measuring the same span of time. For example, figure 6.1 illustrates these confounds in a variety of substantive areas. Thus the developmental model is a special case of a more general time-confound model.

The unhappy corollary is that we can be caught up in secondary confounds without being aware of it if our variables are substantially correlated with the confounded time-defined variables. Unfortunately, such cases are typical in Western societies, which have chronological age norms for many role changes. The special and intriguing cases of age-set and generation-set societies can provide valuable limiting cases, both perfectly confounded and essentially independent. Even in the United States, secular changes are disentangling some confounds before our eyes: for example, there is now a sizable population of middle-aged women who are entering college along with their daughters' cohort. But for most of our studies of age and role transitions, age still enters into confound upon confound.

Cohort and Social Timetables

The cohort context of individual life histories is now widely recognized. However, the cohort consequences of various timetables have received little recognition. Nevertheless, they can be critical. In this sense, timing of parenthood determines a child's cohort context. In my study of paternal timing, this context is by far the most important factor in accounting for differences in both the number and kind of parenting conflicts with adolescents and young adult children. For example, parents of children who were of college age during the upheavals of the late 1960s and early '70s experienced an unprecedented set of problems: conflicts not only increased in sheer numbers, but their content was unique.

For this generation of fathers, timing was critical: if they were very early or very late, their children were either too old or too young to be caught up in the worst of the disturbances and they escaped the escalated conflicts. Furthermore, parents of this cohort of children fear that a constricting job market may add to the years of children's dependence--an unfortunate result for parents and children. Thus one important aspect of many social timetables is their determination of the historical experience of role alters, both in the present and in the future.

Implications for Anthropology

What do cohort effects and the problem of time confounds mean for anthropologists? First, in common with all gerontologists, we must be very sensitive to the possibility of confusing the effects of age with the effects of cohort membership. Unless we are able to conduct repeated studies of subsequent cohorts at intervals of several years, we cannot directly reject this alternative explanation. Our only recourse is to collect evidence bearing on its likelihood. This means that we should always identify social changes and their associated cohorts and that we should estimate the probability that these altered circumstances have affected our results. We may be able to assert confidently that, in any given instance, there were no significant historical differences in experiences among, say, 55- to 75-year-old men; this would support the conclusion that age differences within this group of men were due to age, not cohort membership (Gutmann 1977).

A second and related problem is that cohort differences restrict our ability to generalize results: we can speak only of one cohort at a time. But since anthropologists are among the world's most reluctant and history-conscious generalizers, I doubt that this problem is serious. We must merely keep in mind that cross-cohort generalization may be fully as dangerous as cross-cultural generalization and that tempero-centrism is simply a variant of ethno-centrism.

Third, the meshing of history and social timetables raises a series of complex interaction problems, which are underconceptualized and seldom studied. Anthropologists, accustomed to handling complex meshings of this kind, can make significant contributions to this area, both in research within complex societies and in comparative studies.

In regard to the time-confound problem, the best solution is to avoid time-defined variables whenever possible and to search for measures that better reflect what we now index imprecisely by time. Experience of fathering, for example, is more accurately measured by number of children times their ages (a kind of experience-years measure) than by the customary age-of-eldest-child. In matrilineal societies, might number of nephew-years be the analogous measure? Trying out such indices offers a way out of the confounds and can only improve the specificity of our research. Futhermore, determining ages accurately has been a problem for many anthropologists; we should seize the opportunity to convert this fault into a virtue by devising more meaningful and utlimately more valuable life-course indicators than the mere passage of time.

SUMMARY

Research into the linkage of age to transitions in the life course is beset by problems inherent in three sets of overlapping conceptual areas: age-role transitions, the multidimensional life course, and normative social timetables. Some help is offered by (1) the notion of a role course; (2) distinguishing among timetables in terms of the degree to which they are shared; and (3) sensitivity to cohort effects and the analytic problems posed by multiple time-defined variables. But this is only a beginning; innumerable issues remain to be clarified.

Unavoidably, techniques of measurement are relatively undeveloped, for they must await conceptual progress. Given the state of the art, excessive concern about measurement is premature; we require a fuller exposition of the meaning and range of variables involved. Focused qualitative research should greatly improve our understanding in this complex area.

NOTES

The author gratefully acknowledges the support of NIA grant AG00097 and NIHM grant 29657 for research discussed in this chapter. Portions of this chapter were presented in the symposium The Art of Research at the annual meetings of the American Anthropological Association, Washington, D.C., December 1982.

FIGURE 6.1 Functional Equivalents of Confound Model Components

Component Meaning	General Experience	Specific Experience	Current Experience
Developmental Model	Cohort	Chronological age	Time of testing (period)
Role-Timing Model			
Parenting	Chronological age	Timing of parenthood	Age of first born child
Marriage	Cohort or chronological age	Timing of marriage	Years in marriage
Work	Chronological age	Timing of career	Years in career
	Organizational age	Timing of promotion	Years in rank

Source: Nydegger 1981b.

BIBLIOGRAPHY

Aldous, J. 1978. Family Careers: Developmental Change in Families. New York: Wiley.

Back, K. 1980. "Mathematics and the Poetry of Human Life and Points in-Between." In Life-Course: Integrative Theories and Exemplary Populations, ed. K. Back. AAAS Selected Symposium 41. Washington, D.C.: AAAS, pp. 157-69.

Back, K., and J. Morris. 1974. "Perception of Self and the Study of Whole Lives." In Normal Aging II, ed. E. Palmore. Durham: Duke University Press, pp. 216-21.

Baltes, P. 1968. "Longitudinal and Cross-Sectional Sequences in the Study of Age and Generation Effects." Human Development 11:145-71.

Baltes, P., H. Reese, and L. Lipsitt. 1980. "Life-Span Developmental Psychology." Annual Review of Psychology 31:65-110.

Bandura, A. 1982. "The Psychology of Chance Encounters and Life Paths." American Psychologist 37:747-55.

Bengtson, V., and N. Cutler. 1976. "Generations and Intergenerational Relations." In Handbook of Aging and the Social Sciences, ed. R. Binstock and E. Shanas. New York: Van Nostrand, pp. 130-59.

Biddle, B., and E. Thomas. 1966. Role Theory. New York: Wiley.

Birren, J. 1959. "Principles of Research in Aging." In Handbook of Aging and the Individual, ed. J. Birren. Chicago: University of Chicago Press, pp. 3-42.

Block, J. 1971. Lives through Time. Berkeley, Calif: Bancroft.

Botwinick, J. 1977. "Intellectual Abilities." In Handbook of the Psychology of Aging, ed. J. Birren and K. W. Schaie. New York: Van Nostrand, pp. 580-605.

Brim, O., and C. Ryff. 1980. "On the Properties of Life Events." In Life-Span Development and Behavior, vol. 3, ed. P. Baltes and O. Brim, New York: Academic Press, pp. 367-88.

Bronfenbrenner, U. 1977. "Toward an Experimental Ecology of Human Development." American Psychologist 32:513-31.

Cain, L., Jr. 1964. "Life Course and Social Structure." In Handbook of Modern Sociology, ed. R. Faris. Chicago: Rand McNally.

Clausen, J. 1972. "The Life Course of Individuals." In Aging and Society, vol. 3, ed. M. Riley, M. Johnson, and A. Foner. New York: Russell Sage, pp. 457-514.

Cowgill, D., and L. Holmes. 1972. Aging and Modernization. New York: Appleton-Century-Crofts.

Datan, Nancy, and Leon Ginsberg. 1975. Life-Span Developmental Psychology: Normative Life-Crises. New York: Academic Press.

Demos, John, and S. S. Boocock. 1978. "Turning Points: Historical and Sociological Essays on the Family." Amercan Journal of Sociology 84 (supp.).

Dohrenwend, B. S., and B. P. Dohrenwend, ed. 1974. Stressful Life Events: Their Nature and Effects. New York: Wiley.

Dowd, J. 1975. "Aging as Exchange: A Preface to Theory." Journal of Gerontology 30:584-94.

Eckert, J. K. 1978. "Experiential Cohorts among American Men." Paper presented at meeting of the Gerontological Society, Dallas.

____. 1979. The Unseen Elderly. San Diego: Campanile.

Eichorn, D., et al., eds. 1981. Present and Past in Middle Life. New York: Academic Press.

Elder, G., Jr. 1974. Children of the Great Depression. Chicago: University of Chicago Press.

____. 1975. "Age Differentiation and the Life Course." In Annual Review of Sociology, vol. 1, ed. Alex Inkeles. pp. 165-90.

____. 1978. "Family History and the Life Course." In Transitions, ed. T. Hareven. New York: Academic Press, pp. 17-64.

____. 1979. "Historical Change in Life Patterns and Personality." In Life-Span Development and Behavior, vol. 2, ed. P. Baltes and O. Brim, Jr. New York: Academic Press, pp. 118-59.

Estes, Richard, and Harold Wilensky. 1978. "Life Cycle Squeeze and the Morale Curve." Social Problems 25:277-92.

Field, D. 1979. "Retrospective Reports of Personal Events in the Lives of Elderly People." Paper presented at International Society for the Study of Behavioral Development meetings, Stockholm.

Foner, Anne, and David Kertzer. 1978. "Transitions over the Life Course: Lessons from Age-Set Societies." American Journal of Sociology 83:1081-1104.

Fry, Christine. 1980a. "Cultural Dimensions of Age: A Multidimensional Scaling Analysis." In Aging in Culture and Society, ed. C. Fry. Brooklyn, N. Y.: Bergin, pp. 42-64.

____. ed. 1980b. Aging in Culture and Society. Brookly, N. Y.: Bergin.

____. ed. 1981. Dimensions: Aging, Culture, and Health. Brooklyn, N. Y.: Bergin.

George, Linda. 1980. Role Transitions in Later Life. Belmont, Calif: Wadsworth.

Gergen, K. 1980. "The Emerging Crisis in Life-Span Developmental Theory." In Life-Span Development and Behavior, vol. 3, ed. P. Baltes and O. Brim, Jr. New York: Academic Press, pp. 31-63.

Glaser, B., and A. Strauss. 1971. Status Passage. Chicago: Aldine-Atherton.

Goffman, E. 1958. Presentation of Self in Everyday Life. Edinburgh: University of Edinburgh Press.

Goodenough, W. 1965. "Rethinking 'Status' and 'Role'." In The Relevance of Models for Social Anthropology, ed. M. Banton. London: Tavistock, pp. 1-24.

Goody, J. 1976. "Aging in Nonindustrial Societies." In Handbook of Aging and the Social Sciences, ed. R. Binstock and E. Shanas. New York: Van Nostrand, pp. 117-29.

Gordon, C. 1972. "Role and Value Development across the Life Cycle." In Role: Sociological Studies, vol. 4, ed. J. A. Jackson. London: Cambridge University Press, pp. 65-105.

Gunderson, E. K. E. and R. H. Rahe, eds. 1974. Life Stress and Illness. Springfield, Ill.: Charles C Thomas.

Gutmann, D. 1977. "The Cross-Cultural Perspective: Notes toward a Comparative Psychology of Aging." In Handbook of the Psychology of Aging, ed. J. Birren and K. W. Schaie. New York: Van Nostrand, pp. 302-26.

Haberman, S. 1978, 1979. Analysis of Qualitative Data, vols. 1, 2. New York: Academic Press.

Hagestad, Gunhild, and Bernice Neugarten. 1985. "Age and the Life Course." In Handbook of Aging and the Social Sciences, ed. E. Shanas and R. Binstock (rev. 2nd ed.). New York: Van Nostrand, pp. 35-61.

Hareven, Tamara, ed. 1978. Transitions: The Family and the Life Course in Historical Perspective. New York: Academic Press.

_____. 1981. "Historical Changes in The Timing of Family Transitions." In Aging: Stability and Change in the Family, ed. R. Fogel et al. New York: Academic.

Hogan, Dennis. 1978. "The Variable Order of Events in the Life Course." American Sociological Review 43:573-86.

_____. 1981. Transitions and Social Change. New York: Academic.

Hollander, M. and D. Wolfe. 1973. Nonparametric Statistical Methods. New York: Wiley.

Holmes, T. H. and R. H. Rahe. 1967. "The Social Readjustment Rating Scale." Journal of Psychosomatic Research 11:213-18.

Hudson, R., and R. Binstock. 1976. "Political Systems and Aging." In Handbook of Aging and the Social Sciences, ed. R. Binstock and E. Shanas. New York: Van Nostrand, pp. 369-400.

Hultsch, D., and T. Hickey. 1978. "External Validity in the Study of Human Development: Theoretical and Methodological Issues." Human Development 21:76-91.

Hultsch, David, and Judy Plemons. 1979. "Life Events and Life-Span Development." In Life-Span Development and Behavior, vol. 2, ed. P. Baltes and O. Brim. New York: Academic Press, pp. 1-36.

Johnson, M. 1982. "Personal Biography and Group Experience: A Methodological Innovation." Paper presented at World Congress of Sociolgy, Mexico City.

_____. 1983. "Professional Careers and Biographies." In The Sociolgoy of the Professions, ed. R. Dingwall and P. Lewis. New York: St. Martin's, pp. 242-62.

Jones, M. C., et al., eds. 1971. The Course of Human Development. Waltham, Mass.: Xerox College Pub.

Klein, D., S. Jorgensen, and B. Miller. 1979. "Research Methods and Developmental Reciprocity in Families." In R. Lerner and G. Spanier, eds, Child Influences on Marital and Family Interaction. New York: Academic.

Kluckhohn, Clyde, and H. A. Murray. 1948. "Personality Formation: The Determinants." In Personality in Nature, Society, and Culture, ed. C. Kluckhohn and H. A. Murray. New York: Alfred Knopf.

Langness, L. L., and G. Frank. 1981. Lives: An Anthropological Approach to Biography. Novato, Calif.: Chandler & Sharp.

Linton, R. 1936. The Study of Man. New York: Appleton-Century.

Lowenthal, Marjorie, Majda Thurnher, and David Chiriboga. 1975. Four Stages of Life. San Francisco: Jossey-Bass.

Maas, H., and J. Kuypers. 1974. From Thirty to Seventy. San Francisco: Jossey-Bass.

Mannheim, K. 1952. "The Problem of Generations." In Essays in the Sociology of Knowledge, ed. K. Mannheim. New York: Oxford University Press.

Matthews, S. 1983. "Analyzing Topical Oral Biographies of Old People: The Case of Friendship." Research on Aging 5:569-89.

Merton, R. 1957. Social Theory and Social Structure. New York: Free Press.

Migdal, Susan, Ronald Abeles, and Lonnie Sherrod. 1981. An Inventory of Longitudinal Studies of Middle and Old Age. New York: Social Science Research Council.

Mines, Mattison. 1981. "Indian Transitions: A Comparative Analysis of Adult Stages of Development." Ethos 9:95-121.

Modell, John, and Tamara Hareven. 1978. "Transitions: Patterns of Timing." In Transitions: The Family and the Life Course In Historical Perspective, ed. T. Hareven. New York: Academic Press, pp. 245-69.

Myerhoff, Barbara. 1980. "Life History among the Elderly: Performance, Visibility and Remembering." In Life Course: Integrative Theories and Exemplary Populations, ed. Kurt Back. AAAS Selected Symposium No. 41. New York: Praeger.

Myerhoff, B., and A. Simic. 1978. Life's Career: Aging. Beverly Hills, Calif.: Sage.

Nesselroade, J., and P. Baltes. 1979. Longitudinal Research in the Study of Behavior and Development. New York: Academic Press.

Neugarten, B., J. Moore, and J. Lowe. 1968. "Age Norms, Age Constraints, and Adult Socialization." In Middle Age and Aging, ed. B. Neugarten. Chicago: University of Chicago Press.

Neugarten, B., and G. O. Hagestad. 1976. "Age and the Life Course." In Handbook of Aging and the Social Sciences, R. H. Bunstock and E. Shanas, eds. New York: Van Nostrand Reinhold.

Nydegger, C. 1977. "Multiple Cohort Membership." Paper presented at meetings of the Gerontological Society. San Francisco.

_____. 1981a. "Gerontology and Anthropology." In Dimensions: Aging, Culture, and Health, ed. C. Fry. Brooklyn, N. Y.: Bergin.

_____. 1981b. "On Being Caught Up in Time." Human Development 24:1-12.

Nydegger, C., L. Mitteness, and J. O'Neil. 1983. "Experiencing Social Generations: Phenomenal Dimensions." Research on Aging 5:527-46.

Plath, David. 1980. "Contours of Consociation: Lessons from A Japanese Narrative." In Life-Span Development ad Behavior, vol. 3, ed. P. Baltes and O. Brim. New York: Academic Press. pp. 287-305.

Proshansky, H. M. 1976. "Environmental Psychology and the Real World." American Psychologist 31:303-10.

Reese, H. W., and M. A. Smyer. 1983. "The Dimensionalization of Life Events." In Life-Span Developmental Psychology: Non-Normative Life Events, ed. E. J. Callahan and K. McCluskey. New York: Academic Press.

Riegel, K. 1979. Foundations of Dialectical Psychology. New York: Academic Press.

Riley, M. 1976. "Age Strata in Social Systems." In Handbook of Aging and the Social Sciences, ed. R. Binstock and E. Shanas. New York: Van Nostrand, pp. 189-217.

Riley, M., et al. 1972. Aging and Society, vol. 3. New York: Russell Sage.

Rosow, I. 1976. "Status and Role Change through the Life Span." In Handbook of Aging and the Social Sciences, ed. R. Binstock and E. Shanas. New York: Van Nostrand, pp. 457-82.

____. 1978. "What is a Cohort and Why?" Human Development 21:65-75.

Ross, J. 1977. Old People, New Lives. Chicago: University of Chicago Press.

Roth, J. 1963. Timetables: Structuring the Passage of Time in Hospital Treatment and Other Careers. Indianapolis, Ind.: Bobbs Merrill.

Runyan, William. 1980. "A Stage-State Analysis of the Life Course." Journal of Personality and Social Psychology. 38:951-62.

Ryder, N. B. 1965. "The Cohort as a Concept in the Study of Social Change." American Sociological Review 30:843-61.

Sarbin, T., and V. Allen. 1968. "Role Theory." In Handbook of Social Psychology, vol. 1, ed. G. Lindzey and E. Aronson. Reading, Mass: Addison-Wesley, pp. 488-567.

Schaie, J. K. 1965. "A General Model for the Study of Developmental Problems." Psychological Bulletin 64:92-107.

Sokolovsky, Jay, and Carl Cohen. 1981. "Being Old in the Inner City: Support Systems of the SRO Aged." In Dimensions: Aging, Culture, and Health, ed. C. Fry. Brooklyn, N. Y.: Bergin, pp. 163-84.

Spanier, G., and W. Sauer. 1979. "An Empirical Evaluation of the Family Life Cycle." Journal of Marriage and the Family 41:27-38.

Streib, G. 1976. "Social Stratification and Aging." In Handbook of Aging and the Social Sciences, ed. R. Binstock and E. Shanas, New York: Van Nostrand, pp. 160-85.

Thomae, H. 1979. "The Concept of Development and Life-Span Developmental Psychology." In Life-Span Development and Behavior, vol. 2, ed. P. Baltes and O. Brim, Jr. New York: Academic Press, pp. 281-312.

Tuma, N. B., M. T. Hannan, and L. P. Groeneveld. 1979. "Dynamic Analysis of Event Histories." American Journal of Sociology 84:820-54.

Uhlenberg, Peter. 1974. "Cohort Variations in Family Life Cycle Experiences of U.S. Females." Journal of Marriage and the Family 36:284-92.

van Gennep, A. 1960. Rites of Passage. Chicago: University of Chicago Press.

Waring, J. 1975. "Social Replenishment and Social Change." American Behavioral Scientist 19:237-55.

Wohlwill, J. 1970. "The Age Variable in Psychological Research." Psychological Review 77:49-64.

Yarrow, M., J. Campbell, and R. Burton. 1970. Recollections of Childhood: A Study of the Retrospective Method. Society for Research in Child Development Monographs, No. 35.

7
Ritualization of the Life Cycle

JOHN T. HINNANT
Department of Anthropology
Michigan State University

INTRODUCTION

Ritual is a means for communicating the most profound truths of a culture to its members. Among different forms of ritual, those marking the stages of life convey the deepest conceptualization of the meaning of existence. All cultures have some degree of ritualization of birth, marriage, and death, and a very large number also mark the transition from childhood to adulthood. A portion of this group marks even finer divisions of life with rite-of-passage ceremonies that dramatically separate individuals from their previous identity and provide them with the cultural knowledge for moving to the next higher level of life. That the later stages of life may be seen as "higher" rather than merely older is often due to the way a culture communicates an idealized view of life. As Baxter and Almagor have eloquently stated, "Age systems are a device to make the cruel descent through life to decay appear as if it were an ascent to a superior, because senior, condition" (1978:24).

Researchers who study aging often concentrate on behavioral, statistical, and institutional aspects of the later stages of life, but frequently ignore the cultural reality through which people learn to perceive the course of their lives. This chapter will present a methodology for investigating the ritualization of this cultural reality. The ultimate intent is to learn about aging, but (as will be argued later) it is almost impossible to look at the ritualization of only one phase of life in isolation.

163

Fieldworkers conducting research in different parts of the world will find varying degrees of elaboration of life-cycle ritualization. In order to be appropriate to the full range of field situations, this chapter will address itself, initially, to the more elaborate types of age organization and ritual. The specific techniques for analyzing ritual discussed in the middle sections may be useful to the study of age ritual in any society, including our own. The final section of the chapter is in part directed to the study of aging in Third World countries, but it also addresses certain general issues.

CULTURAL SYSTEMS BASED ON AGE

A relatively small number of the world's societies[1] have developed explicit models for the aging process, through systems of age grading, in which the male[2] life cycle is divided into a sequence of distinct phases, or *grades*, punctuated by rites of passage. Generally, individuals are initiated in groups that are referred to as *age sets*.[3] The term *age class* refers to all of the age sets introduced into the system during a given initiation period. Initiation is not triggered by exact biological age, but by societally defined appropriate age range (van Gennep 1960). This is due in part to the fact that initiation ceremonies are held during restricted periods every few years. All who are within the general range of the appropriate age are initiated together, and then the initiation period is closed until the next class of age sets enters the system.[4] The length of time an age class remains within a given grade is culturally variable.

A few cultures in northeastern Africa have evolved a complex variant of age grading, known as *generation grading*. In these cases, initiation into the system is controlled not by the age of initiates, but by a fixed rule that all of a man's sons must be initiated into the system a set period of time after the father. For instance, in the case of the Guji Oromo, of Ethiopia (Hinnant 1978), all of a man's sons must be initiated into the system forty years after him. Generation-grading systems are highly unstable demographically and must have rules restricting the number of years men can legitimately sire children. Otherwise, the age span of initiates would make it impossible for them all to play the appropriate roles of the various grades.[5] The effectiveness of these rules is often minimal, however.

Even in the tortuous case of generation grading, initiates pass together through a hierarchy of grades that are entered through a succession of rites of passage. These ceremonies provide initiates with vital information for the succeeding stages of life. As van

Gennep (1960) has demonstrated, initiates passing through these ceremonies are symbolically stripped of their previous identity, go through a period of transition, and then are reincorporated into society with a new, older, social identity. The rituals, as Turner (1969:94-203) has further shown, offer initiates the most profound cosmological meanings of their culture, while at the same time providing more mundane instruction about the next stage of life. Rituals compel initiates to step back from the petty affairs of daily life and to enter the realm of a culturally defined eternal order that is structured very differently from daily life. During these ceremonies myth is more "true" than the "truths" of the village or cattle camp. Turner (1969:94-165) states that the shared experience of rite-of-passage rituals provides those who are initiated together a common experience of statuslessness (communitas) and shared insights, which become the basis of the continuing relationship among them.

GENERAL CHARACTERISTICS OF LIFE CYCLE RITUALS

Life cycle rituals provide members of a culture with a rich and detailed model for the meaning of each stage of life. For the researcher, however, these rituals can be a perplexing mystery. On first viewing the ritual of another culture, the researcher may find that nothing is comprehensible. There are several reasons for this. Rituals are clearly dramatic events which are set off in time from the normal flow of daily affairs. The symbolism of ritual contains greatly condensed meaning, in that verbal symbols often have a poetic compactness that is different from daily speech. In addition, much of ritual communication involves nonverbal communications such as dance and the manipulation of objects, which themselves are charged with meaning. If the researcher has not grown up in the culture under investigation and has not fully mastered the language, he may feel himself to be at a distinct disadvantage. This paper will attempt to reduce that disadvantage by suggesting a number of frameworks for the observation and analysis of ritual. While no effort will be made to present a set of laboratory procedures, an attempt will be made to direct the investigator's attention to fruitful areas of inquiry.

Before discussing specific issues, it will be useful to mention a few general characteristics of life cycle rituals.

Performance

The performance of a ritual does not progress in a linear manner.

Rather, it is useful to think of a ritual as being like a play in many acts (or a poem in many verses). There is a central theme (here, transition), but each "act" of the ritual explores a different dimension of that theme. For example, life cycle rituals mark the changing relationships between initiates, kinsmen, and other members of the community, as well as alterations in their political, economic, and religious status. Even sexual identity may be portrayed differently at various stages of life-cycle ritual. The "acts" of a ritual may be separated by periods of secular time when participants shift back to discussing daily affairs and seem to have quite forgotten the ceremony. Thematic shifts in the ritual may otherwise be marked by different actors taking over the performance, or by music or dance. When the researcher reviews data from a completed ritual it may become apparent that there is a fair amount of redundancy among the acts, but that this repetitiveness adds emphasis to the symbolic message.

Variations in Ritual Performance

No two performances of a given ritual are identical. The performers change, there are regional variations, and some rituals are simply botched. Variability may at first be annoying but should actually be the basis for fruitful questioning. When informants are asked to explain why differences occur, they are often led to a more philosophical commentary on the meaning of the ritual as a whole. Botched rituals are especially interesting. They tend to cause much discussion and criticism, which may contain valuable clues about meaning.

In the instance of one botched Guji rite-of-passage ritual, a somewhat unusual man (who lived with his sons apart from his two wives) seemed to deliberately mismanage every phase of a rite-of-passage ceremony marking his promotion to more senior elderhood (*dori*). Observation of two previous instances of this ritual had yielded much information, but the many days of gossip and criticism after this performance led to a much greater appreciation of the implications of ritual for the future destiny of its participants, and for their status as competent members of society.

Stages of Transition

The process of the unfolding of life-cycle ritual may be usefully thought of in terms of Arnold von Gennep's (1960) classic stages of separation, transition, and reincorporation. The separation phase is marked by symbols of the stripping or death of an old status. Washing with water, blood, or other substance, stripping of clothing and jewelry, shaving of the head, or other symbols of removal of identity are characteristic. As Turner (1969) has pointed out, in societies in which initiates pass through transition together, they are shorn of their individualistic statuses and thereby come to share an identity of diffuse solidarity or communitas.

Transition is a time of education. Initiates enter into a period in which their new role in life is presented to them in a dramatic context, with instruction by individuals of high ritual status. Initiates are often exposed to symbolic statements about the philosophical dilemmas of each stage of life. In this state they may be vulnerable to ritual pollution by the uninitiated and may in turn be dangerous to them. Reincorporation into society with a new status involves putting on the raiment of that status in the fullest sense, and being presented to society at large, usually in a festive setting.

The play-in-many-acts quality of ritual is especially noticeable in the stages of transition. Each act of a life-cycle may employ symbols of each stage of transition, or may concentrate on only one. Initiates may be shorn of past identity in many aspects-- bathing, removal of hair, ritual nudity--each employed in a different part of the ceremony. Instruction most likely will occur in most acts, but the instruction may, by turns, emphasize secular roles and new ritual relations with divinity. The phase of reincorporation in the later stages of life may emphasize the religious nature of senior roles and the shedding of secular responsibility. Newly made priests, for example, may be presented as the earthly manifestations of divinity. When life-passage rituals are viewed in toto for a given society, it may become clear that the overall emphasis on one or another of van Gennep's stages varies throughout the sequence (with, for example, less emphasis being given to the preliminal phase in promotion from junior to senior elder than in either adulthood initiation or death ritual), and that this may be an important clue to the relative message of each ritual.

Schedule of Life-Cycle Rituals

One of the more frustrating aspects of life-cycle rituals may be the infrequency of their performance. In societies in which people pass through the ceremonies in groups, a number of years may pass between occurrences of the rituals. Even then, the rituals may be staggered, with some stages of the life cycle being initiated years after other stages. For a researcher attempting to investigate these ceremonies, only a part of the sequence may be available during the fieldwork period, and there may be only a few performances of each ritual in the entire society. In this case the fieldworker will have to build an understanding of missed rituals by interviews with knowledgeable informants, and will have to prepare carefully for the rituals that can be observed. The ceremonies marking birth, marriage, and death are of course performed on an individual basis, and it is far easier to see a number of instances of each.

PREPARATION FOR THE OBSERVATION OF RITUAL

Since fieldworkers may have very few opportunities to observe life-cycle rituals, they need to prepare carefully for those they do see. If it is at all possible, a variety of participants in an upcoming ritual should be interviewed in advance so that the observer will at least know the broad outlines of what to anticipate. Those interviewed should include initiates, the sponsor of the ceremony and the sponsor's spouse, any ritual experts who may be responsible for the proper performance of sacred action, and the person actually responsible for the overall performance. From them it should be possible to ascertain the important stages of the ritual actions and their general meaning, specifics of who must attend (kinsmen, affines, age-mates, neighbors, priests), and how these people are related to one another.

Researchers working in another culture often have an assistant from that culture who grew up in the local area. The assistant can be most helpful in collecting information about a ritual. First, the assistant should be trained in the techniques of careful observation and note taking. Second, if camera and tape recorder are permitted, the assistant should be trained in their use. During the performance the assistant should periodically be allowed to work independently, recording and photographing what he or she thinks is important. Because of the assistant's cultural knowledge and sensitivity to the nuance of language, it is likely that important information will be collected that the researcher would have missed.

During the performance, everyone collecting information should make frequent notations of the time, both when writing notes and when taping. Otherwise, attempts at reconstructing the ceremony from different data sources will be chaotic. Also, the timing of ritual action is consequential, as will be seen below.

FRAMES FOR OBSERVING RITUAL ACTION

It is crucial to view rituals analytically while they are occurring. The stages of transition discussed above are major aids in this direction. In addition, several specific observational frames are important.

Space

The place where the ceremony is held may well be conceptually divided into different zones. The most basic distinctions are the geographical directions (compass points), right and left[6] (which are usually given different moral values), center-periphery (or distance from some focal point such as a shrine or hearth), and inside or outside a bounded space. Certain segments of a ceremonial area may be assigned by gender or age of performers. The assignment of different categories of people to a simple set of contrasted ritual spaces is often employed to make profound statements about the place in society of individuals and groups, and about transitions as performers are moved about in ritual space.

The fieldworker should learn in advance the zones of a ceremonial stage and should make drawings of the locations of actors at frequent intervals. A major set of communicative acts may involve the joining and separation of the initiate and representatives of different kin and generational groups, as well as the position of initiates relative to the sacred center of ritual space.

Time

Time is central to the performance of ritual along many dimensions. First, in societies in which there are group initiations (whether they consist of an elaborate set of age-grade rituals or simply the periodic initiation of children into adulthood) the timing of the onset of the rituals should be investigated. Is an elaborate calendrical system used, or is a simple counting of years or the availability of initiates the basis? Are the phases of the moon assigned values (completeness, or fatness and abundance), with different life-cycle rituals performed in different phases? It is also important to learn who has the responsibility for setting the date for rituals to occur. This may be a high-status position for a senior person.

The time during which a ritual actually transpires is often charged with meaning. Dusk and dawn are times used to bring about human transitions of status. The timing of acts during rituals, and those who control the timing, may provide important clues to meaning. The subjective sense of shared time during ritual (and the different types of time during song, dance, chants, and so on) may be a key part of the shared communication of ritual.

The nature of time during the life cycle itself is often given profound meaning. In many societies life is not thought of as a linear course but as a cycle, with the beginning and end somewhat mirroring each other. Expressed in terms of generations, the childhood and grandparental generations are seen as being alike as the ends of existence, and as periods without secular power (but possibly with greater sanctity, or "innocence"), whereas the parental generation, caught up in economic and political affairs, is seen as being very different. In rituals there may be periods in which this is emphasized by separating the generations or denying one or another the use of areas of ritual space.

Gender

The culturally defined differences between male and female at each stage of the life cycle not only define appropriate behavior and responsibility, but also serve as metaphors for social values and cosmological forces. Gender is often combined with other symbolic oppositions such as right and left, sky and earth, and culture and nature to make a wide range of symbolic statements.[7]

In many cultures gender differentiation in ritual will portray men and women as belonging to different cultural domains. Men are presented as directors of the public realm of politics, economics, and major areas of ritual. In most traditional cultures men are also the keepers of ritual knowledge, myth, and the paraphernalia of the major divinities. Women are portrayed as controlling the domestic domain of the household and a large part of food production. Often there is ritual knowledge controlled by women, but it is generally concerned with curing rather than major propitiatory ceremonies or rites of passage. The actual behavior of women (for example, in controlling markets) may be considerably at variance with their portrayal in ritual.

In addition, as mentioned earlier, in most societies formalized age-grade systems are for men only. This is explained by Kertzer and Madison in the following way:

Aging has different implications for male and females, the nature, sequence and timing of the allocation of social roles to males and females through their life course differ. This sexual quality has led to a lack of structural parallel between the institutionalization of aging men through age-set systems and the weakness of age as an organizing principle for women in those same societies. In this light, the seeming monopoly by men of age-set systems is simply the dramatic expression in societies which employ age as an explicit principle of social groupings of the universal principle that social processes of aging are sex-specific. (1981:127).

During the life cycle and its ritualization, the gender of individuals may be seen to change considerably. For males, often the beginning and end of life may lack the strong display of "masculinity" of the middle of life. For females, the transition to strong "femininity" may begin with an adulthood ceremony, be enhanced with the move from paternal to husband's house, and finally be seen as fully developed at childbirth. In some cultures women at the end of life may be conceptualized as much more like elder men in their social role than they ever were like men previously.

In the observation of ritual and of individuals in daily life, contrasts and similarities in costume between the sexes and between different generations of the same sex should be carefully observed. Men and women should also be questioned separately about their perceptions of the meaning of rituals.

Social Relations

The passage through the life cycle involves continual realignments among people. These changes often find expression in the sequence of life-cycle rituals.

In the case of males, the life-cycle sequence shows the evolution of male initiates from dependence on the maternal-domestic realm to the paternal-societal realm, followed by independence and authority expressed in terms of age-mates and society at large, and finally the gradual growth of dependence on junior generations for physical support. Since life-cycle ceremonies involve several generations of kin and representatives from the larger society in any given ceremony, there may be a complex play of statements and actions centering around the realignment of social roles and responsibilities. The acting out of these changes can vary from rather poignant dialogue between kin to the exchange of objects indicating new social alignments.

In many traditional cultures, realignments in women's roles will be between kin and affines, with the adulthood and marriage ceremonies expressing these changes.

In observing life-cycle rituals, the symbolic commentary on role change is easy to overlook. It usually lacks the dramatic force of head shaving, scarification, animal sacrifice, and other compelling acts that define other aspects of transition. Yet role-change symbolism yields some of the most important insights into proper conduct in daily life. It is therefore crucial to learn the relationships among the actors in a ritual, and to think through ritual action in terms of these relations. A well-trained local assistant can be especially valuable here, since he or she will be more likely than the investigator to see ritual interactions in terms of concrete social relations, rather than as more abtract conceptualizations.

Exchange

It is an anthropological truism that social relations are often defined by systems of exchange. During life-cycle rituals, exchanges may take place at various points in the performance, and these should all be investigated. It is therefore important to arrive early at ceremonies, to observe who brings food and other gifts. During the ceremony certain people may give food to one another, or exchange other objects. In addition, gifts may be promised for after the ceremony; this is the case in age-grade ceremonies in certain pastoral societies when initiates into the junior grades are promised cattle for their herds by their fathers and other senior kinsmen.

Food and Festivity

Life-cycle ceremonies generally involve the consumption of large quantities of food. The idea of abundance is often important for rituals that, in part, are designed to promote success in later stages of life. In fact, the timing of these ceremonies may partially depend on bountiful harvests and may be delayed in years of drought and disease. The specific foods eaten on these occasions may have undergone preparations that are peculiar to the ceremonies.

Food restrictions may also be important for distinctions among stages of life. In some cultures, people at various stages of the life cycle are required to eat specific foods and to refrain from others. In a sense, the food restrictions are part of the definition of the life cycle. These restrictions even help define social associations, since people are more likely to eat with those who have the same food restrictions.[8] It is therefore important not only to observe what people consume during ceremonies according to their sex and generation, but also to investigate the allowed foods for the entire life cycle.

Additional Symbolic Distinctions

In a given ceremony, there will be other types of symbols in addition to those just discussed. Many objects will be manipulated or exchanged, including not only manufactured items but also various plant and animal products. These objects, their names and ritual uses, should of course be noted during the ceremony, and informants should be questioned later about their meaning. It is important to learn their use in nonritual contexts.[9]

Another key attribute of ritual symbols is color. Cultures employ sets of contrasting colors in ritual, and each color is rich in symbolic meaning. It often happens that objects are used ritually because of their own color, or objects are given a new color to add new dimensions to the meaning they already have.[10]

Turner (1967b) points out that some ritual symbols are polysemic; that is, a great deal of meaning is condensed in one symbol, and this meaninq is "unpacked" in a multiplicity of ritual contexts. Other symbols are instrumental, being used primarily to facilitate the sequence of actions in a ceremony. The meaning of symbols can be learned by asking informants and by examining the range of contexts in which they occcur. This topic will be discussed later.

INDIVIDUAL VS. GROUP CEREMONIES

The discussion of observational frames is intended to apply both to ceremonies in which groups of coevals are initiated together and to the individual ceremonies marking birth, death, and possibly other life stages. (In Western cultures, of course, the individual ceremonies that go with marriage are predominant.) It is useful to make special mention of birth and death ceremonies.

The importance of birth ritual for aging is that birth and death rituals mirror each other along certain dimensions. Birth ritual involves the creation of a new social person, an actor who will stand in a particular set of relationships to people already living and who will be destined to play certain other predetermined social roles. In contrast, death ritual involves, in part, the dissolution of a social person. There are now gaps in the kinship and community structures, and these must be acknowledged and repaired. Birth and death ritual thus become commentaries on each other.

Death rituals also provide an important commentary on the later stages of life. Depending on the conceptualization of the afterlife, death ritual may be seen as a rite of passage into another level of existence, that of ancestor who will continue to influence the group. Or the dead person may be reborn into another generation of the group. In some cases, at death the individual passes beyond direct influence on the living. In each case mortuary ritual will reflect the regard, concern, and possibly fear the living have for the dead and for those near the end of life.

When the kin and affines gather for death ritual at burial, the goods and possibly the special statuses of the dead person are divided. The researcher can learn a great deal about the conditions of old age from this process. Was the newly dead person devoid of property and fully dependent on younger generations, or was he still controlling valuable resources needed by the living?

The full expression of death ritual may not be confined to the time of burial. In some cultures secondary burial takes place long after the time of death. Each stage of mortuary ritual can provide important insights into the status of the eldest living generation.[11]

INDIGENOUS INTERPRETATION OF RITUAL

The observation of a ritual should produce a large amount of data describing the ritual action, along with diagrams of actors' movements in ritual space, short genealogies of the relationships among actors, photographs, tapes, and so on. The next step is to return to those participants who were interviewed before the ceremony and to discuss the ritual from beginning to end (a process that might involve several interviews with each informant). It is at this point that the actors' own understanding of what the ritual communicated can be learned. A discussion of the ritual in terms of the observational frames presented earlier will be most useful in directing an informant through each stage of the ceremony, and in convincing informants that the investigator is genuinely interested in fully understanding the ritual. The richness of observational data should permit asking the highly specific questions that an informant can most easily answer. Why did the junior and senior age sets leave the ceremonial grounds when members of the middle age set had their heads shaved? Why was the beginning of the ceremony delayed until actor X arrived? Why at a particular point did the man being interviewed have to locate his eldest sister and give her a container of milk? Why that kind of container?

In addition to the highly structured interviews aimed at exegesis of ritual symbols, it is important to learn the personal reactions of a range of participants to the specific ceremony. Was the ceremony successful in comparison with others seen by the informant? How will the initiate be different after the ceremony? Will the initiate associate with different people? Will the initiate treat this informant differently? People interviewed for personal reactions should include those mentioned earlier as well as participants of both sexes and a wide variety of ages. These additional informants should be asked enough general questions about the meaning of the ritual to determine their level of understanding. It will soon become apparent that there is a wide range of appreciation of a ceremony by age and sex. It is important to determine what is communicated to the heterogeneous audience by life-cycle ritual. One of the faults of the general age-grade literature is that it concentrates on initiates, to the exclusion of others. In fact, everyone learns about what to anticipate in the later stages of life by being involved in the ceremonies. Researchers wishing to learn about aging should also ask the young how they perceive senior-level ceremonies. The results may provide important clues to how the young think about the course of their own lives, and how they treat older people.

THE ROLE OF OLDER PEOPLE IN RITUAL

In terms of the study of aging, it is especially important to ascertain the role of older people in ritual. In many cultures the control of ritual is in their hands, and it is they who mediate between earthly and divine powers. An investigator concentrating solely on the secular role of this age range might misperceive old people as having little importance for society. For this reason it is necessary at least to inquire about the significant ritual roles in all types of ceremonialism, not just age-related performances.

Frequently, the cultural model of older people is that they have passed through secular concerns, have mastered them, and are now at a more pure stage of life, one more like divinity. For example, in the Guji Oromo generation grading system (Hinnant 1978), each higher grade is a step toward priesthood. Finally, after the *gada* grade of greatest secular authority, a man should transfer most of his property to his sons and live primarily for religious activities. It is these *yuba* priests who direct the full sequence of rites of passage, terminating with mortuary ritual, which is considered the most dangerous of all ceremonies. In addition to these ceremonies, *yubas* are actors in a variety of propitiatory ceremonies. Yet, in daily life they appear to have a minimal social role, and are often dependent on adult children for survival.

Similar ritual importance for the old has been reported elsewhere. For instance, Pamela Amoss, in discussing the role of elders in Coast Salish society, has divided the historical transition in the role of ritual expert ino three stages. First, during aboriginal times, the elders were the controllers of ritual knowledge. During the second period, that of culture contact and the growing importance of the Shaker church, the old system of ritual knowledge and control fell into disuse. In the final stage, the old ways have become a key part of cultural identity, as have the ritual powers of the old. Amoss says of the Coast Salish elders:

> The two avenues of religious expression that are most "indian" and in which the elders are most important are the Winter Dancing and the Shaker Church. Both exalt knowledge of the old ways and the older people as vessels of that knowledge. Both systems maintain that a person grows in power as he or she learns how to cooperate with the spirit, whether a guardian spirit or the Holy Spirit which inspires Shakers. Since older people have been practicing this cooperation longer, they are spiritually stronger than young people. Furthermore, survival to old age is itself taken as evidence of good spiritual connections. (Amoss 1981:57)

As Amoss' statement implies, it is as important to study the role of the old in the Shaker Church ritual as in the recreated winter dance. In both instances, old people are innovating rituals to be performed by the whole society. Biesele and Howell (1981), in discussing the role of old people in !Kung society, indicate that elders are central to curing ritual because of their ritual knowledge and the efficacy of their medicine spirits. There may be cases in which the old have finally lost power due to rapid social change, but this should never be assumed without investigation.

ANALYSIS

The analysis of ritual symbols depends in part on the researcher's perspective on theories of symbolism and meaning. There is a vast (and growing) literature on this topic,[12] and it is not the intention here to suggest a particular orientation. Whatever the researcher's perspective, there are certain goals of analysis in terms of the life cycle and aging.

First, a consideration of the sequence of life-cycle rituals in a society or ethnic group should reveal the formal (idealized) models for the sequence of roles an individual will play in the larger society. In terms of aging, is the individual directed to give up secular economic concerns and involve himself or herself in religion? Is old age seen as a decline, or as a purification of spirit from which state the individual is uniquely able to serve as priest and ritual expert? What does death ritual indicate about the ability of ancestors to influence the living, and how does this affect the perception of older people?

Second, the set of life-cycle rituals should present a normative model for the changing relationships between an individual and his or her kin, affines, and peers. At each stage of life one or another of these groups assumes central importance, and the ritual sequence should indicate the overall pattern of changes.

Third, the analysis should indicate the changing nature of the definition of gender and proper relationships between sexes at each stage. The strong emphasis on sharp gender differentiation may be in effect only for the central part of the life cycle, or may be in effect from earliest child training.

Fourth, and most abstractly, the sequence of life-cycle rituals should reveal the complex metaphorical relationships among the individual, divinities, and cosmological forms that control human destiny. Some life-cycle ritual sequences provide a path between levels of ability to supplicate divinity for the rewards of abundance and healthy long life.

Fifth, in terms of aging, the rituals should reveal the extent to which the end of life is conceptualized as a mirror image of its beginning and of the ultimate worth of the individual at the end of existence. In addition, it may happen that the most important social role of older people is to be ritual experts and directors of life-cycle ceremonies for those more junior.

Turning to the analysis itself, it should be carried out in terms of major ritual themes. It is virtually certain that van Gennep's tripartite system of separation, transition, and reincorporation will be clearly discernible. But what are the additional themes in the various "acts" of the ritual? What makes transition in this particular society distinctive? The contribution of many specific symbols to these themes should be fairly clear also. However, there will no doubt be apparent changes in the meaning of symbols among the different life-cycle rituals, and there will be symbols for which no meaning is apparent. In both cases, much of the meaning of a symbol can be learned by comparing the contexts in which it occurs.

An invaluable aid to discovering the full set of contexts of specific symbols in a set of field notes is the construction of a symbolism index. Presumably, the field notes from an ethnographic study of aging contain data concerning a wide variety of topics in addition to ritual. The full set of notes should be organized by topic and further ordered by the date on which they were recorded. The symbolism index involves preparing a large note card for each ritual symbol (blood, special foods, the use of a particular species of wood) and noting all occurrences of the symbols in the corpus of notes. Each card should contain a brief summary of each occurrence of that symbol and the topic and date reference by which the full statement may be found in the full corpus of field notes. The construction of an index obviously takes time, but is worth the effort in that it allows the most complete use of collected data for understanding the relationships among ritual symbols.

FINAL ISSUES

It is important to understand that the role of life-cycle ritual is not to provide an exact script for social action but to create a more philosophical ideal for proper action and proper relationships at each stage of life. Just as the study of social action is not fully adequate for assessing the cultural meaning of the life cycle in a particular society, the study of ritual is also not fully adequate for understanding social action. It is not the purpose of this paper to discuss the specific methodology for studying social action, but a few comments are in order on the relationships among ritual, action, and individuals' subjective perceptions of aging.

One failing of the general anthropological literature on age grading is that it does not attempt to present the individual's understanding of aging per se. Does the individual evaluate his or her life in terms of the standards imparted in ritual or in terms of other, perhaps more immediate, criteria? One means of assessing the individual's perceptions is that of the life review (Butler 1968). Butler asserts that there is a general pattern of reassessment of life experience by the elderly in terms of relative success and even moral worth. This often-piecemeal evaluation leads to a final subjective view of the total life course of each individual. Researchers have been able to serve as audiences for this assessment and thereby to learn the retrospective subjective reaction to each phase of life. If the life review is indeed a cross-cultural universal, it can be employed in traditional societies (including those with age grading) to assess the self-perception of older informants whose lives presumably continue to be highly valued. In cases in which the very old are venerated as near-ancestors, does this final "retirement" become the ultimate progression in life, and does life thus end without the sense of loss of significant function that may come with retirement from the workforce in the West?

Another major topic for investigation in the relationships between life-cycle ritual and social action is the effect of age grading (which may be present in one degree or another in a given society) on relationships within the family. Potentially, age-grade organization can prevent many of the intergenerational conflicts that beset families as the male head of the family grows old.

Among these potential areas of conflict are the time of succession to hereditary office of adult sons; the point at which control of economic resources passes from father to sons; and, in the case of polygamy, the point at which fathers cease to use family wealth to acquire new brides, and sons are then able to use these resources for their own marriages. Should the individual attempt to retain the prerogatives of earlier grades, the sanctioning of this inappropriate conduct may well come from age-mates, thus removing the intrafamily conflict to a larger social arena. Throughout life the individual has in part been socialized by age-mates; and in the final stages of life it is possibly they who ensure that the succession of generations will be a smooth one.

Another major issue in the relationship between ritual and social action is the different life cycle of the two sexes. Generally, the more elaborate ritualization of the life cycle, and especially formalized age-grading, is the province of males. The life cycle of females in these systems needs to be investigated. Typically, women pass through ceremonies marking birth, the end of childhood, marriage, and finally death. However, their fathers and husbands may be passing through a much more elaborate set of rituals and statuses. The question here is whether women perceive their life cycle in terms of a set of stages separate from their husbands' or whether they see themselves as being carried along with their husbands' sequence of age-grades. It should be possible to tap the semantic domains in which women define their lives using the card-sort method discussed by Fry (Chap. 5). Based on participant observation of adult activities, a set of cards could be designed to portray activities which are female specific, male specific (as a control), and finally age-grade related, shared by males and females (such as age-grade rituals and other occasions when women are expected to be present and active). Women and men could then be asked which cards show things important to their lives. The ultimate purpose of separate card sorts for males and females is to determine whether men and women operate in separate semantic domains when viewing the course and meaning of life, and ultimately whether they view the last stages of life in radically different ways.

In contemporary Third World countries, specific ethnic groups are often divided between those who still carry on the traditional way of life to some extent and those who live in the modernizing sector. Whenever possible, it is important to conduct comparative studies of aging in these two sectors. Often the traditional/modern distinction will coincide with rural/urban, but there are many cases in which part of the rural sector has been subjected to development projects of various sorts. In either case the role sequence contained in the age-grade system will most likely have been superseded by other, probably less well defined, social roles for the life cycle. The status of the elderly in the modernizing sector of Third World countries and their perception of that status are areas that require investigation. The same techniques, including the life review and card sorts, should be employed here. The cards used in the traditional sector should first be administered to determine whether the old semantic domain carries over in any sense. Then a second set of cards can be administered, one that reflects the apparent sequence of life in the rapidly changing sector. By such techniques it may be possible to comprehend the plight of those who in the past would have represented the collective wisdom of their people, but who now may well feel marginal. They may in fact be on the periphery of local government concern in social planning, in addition to having lost their central role in the family. In a more optimistic vein, it may be the case that explicit age-grading and the support of peers may facilitate the adaptation of older people to social change by using traditional cultural institutions.

NOTES

1. They are located in East Africa, West Africa, Taiwan, and in North and South America among a minority of American Indian groups. See Stewart (1977:115-124).

2. Most formalized age-grade systems are for men only. Generally, women pass through the ritualized transitions of birth, marriage, childbirth, and death, but do so individually. The only mass initiation usually occurs in those societies having adulthood ceremonies for women. For a discussion of the exceptional cases in which there are formalized age-grades for women, see Kertzer and Madison (1981). Also see the discussion of the issue later in this chapter.

3. The distinction between grade and age set was first made by Radcliffe-Brown (1929). See also Stewart (1977) for a discussion of terminology.

4. Also van Gennep (1960) pointed out long ago that the term *puberty rite* for teenage initiation into age-grade systems is inappropriate. The moment of physiological puberty is impossible to define for males or females (unless first menses is selected in the case of females).

5. Additional rules may require that a child born "too late" to fit into the beginning generation grade be adopted by a father of the

correct age for that child. For discussion of the generation-grade puzzle, see Stewart (1977), Legesse (1973), and the essays by Baxter and Hinnant in Age, Generation and Time (Baxter and Almagor 1978).

6. See Needham (1973), "Introduction," and the following chapters for a discussion of the symbolic dichotomies centering on right and left.

7. See La Fontaine's (1978) introductory statement for a general discussion of the relationships between age and sex. The following chapters and bibliographies are also useful.

8. The classic study of the use of food prohibitions to define and separate social groups is A. R. Radcliffe-Brown's The Andaman Islanders (1922, especially chap. 5). For a more recent ethnographic example of the cultural use of food prohibitions, see Edwin L. Schieffelin, The Sorrow of the Lonely and the Burning of the Dancers (1976, especially chap. 3).

9. For instance, in the case of the Guji Oromo, certain tree species are venerated and have myths associated with them (such as stories of warriors' camping under trees of a given species before winning a major battle). Rituals are held beneath trees of these species, and they are also used in a number of contexts in upper-level life-cycle ceremonies. Acacia limbs are piled on the graves of the dead to keep hyenas from digging up the bodies, and this wood is used ritually only to express the most negative meanings. Flowering shrubs, the nectar of which is collected by bees, are used ritually to make people "sweet for each other." Yoghurt is drunk by specific groups in ceremonies to make their members "thick with each other" in friendship or alliance.

10. Three articles concerning the cultural use of contrastive color categories are particularly relevant. Marshall Sahlins's "Colors and Cultures" (1977) discusses the general relationships among color, meaning, and the biological constraints on color perception. The remaining two articles, Victor Turner's "Color Classification in Ndembu Ritual" (1967a) and Harold Conklin's "Hanunoo Color Categories" (1955), discuss color categorization in terms of specific societies but with reference to larger cultural issues.

11. For a general discussion of the varieties of death ritual and for bibliographies, see Celebrations of Death, edited by Huntington and Metcalf (1979).

12. In addition to the sources already mentioned, the reader Symbolic Anthropology (Dolgin, et al., 1977) contains an excellent bibliography on the analysis of ritual.

BIBLIOGRAPHY

Amoss, Pamela T. 1981. "Cultural Centrality and Prestige for the Elderly: The Coast Salish Case." In Dimensions: Aging, Culture and Health, ed. Christine L. Fry. New York: Praeger, p. 47-63.

Baxter, P. T. W. 1978. "Boran Age-Sets and Generations-Sets: Gada, a Puzzle or a Maze?" In Age, Generation and Time: Some Features of East African Age Organizations. Ed. P. T. W. Baxter and Uri Almagor. London: C. Hurst, pp. 151-82.

Baxter, P. T. W. and Uri Almagor, eds. 1978. Age, Generation and Time: Some Features of East African Age Organizations. London: C. Hurst.

Biesele, Megan, and Nancy Howell. 1981. "'The Old People Give You Life.' Aging among !Kung Hunter-Gatherers." In Other Ways of Growing Old, ed. Pamela T. Amoss and Stevan Harrell. Stanford, Calif.: Stanford University Press, pp. 77-98.

Butler, Robert N. 1968. "The Life Review: An Interpretation of Reminiscences of the Aged." In Middle Age and Aging, ed. Bernice L. Neugarten. Chicago: University of Chicago Press.

Conklin, Harold C. 1955. "Hanunoo Color Categories." Southwestern Journal of Anthropology.

Dolgin, Janet L., David S. Kemnitzer, and David M. Schneider, eds. 1977. Symbolic Anthropology: A Reader in the Study of Symbols and Meanings. New York: Columbia University Press.

Hinnant, John. 1978. "The Guji: Gada as a Ritual System." In Age, Generation and Time, eds. P. T. W. Baxter and Uri Almagor. London: C. Hurst, pp. 207-43.

Huntington, Richard, and Peter Metcalf. 1979. Celebration of Death: The Anthropology of Mortuary Ritual. London: Cambridge University Press.

Kertzer, David I., and Oker B. B. Madison. 1981. "Women's Age-Set Systems in Africa: The Latuka of Southern Sudan." In Dimensions: Aging, Culture and Health, ed. Christine L. Fry. New York: Praeger, pp. 109-43.

Kirk, Lorraine, and Michael Burton. 1977. "Meaning and Context: A Study of Contextual Shifts in Meaning of Masai Personality Descriptors." American Ethnologist 4(4):734-61.

184 Methods for Old-Age Research

La Fontaine, J. S. 1978. Sex and Age as Principles of Social Differentiation. New York: Academic Press.

Legesse, Asmarom. 1973. Gada: Three Approaches to the Study of African Society. New York: Free Press.

Needham, Rodney. 1973. Right and Left: Essays on Dual Symbolic Classification. Chicago: University of Chicago Press.

Radcliffe-Brown, A. F. 1922. The Andaman Islanders. Glencoe, Ill.: Free Press.

———. 1929. "Age Organization Terminology." Man 29:21.

Sahlins, Marshall. 1977. "Colors and Cultures." Reprinted in Symbolic Anthropology: A Reader in the Study of Symbols and Meanings, ed. Janet L. Dolgin, David S. Kemnitzer, and David M. Schneider. New York: Columbia University Press, pp. 165-80.

Schieffelin, Edward L. 1976. The Sorrow of the Lonely and the Burning of the Dancers. New York: St. Martin's Press.

Stewart, Frank Henderson. 1977. Fundamentals of Age-Group Systems. New York: Academic Press.

Turner, Victor W. 1967a. "Color Classification in Ndembu Ritual: A Problem in Primitive Classification." Reprinted in The Forest of Symbols. Ithaca: Cornell University Press, pp. 59-92.

———. 1967b. "Symbols in Ndembu Ritual." Reprinted in The Forest of Symbols. Ithaca: Cornell University Press.

———. 1969. The Ritual Process: Structure and Anti-Structure. Chicago: Aldine.

van Gennep, Arnold. 1960. The Rites of Passage. Chicago: University of Chicago Press.

8
Cross-Cultural Use
of Life History Methods in Gerontology

GELYA FRANK
Department of
Occupational Therapy
University of
Southern California

ROSAMOND M. VANDERBURGH
Department of Anthropology
University of Toronto

COLLABORATING WITH THE ELDERLY TO CREATE MEANING

Rather than talk about simply "collecting" or "recording" life histories with old people, we would like to stress the increasingly current view that each life history is only one of many possible versions. In part this is because the method involves a creative relationship between the researcher and the person whose life story is being told. For this reason, the best guides on how to write life histories are the works themselves, since each represents an accommodation to several factors, not least of which is the personal collaboration. What we are seeing more and more in life history work is the interweaving of facts and interpretations by the anthropologist along with the recorded narratives of the informant. At stake here is the idea, one for which we are indebted to sociolinguistics, that what gets told depends a great deal on whom it is being told to and on what occasion.

The reliance on subjective reports for data in the social sciences has been criticized because what people say does not necessarily tally with what they do (Deutscher 1970). Myerhoff's *Number Our Days* (1978) testifies to the power of life histories when the observations and narratives on which they are based have been carefully weighed and refined over time. Myerhoff's use of a "critical incident" approach is an excellent frame in this respect (see also Edgerton and Langness 1978). Like the case approach to legal conflict in non-Western societies developed by the Manchester social anthropologists, Myerhoff's work captures the drama of temporal existence in a world of give-and-take with other people.

As in all good ethnography, life histories of the elderly in this and other societies ought first to ask the question: What opportunities does the culture itself ordinarily offer individuals to talk about themselves and to perform ritual and other acts in which the self is reflected? Subjectivity does not always take an ego-centered form: When poet Deena Metzger video-taped an interview with a 72-year-old Jewish musician as part of the documentation for a spinoff of Myerhoff's Venice study, this man spoke at length about the talents of his three children, who also made the arts their career. "Mr. Mekler," his interviewer interjected softly, "tell me about *yourself*." At this, the musician insisted, "My children *are* myself." As a good life historian should, Metzger acknowledged his point with a nod of understanding and let him present himself in his own way in this brief life-history session. Cross-cultural differences in subjectivity may be quite unfathomable at first, as shown by R. Rosaldo's (1976) life history of Tukbaw, a middle-aged Ilongot tribesman in the Philippines. Despite his astuteness in personal matters and his eloquence in tribal affairs, Tukbaw's narrative lacked psychological depth and inner reflection. While it was not unusual for an Ilongot to tell stories, it was strange for them to be centered around himself. Motivated by his growing friendship with Rosaldo, Tukbaw was able to construct a first-person account of his life, but it was not for him a conventional mode of expression. This is the process, as Crapanzano (1977) puts it, of negotiating the life history. Through successive versions the life historian arrives at an understanding of what another's experience is really like.

Clearly the life history has more to offer than a list of events. As linguist Linde (1985) phrases it, the life story is a narrative rather than a chronicle; in it resides the evaluation of one's own existence. The story-telling aspect of the life history is frankly looked upon as the element that gives this method its power to convey a sense of what it is to be human. Existence, as Heidegger (1962) characterized it, always has a temporal dimension extending forward and back. Not only do people find meaning in their past, but they anticipate a future. Especially as one gets old, the horizon of this future--death--becomes visible. One means of anticipating death, reconciling with it, and anticipating a future beyond one's own corporeal demise is through the creation of memorials for those who remain behind. Hilda Kuper suggests (personal communication, 1980) that an old person's self-perceptions might be considered in terms of cultural expectations about death: Will the person's spirit live on in this or another world? If so, what will be his or her place within it? L. L. Langness (personal communication, 1980) mentions in this regard the Bena Bena custom in the New Guinea Highlands of holding funerals for the very old before they die. Eulogies and displays of grief assure the old people that they have been valued and at the same time suggest to them, Langness thinks, that they should depart and not return as spirits.

The life history offers individuals the opportunity to tell their story, and in doing so, to consider their existence as a whole and discover its significance (cf. Butler 1968). This is not necessarily an opportunity that otherwise comes along. James Sewid, the subject of Spradley's study of a contemporary Kwakiutl chief in midlife, remarked on seeing the finished manuscript, "I think it is a wonderful life. . . . I didn't realize it, I didn't think nothing of it before now. . . . I only wish that I live another few years and then I can make another, what we have left out when the book closes, what happens in the future" (1969:288). The life history collaboration is an often difficult but unusually gratifying process for both partners. Where the elderly are concerned, the interest of an outsider in their lives can be a valuable and validating gift. Also a gift is the chance the life history gives them to speak for themselves, and, as Myerhoff (1978, 1980) effectively puts it, re-membering and re-collecting the elements of so many years' experience. Finally there is the gift of creating for those who follow, a testimony of life's personal meaning.

The Life History Process

Exactly what is involved in the selection of informants for a life history? The training of life historians? The eliciting, recording, and writing of life histories? Their analysis and interpretation? The comparison of life history materials? Many of the key issues in the systematic and scientific use of life histories have been articulated by Dollard (1935), Allport (1942), and Kluckhohn (1945; see also 1949). Their works are still valuable, as is the comprehensive review of the literature, guide to field methods, and suggestions for analysis by Langness (1965). Bringing Langness's overview up to date, Langness and Frank (1981) discuss innovations of the last fifteen years in the analysis and interpretation of life histories, as well as ethical and moral considerations in reporting highly personal materials. Some of the more current issues are raised, too, in a review (1979) of the life-history literature by Frank.

The procedures for taking life histories depend mainly on the overall research strategy, which may be retrospective or contemporaneous. *Retrospective* life histories reconstruct a life from memory. Some of the data can be objectively verified through records or interviews with significant others. The elaboration over time of psychological defenses to the events recalled, and the shifts in general in the recall of things past, raise problems of reliability and validity that must be accounted for. However, the taking of retrospective life histories can be accomplished relatively efficiently with respect to time, and thus is productive when the research design involves interviewing many informants. Looked at as projective documents, retrospective narratives provide an index to how individuals feel about events in their past but not necessarily to how they felt at the time or to what really happened.

Contemporaneous life histories document a daily life in progress from the point of view not only of the subject but the researcher, who makes observations and collects reports from others, besides taping narratives by the subject about current and past events. Such accounts let us see the complexity of lives and often a quality of indeterminancy in experience from day to day. The more intensive participation called for by this method makes it most feasible when used with a small sample or when a team of fieldworkers is available.

Because of cultural variations in the concept of the self and in styles of self-presentation, "emic" and "etic" categories should be distinguished as much as possible at the start of a life history project (see Fry, chap. 5 in this volume, for a discussion of these terms). In other words, the researcher's preparation for subjective life-history work should be grounded in the native theories of the emotions and of the self (e.g., Briggs 1970; Levy 1973; Myers 1979; M. Rosaldo 1980).

For the most part, the selection of life-history subjects is made on the basis of what Honigmann (1970) calls "non-probability judgment sampling," just as are the informants and settings usually studied by ethnographers. This means that the life historian has a rationale for pinpointing a particular informant, which can and should be made explicit (see Keith, chap. 1 in this volume). When life histories are collected in a context where other methods more easily quantified are in use, the selection of subjects can be made quite rigorous. Measures of functionality, social integration, or shifts in status and role (see in this volume Beall & Eckert, chap. 2; Sokolovsky, chap. 10; Nydegger, chap. 9) can identify those individuals who differ strongly along salient dimensions as candidates for more intensive study. Those individuals whose profiles conform to a typical pattern, and those whose profiles are the most marginal, call for the kind of intensive description that a life history can offer. However, as Aberle (cited by Mintz 1979) argues, even one individual's life history, and that person a deviant, will represent a position in a social system and may be interpreted with respect to cultural values and social norms. Full-length life histories sometimes take years to complete; Kuper's (1978) biography of Sobhuza I is one worth looking at for the craft with which this unique figure she knew for over 40 years is portrayed in the context of a lifetime of political struggle for Swazi land and independence. Kuper's advice to those who would consider writing a biography is, "Choose someone who *fascinates* you!"

APPLYING THE LIFE HISTORY METHOD CROSS-CULTURALLY: CANADIAN INDIAN ELDERS

The role of the ethnographer as seeker-of-wisdom from elders is particularly congruent with Anicinabe culture. The Anicinabe (Ojibwa-Odawa-Potawatomi) of Southern Ontario traditionally use experiences from their own lives to illustrate their teachings to younger generations. In our discussion of the life history method in cross-cultural settings, research conducted by Vanderburgh from 1965 to the present at two Anicinabe reserve communities, Cape Croker and Wikwemikong Unceded Indian Reserve, will provide most of the data.[1] Some of the data come as well from Anicinabe in the urban setting of Toronto.

In 1974-75, most the members of the Cape Croker band who were then age 65 or older were interviewed. From a possible sample of forty-one elders, thirty-three life histories were collected, using a loosely structured interview schedule to provide a consistent framework. Each participant was interviewed at least twice, and many were interviewed in greater depth. The number and length of the interviews depended upon such factors as health (including memory), ability to speak English, and reaction to the life-history interview process.

This work, along with prior research on the life history of an Anicinabe woman elder (Vanderburgh 1977), led to the researcher's theoretical interest in the problem of how the traditional elder's role has been both maintained and changed over time.[2] Although certain aspects of traditional elderhood seem to have been retained over time, major shifts of emphasis have occurred during the modernization process. The information-transmitting function of elders, proposed by some theorists to be disappearing under the impact of modernization, was found to be still in operation among the Anicinabe, although there have been changes in the context in which elders transmit information (Vanderburgh 1982).[3] The tradition of using experiences from their own lives to teach the young predisposes Anicinabe elders to appreciate the life history method and to cooperate with the ethnographer. The techniques outlined below may prove less workable for data collection, interpretation, and analysis in other cultural settings.

Factors in the Selection of Informants

The most significant factor in the selection of informants must be the researcher's theoretical/topical interests. In 1974-75, when Vanderburgh attempted to interview all of the elders at Cape Croker, she was at the first stage of using the method to arrive at an understanding of information transmission in the community (see Stage 1 in Keith, chap. 1 in this volume). As research goals took a more specific direction informants were chosen more selectively. Women were selected because ongoing reviews of life history data revealed that women play an extremely important role in initiating change in Anicinabe reserve communities. Also, earlier work with Verna Johnston on change at the microlevel through the analysis of role adaptation (Vanderburgh 1977) had underlined the significance of elders as role models and teachers in hers and other Anicinabe communities. In selecting informants for the work in progress, *Tomorrow's Elders*, women were sought who had undergone socializing experiences with traditional elders known to the ethnographer and who had been "life historied" already, or who were still available for interview.

Pragmatic considerations also enter into the selection of informants. Frank (1980) indicates the difficulty of using interpreters in the collection of such highly personal data. If the researcher is not fluent in the native language and wishes to avoid using an interpreter, it is necessary to find an informant who, in addition to fitting the theoretical framework of the project, can speak the language of the researcher. Although most of the Anicinabe elders from Cape Croker had been exposed to the English language in school, there was great variation in their ability to use English in conversation. Informants who were fluent in English were invariably selected and as a result, when reviewing the data for analysis, it was discovered that all these informants had either undergone considerable off-reserve experience during their lives, or else came from homes where an adult responsible for socializing them spoke English. Selection of informants on a purely pragmatic basis then, can influence research results, and the researcher should be aware of this. The language problem can be dealt with through an interpreter, especially where the research design calls for the collection of multiple life histories. For in-depth, long-term research, however, it is advisable to heed Frank's warning, as the closer relationship between informant and ethnographer that derives from direct interviewing is an important dimension of the life-history method.

When one is working with elders a potential informant's health, and particularly memory, are factors to be considered. The individual who feels that his or her memory is failing is not apt to be cooperative when asked to undertake a *retrospective* life history, but may be perfectly comfortable with a *contemporaneous* approach emphasizing participant observation. If the research goal is retrospective, and the selected informant turns out to have a problem with long-term memory, it is less frustrating for both ethnographer and informant to switch informants.

Another significant factor in the selection of informants is the degree to which a potential informant understands the goals of the research project. Where the ethnographer is working within a literate culture, or with a literate informant, it is possible to offer published life histories for examination as examples of the end product. It is important that the informant understand clearly the goals of the research, for the ethnographer will presumably wish to obtain authorization for the publication of at least some of the data. Where the ethnographer is dealing with a number of informants in a single community, it may also be important to present the research goals regarding theory and eventual publication at a community level to ensure cooperation and satisfy ethical considerations. Before many of the elders at Cape Croker were approached, the project was explained at a band council meeting. Councillors questioned the anthropologist closely until each was satisfied. A formal statement of approval was then requested, and the resulting band council resolution gave the researcher permission to work in the community within carefully specified guidelines that recapitulated her explanations. Clearly the scope of the research would have been restricted had less open explanations been offered.

Setting the "Dimensions" of a Life

Mandelbaum's (1973) concept of the dimensions of a life is helpful in outlining the first step in the life history method. Of his five dimensions ("biological," "cultural," "social," "psychosocial," and "unique") the cultural and social will be of general significance no matter what the particular theoretical interests of the researcher. The cultural dimension, according to Mandelbaum, reflects the "mutual expectations, understandings, and behavior patterns held by the people among whom a person grows up and in whose society he becomes a participant" (1973:180). The social dimension emphasizes "real relations in the course of which the actors may alter the roles, change the nature of the choices, and shift the cultural definitions" (1973:180). Mandelbaum's "biological", "psycho-social," and "unique" dimensions may also prove useful to gerontological studies in certain theoretical contexts.

In most Anicinabe communities, much can be learned about the cultural dimension before beginning actual work with an informant. Archival research provides historical details, and with band council permission current statistics will be made available through the agent's office. It proved useful to review the ethnographic literature on the Ojibwa, Odawa, and Potawatomi, and to keep a sort of cultural outline in mind when actual interviewing of elders began. Parts of the "cultural scenario" (Mandelbaum 1973:180) that emerged at Cape Croker could be related to and understood through this mental outline, and questions could be phrased so as to be easily comprehensible to informants.

Before actually beginning to interview elders, it proved helpful to map the community, noting landmarks and asking for local names for the various roads, bluffs, streams, etc. This gave a spatial background to the emerging cultural dimension that was useful as a referent during interviewing. As well, the construction of a unique, personal map that reflected the spatial aspect of each informant's participation in his or her community was attempted. This was accomplished by driving the elder slowly around the reserve and recording the places that had been significant in his or her life. In addition to information about places where the informant had lived, genealogical details often emerged or were clarified, and social networks were made explicit by the linking of places with significant people.

The basic step in setting the social dimension of a life is the preparation of a genealogy with the informant. This is particularly important when the ethnographer is working in a kin-based community and with people from a predominately oral tradition, who rely on memory more than on records to trace family relationships. Such a tradition is still strong among the Anicinabe in spite of decades of exposure to formal Western education, and kinship is still the basis of the reserve community's social organization. At Cape Croker most genealogies were linked at some generational level or another, enabling questions to be phrased in terms of already familiar aspects of the social dimension. The genealogical method prescribed by Rivers (1910) remains the key reference for setting this aspect of the social dimension.

Developing a Protocol

The theoretical/topical orientation of the research will be a key factor in the development of a protocol. Because of the interest in cultural transmission across the generations, questions about the languages spoken in the home and about formal schooling were included in the interview schedule. Information on how the adults responsible for socialization in the informant's life had made their living was also important in ascertaining whether a link existed between the type of information transmitted (e.g., the alphabet vs. Anicinabe legends) and the mode in which the information was transmitted (e.g., at school by a teacher vs. in the home by elders). Another concern was the transmission of specific skills (e.g., midwifery). A question on place of birth was included, and, if the informant had been born at home, which was generally the case, the presence or absence of a doctor or midwife was ascertained. Female informants always followed their response to this question with a discussion of their own experiences in childbirth, and it was possible to trace the transmission of midwife skills in the community. The question thus proved to be useful in generating information not formally sought in the interview schedule.

Following even a relatively informal interview schedule based on the researcher's particular theoretical/topical interests will ensure a degree of comparability when dealing with more than one informant. However, the step of setting the cultural and social dimensions of the community should precede the design of even the most loosely structured interview schedule. As Pelto and Pelto (1978:79-81) point out, the preliminary work--"setting the dimensions"--will help to define significant questions for structured interviews, as well as to identify community-appropriate terminology for the questions to be asked.

As the researcher begins to develop an appropriate protocol, various kinds of resources may be utilized. Family photograph albums can be useful in understanding the social dimensions of a life, and in filling gaps in a genealogy.[5] They also serve as mnemonic devices, even for elders with excellent memories. Too, the cultural dimension can be illuminated through photographs, as when a collection of very old snapshots at Cape Croker served as the basis for discussions of logging and milling of boards, maple syrup making, and funerals.

Other informal records may also be helpful in suggesting questions to be asked as well as in setting the cultural and social dimensions of a life. Often individuals keep scrapbooks where significant family and community events are memorialized. At Cape Croker, connunity news events are covered in local off-reserve newspapers, and clippings of such coverage for ned the bulk of the three sets of scrapbooks to which the researcher was given access. As well, the books contained fall fair schedules, school commencement programs, wedding invitations, cards of condolence, etc. In this way, the ethnologist learned of record catches of lake trout and sturgeon, of the marksmanship displayed by a local woman who shot a marauding bear, and of a great blizzard that isolated the community for over a week and brought to the fore traditional patterns of sharing and mutual aia.

More formal records--such as those of the Indian agent, the band council, and the various churches on the reserve--provided demographic information that proved helpful in suggesting questions on diet and health relating to traditional livelihood skills passed on by elders. It was noticed that the number of living individuals in the elder generation (65 years and older) and the succeeding generation (45-65 years) was approximately the same, and the investigator began to look at such variables as longevity, disease, and diet. In the final analysis, a link between a diet based on traditional foods and longevity was indicated.

In research settings where historic demographic data is not available, visits to cemeteries with knowledgeable elders may provide useful information. Although at Cape Croker many graves are unmarked, elders could remember who was buried where, their approximate age at death, and, in a surprising number of cases, the cause of death, as well as details of the person's life-style.[6] It was noticed that certain graves were regularly avoided, or verbal greeting was offered to the dead followed by an apology for the disturbance. This behavior suggested questions about specialized supernatural knowledge and its transmission.

The development of a protocol is thus an ongoing process during the collection of life history data. An approach that works with one informant may not work with another, due to such variables in the social dimension as gender and family background. To verify data, it is helpful to seek out other members of the community identified by the informant as significant in his or her life, and ask for their perceptions of events and relationships described by the informant. This should be done with the knowledge of the informant, however. Such consultation with significant others underlines the difference between the social and cultural dimensions, on one hand, and the unique dimension of the informant's life, on the other, and it is helpful in the on-going interpretation and analysis that is an essential part of life history methodology, as the researcher evaluates and reconstructs her protocols.

Constructing the Life Sequence

The number and length of interviews necessary in the collection of a life history will depend in part upon the research design, including such factors as the time at the researcher's disposal and the number of informants to be interviewed. As well, the articulateness of the informant and his or her attitude toward the project and the ethnographer will affect both the number and the quality of the interviews. Frank (1980:164) has suggested that "a minimally adequate narrative. . .can usually be taped, in this culture, in two sessions of two hours each." In the Anicinabe context her assessment seems accurate, although in a cross-cultural setting involving the use of the native language or an interpreter, the ethnographer might well find it more realistic to anticipate at least three two-hour sessions. Certainly the life history that is planned to be purely retrospective can be collected in relatively few hours of interviewing, given the prior establishment of at least part of the cultural and social dimensions of the life.

When the life history is planned around a contemporaneous approach, the interview demands will be very different. In working with the native artist Daphne Odjig, one of "Tomorrow's Elders," these two perspectives were combined. A month of participant observation was undertaken, interspersed with some twelve hours of taped interviewing and another six hours of interviewing recorded by note taking. This approach made possible a focus on Daphne as an artist and the relation of her life sequence to the development of her career. On the other hand, the collection of data for the life history of Verna Johnston (Vanderburgh 1977) went on intermittently for three years with taped interviews interspersed with short periods (two to seven days) of participant observation. Then the project was shelved for some six years while Verna Johnston adapted to living with Hodgkin's disease. When she had made that adaptation the work was quickly brought up to date with two taped interviews of two hours each.

The method used by the ethnographer to record life history data will necessarily vary with each informant. Some cultural scenarios are more in tune with research using tape recorders than others. Even within a single community the field worker may find great variation in this respect among her informants. Although many Anicinabe elders are quite comfortable with the tape recorder, others become tense and inarticulate. Failure to recognize and meet the informant's needs can lead to frustration for the researcher who rigidly follows a set interview protocol.

Similarly, the interview setting itself should not be rigidly defined before the social and cultural dimensions of the life have been set. Elders may live with families in a multi-generational situation, alone, or in an institutional setting. Anicinabe elders in the reserve setting seldom have access to transportation, so it was important that the ethnographer had a car to travel about the reserve. Several productive sessions resulted from gathering a number of male elders together. Interviewing elders who lived in a nearby off-reserve nursing home also proved very productive, as Indian people often roomed together. Thus, in a double room or a four-bed ward all residents would be Cape Croker elders, and the resulting interviews were usually very rich. Residents were especially eager to work out their genealogies. They discussed this social dimension of their lives among themselves in order to refresh their memories for the interviews.

Once the interview has progressed through the collection of genealogical data, the problem becomes one of transition from the social dimension to the life sequence itself. A useful technique is to suggest that everyone actually has some "first" or earliest memory, if he or she thinks consciously about it, and to relate the researcher's own first memory. Often these first memories generate a lot of laughter and set the tone for a relaxed interview.

Combining the first memory with the social and cultural dimensions already known to the ethnographer will set the retrospective reconstruction of the life sequence in process. The interview schedule provides a framework to keep in mind as the interviewing progresses, but it should not be permitted to dominate the way in which the informant wishes to relate the life. Anicinabe elders do not hang their lives on dates, and they become exasperated with repeated requests for the precise year of an event. They have no problem in placing life events in the proper sequence, but they use as reference points significant happenings at various levels of the social structure rather than dates. These significant happenings can be at the family, community, national, or world level, and the perceptive researcher will find they offer clues to the scope of the life in question. One female elder whose entire life had been lived on the reserve used primarily family and community referents to order the sequence of events in her life. Her sons' military service in World War II was the only wider referent that she used. One male elder, a long-time resident of Toronto, used many world-level events in organizing the presentation of his life. He referred to the Depression, to World War II, and even to the eruption of Krakatoa in 1883 as a referent for his father's age. His father had been in his early teens during the "year of the miraculous sunrises and sunsets." He told how as an adult he was able, from his father's description, to relate those sunrises and sunsets to an article he read about the volcano's eruption.

People who are relating the story of a life seldom follow the actual sequence of life events. A researcher whose protocol demands sequential accuracy may find this frustrating but should understand that the informant who seems to wander through time, following the development of an event and relating consequences of that event in the community or in the lives of others, is nevertheless performing a valuable task. The informant is providing the researcher with the necessary context in which his or her life unfolded, offering important background data, which help to further define and clarify the dimensions of the life. Further questions can be derived from reviewing this contextual data, and the on-going interpretation and analysis in collecting a life history is aided.

Contextual enrichment is not the sole benefit that is derived from allowing an informant to follow the development of events through time in his or her own way. Interaction between informants and the researcher is smoothed when protocols are relaxed enough to allow informants to impose their own order on their life. The researcher must also be aware that events can be painful even in review, and should be alert for signs of distress. Distress signals vary cross-culturally, and knowledge of the cultural dimension should provide the necessary understanding. Working with the Anicinabe elders, the researcher learned to be aware of long silences, which could be interpreted in a variety of ways. The informant might be reviewing events, sorting information mentally in order to present it with maximum impact (the Anicinabe excel as story-tellers). On the other hand, the informant might be indicating a negative feeling about the interview, a wish to bring it to an end. Often, however, the long silence indicated distress at the review of a painful event. When the informant is able to articulate the distress, the researcher should accept it, express sympathy, and ask whether the informant would like to drop the subject. Anicinabe women elders often found relief in sharing their distress with the researcher.

This sharing aspect of life history work should never be forgotten. Scheduling demands should not be permitted to interfere with the shared process of constructing the story, even where multiple informants are used. The informant is giving something precious; the ethnographer must respond in culturally appropriate ways to indicate awareness of the gift and empathy with the giver (see Langness & Frank 1981:5-6). The quality of the relationship between informant and researcher will affect the quality of the data obtained, and thus the value of the life history (Frank 1985).

While the design of the research project may demand multiple life histories, and so dispose the researcher toward minimal four-hour retrospective life reviews, much can be gained by establishing in-depth, long-lasting relationships with informants. Although this demands more work on the researcher's part (Frank 1980:164-65), the rewards are great in terms of long-range research goals. However, an intimate prolonged association with one family can cause problems in a small faction-ridden community. Where factions based on kinship exist, as at Cape Croker, it is virtually impossible to build a long-lasting set of relationships without becoming identified with a particular kin group.

The maintenance of a long-term relationship, because of the extremely personal and sensitive nature of what is shared, enters the ethical domain when the stage of reporting results is reached.[7] In reporting research it is important not to contribute to the negative image of an informant or to hurt the feelings of members of his or her family. Such a commitment frequently conflicts with professional standards. For example, the most difficult problem in writing Verna Johnston's life history was her relationship with her husband. Cape Croker men, life histories revealed, have always controlled their wives through control of family finances (including real estate and the wife's earnings), and through the authority of the Roman Catholic Church. Verna rebelled against this aspect of the cultural scenario, and left her husband and her community. Since this was her life history, her view of the relationship had to be presented, at the risk of hurting her husband and children. The issue was partly resolved by separating the narrative of Verna's life from the interpretation of that life (see Vanderburgh 1977). In the interpretive section of the text, the husband was presented as a "bound actor" (Mandelbaum 1973:194) within the cultural and social dimensions of his community, and his personal dignity and kindness to the researcher were stressed.[8] One suspects that the conflict between the personal and the professional uses of life history data can never be completely resolved in a long-term informant-ethnographer relationship. The appropriateness of such a relationship will vary cross-culturally. Certainly the mentor role of the elder in North American Indian societies is more congruent with a long-term relationship. Researchers in other cultures may not find established elders' roles so readily adaptable to their professional goals.

Practical as well as ethical problems arise for the ethnographer who uses the life history method cross-culturally. Perhaps the most serious problem is in communication, and this raises the question of using an interpreter when one is needed. On selecting an interpreter to work with elders, try to find a bilingual *elder*. Work first with such an individual on his or her own life history. This will ensure that the interpreter understands the research goals and the process of data collecting, so that he or she can explain and justify them to other elders. A person who has been through the process can convince others to cooperate.

Too, an interpreter who is also an elder generally relates more successfully to other elders. When a bilingual elder is not available, however, look for a bilingual individual in mid-life, someone of the elders' children's generation. Again, work on a life history with the interpreter to ensure comprehension of the project and the process. In certain cultural contexts the sex of the interpreter may be an important factor in gaining access to gender-specific information.

The use of a bilingual member of the grandchild generation in collecting life history data must be approached with caution. Where the cultural scenario calls for a close, mentoring relationship between grandparents and grandchildren, the use of a youthful interpreter may prove successful. Anicinabe elders have always drawn upon their own experiences in the instruction of their young people, so we may predict some success here in the use of a youthful interpreter, although today very few of the young people are bilingual. However, certain topics, notably sexual relationships with whites and births "behind the woodpile" (out of wedlock) were not discussed in front of young people. The problem of communication is never simple.

INTERPRETATION AND ANALYSIS

It is useful to explicitly distinguish between interpretation and analysis. Both processes go on simultaneously during the construction of the life history with the informant and in practice researchers often blend the interpretive and analytical processes in the field. The interpretive process is the attempt to make the meaning of the informant's behavior clear to the researcher and to those who will read her reports, to make sense of the life. This is a special challenge in the cross-cultural context, where the cultural dimensions must be distinguished and spelled out before interpretation can begin. The researcher's interpretations are checked and reformulated through questioning the informant as well as significant others, and are continually being tested when the life history project allows for participant observation. Ultimately the researcher's interpretations should make sense to the informant and others in the community, and should make the life comprehensible to the reader from another culture.

Managing Textual Data

Before either interpretation or analysis can take place, the data must be kept in some kind of order. There are a number of straightforward techniques that may help the life-history researcher to do this. Regular reviews of the interview data are essential. It is seldom possible to transcribe tapes in the field, but it is helpful to listen to the tapes and summarize the highlights in a notebook. Notes taken directly in interviews should also be re-viewed.

In the absence of computer technology for recording and indexing data, crayons or felt-tipped pens may be used to color code all written records.[9] The categories that are coded will reflect particular theoretical/topical interests. When the color code has been established and applied to the records, a card index of all records by code category can be prepared. It is a simple enough matter to add another category (another color), code in another topic, and expand the index. Life history data can be mined in this manner for use in more than one research project.

Too, this system of indexing blends interview and other data, so that scrapbooks, photo albums, archival material, and the ethnographer's journal entries come together under relevant research categories. Where a research design calls for the use of multiple informants, standardized color coding will facilitate analysis. Once the coding and indexing are in place, reviews of the data will generate continuing interpretation, which can be tested through questions as well as participant observation (see Keith, chap. 1 in this volume).

Interpretation and Analysis

Although Mandelbaum's (1973) framework has been presented in the literature as an analytic scheme, it may be more appropriate to think of it as one offering a consistent approach to the interpretation of life histories cross-culturally. Of his life history of Gandhi, Langness and Frank (1981:72) say, "such a framework did indeed help in organizing and understanding an individual's life. . . it remains as probably the most important scheme available for gathering and interpreting the lives of others." Mandelbaum's scheme can help to create a model of a life, not unlike a genealogical diagram or a village map (see Frank 1984 for an example). Such models do have within them a set of theoretical presumptions; Mandelbaum's are drawn from well-established cultural anthropological theories about the relationship between the individual and society. Is the model-building step, then, in itself an analysis?

In our research, when using Mandelbaum's scheme, analysis or a second layer of interpretation has been a distinct step after the model of the life was created. After this model is established, theories may be tested that relate to a predefined research interest (e.g. Vanderburgh's question of whether modernization diminishes the importance of elders' role of transmitting information). Other theoretical constructs may also come to mind inductively or be applied deductively as the model is re-examined. Calling the steps after model building "analysis" or "interpretation" may depend on the following: Are specific propositions from a systematic theory being tested? If so, we would call this analysis. Are further syntheses and explications being elaborated from a range of sources? If so, we would call this interpretation. In practice, analysis and interpretation go hand in hand.

In interpreting Verna Johnston's life to the reader, Vanderburgh (1977) used Mandelbaum's "dimensions," and also his concepts of "turnings" and "adaptations," which will be defined later. When Verna was asked to review and comment on the interpretations, her response was, "Now I understand why I did what I did. . .it all makes sense now." The analytical process relates the life history to the theoretical/topical interests of the researcher. In analyzing Verna's life history, theories were used that could illuminate microlevel change and role adaptation. The most useful theoretical construct in the analysis of this particular life in this particular research context proved to be that of the culture broker (Paine 1970; Press 1969).

The researcher will find that both interpretation and analysis will be facilitated by identifying what Mandelbaum (1973) calls the "turnings" of the life. Turnings are major transitions, "when the person takes on a new set of roles, enters into fresh relations with a new set of people, and acquires a new self-conception" (Mandelbaum 1973:181). The advantage in using such a concept in interpretation and analysis is that, as Mandelbaum points out, it brings together the cultural, social, and psychosocial dimensions of the life. These turnings, or transitions, may be gradual, or abrupt and focused on a single event.

Once the researcher has identified the turnings of the life, continuing review of the data should reveal the informant's adaptations to those turnings. "Adaptation" is the term used by Mandelbaum (after Kluckhohn [1962]) to refer to behavior that contributes to the survival of the individual or the group: "Every person must, in the course of his life, alter some of his established patterns of behavior to cope with new conditions. Each person *changes* his ways in order to maintain *continuity*, whether of group participation or social expectation or self-image or simply survival" (Mandelbaum 1973:181). If the informant's turnings and adaptations are not clear from the data already collected, the reseacher can now frame questions that will generate further data to clarify these points.

The concepts of dimensions, turnings, and adaptations are etic devices for ordering, interpreting, and analyzing data. They can be sharpened and refined by seeking the emic point of view. Anicinabe elders were asked to identify the major decisions they had made that changed the course of their lives. Responses were very revealing. Some listed a number of such decisions, which could be related to already identified turnings or used as clues to identify additional turnings. Others said that they could think of no major decisions that had changed their life courses. When pressed, one woman responded, "No, my life has been a gradual unfolding, I made no major decisions that changed it." This response was so challenging that all her life data were reviewed to check her perception of a gradual unfolding. Thus it became clear that the cultural dimensions of her life had been comfortable for her, and that she had accepted the decisions that others (parents, husband) had made for her as part of the cultural scenario of her community. These decisions by others had actually been the basis of the turnings already identified in her life. Both her turnings and her adaptations have been fully congruent with the cultural dimensions of her reserve, yet this woman has been a significant agent for change in her community. Further questions must now be formulated to identify the locus of change in this life, and a review of life-history data from other elders in her community will help in formulating these questions. The development of a protocol must thus be an ongoing process in the use of the life-history method for gerontological research. Protocols must remain flexible to accommodate not only specific theoretical interests and specific cultural scenarios, but, importantly, the "unique" dimension of informants' lives.

Validating the Life History with Your Informants

When interviewing is finished and the researcher has spent some time interpreting and analyzing the life history data, it is useful to arrange a review session with the informant. In preparation for this session, a life chronology should be drawn up, using data where they are available, and an outline of the life history should be prepared.[10] The review session must be long enough to allow the literate informant to read both the chronology and the outline, and to make any additions or expansions that are deemed necessary. With the nonliterate informant, the review process may be longer, as the researcher will have to pace the interview to the informant's capacity to follow the outline aurally. It is important to assure the informant that the outline is not the finished product, and that the life history in final form will be presented for review before permission is sought for publication.

After reviewing the life outline, and while the retrospective view of the life left by the review process is still in sharp mental focus, the informant can be asked to identify the events he or she perceives as of major significance in the life, and to specify why they were significant. This list can later be compared with the researcher's list of turnings and with the informant's list of the major decisions that changed his or her life course. Again, additional turnings may be identified, or established turnings clarified. In the final analysis of the data within the theoretical framework of the project, both the emic and etic views of the life will be useful.

The last part of the review session deals with the informant's reaction to the shared process of constructing the life history. This step must be distinguished from the presenting of the finished life history to the informant for his or her reaction. The informant's view of the life history process will be one of the tools used by the researcher to evaluate and validate the relevance of protocols to both her theoretical interests and the particular cultural context. One old man at Cape Croker said that the thing he enjoyed most was that the life history work had enhanced his reputation as a lady's man. "They all see me driving around the place with a nice lady, young enough to be my daughter, and they think, lots of get-up-and-go left in that old guy!" Members of the household where the ethnologist boarded corroborated this impression. It was decided that in future life history work with male Anicinabe elders, a professional image would be better maintained by fitting more carefully into the cultural scenario of the community, and arranging for the company of either a native field assistant or an interpreter.

If the informant expresses a positive reaction to the life history process, the researcher is reassured that her methods of establishing and maintaining rapport have been adequate; and explicit questions will reveal whether her understanding of the all-important cultural dimension of the community is also adequate. At Cape Croker comments such as "Doing this with you has made me go back and look at the bad and the good together, and see that there's more good than bad back there," and "It really felt good, you're a good listener, I never had a chance to talk about it all before," validated the use of the life history method with elders. Negative responses, such as "I didn't like being asked about my granny and who she married," indicated that more sensitivity is required on the part of the researcher in phrasing genealogical questions to accommodate the many instances of unmarried motherhood that occurred in all generations.

It will be clear by now that the relating of the life history to the researcher's theoretical/topical interests is a process that begins early in the fieldwork, and continues throughout. When the researcher is working with multiple informants, it is not always possible to do comparative analysis in the field. However, each separate life should be the subject of some degree of analysis during the process of working with the informant.

Whether or not the researcher presents her analysis to the informant with the finished report when seeking authorization to publish may depend upon the degree to which the informant has understood the theoretical goals of the research. The analysis is of interest primarily to other social scientists; Indians who read Verna Johnston's life history find the analysis the least interesting part of the book, and many of them say they haven't read that section.

Verna, however, reviewed the entire manuscript before publication, and requested changes, which were made. She gave written permission to publish the version that was submitted to the publisher and ultimately was published. This step was necessary as a safeguard for both informant and researcher; use of one's life to support a theoretical framework that one finds abhorrent would be distressing to the informant and could leave the researcher open to the charge of having misrepresented the future use of data.

Not all Anicinabe elders may seem sufficiently sophisticated, in terms of the social sciences, to make such precautions necessary. However, the children and ultimately the grandchildren of those elders must also be considered. Verna's daughter was asked to review the manuscript as well, and she requested changes she thought necessary to avoid hurting family members. The analytical framework used in Verna's life history proved to be both understandable and inoffensive to those concerned. If the informant and/or family members should find the theoretical framework offensive, the researcher may wish to present them with the possibility of anonymous reporting. The linked issues of confidentiality and anonymity in life history reporting are reviewed by Langness and Frank (1981, chap. 4).

CONCLUSION

In this chapter, the authors presented a step-by-step guide to the life history method in working with old people in a cross-cultural setting. A framework by Mandelbaum (1973) was employed. Mandelbaum's proposition that this scheme can be used to gather and interpret life histories in any culture can be validated only if further research is undertaken in a broad variety of contexts. It is especially important that this be done with informants little influenced by the Western world-view that informs American anthropology despite our discipline's attempt to transcend its own cultural presumptions. If difficulties and discrepancies in employing the approach are carefully noted, they will be a source of valuable insight into the ways in which lives are actually organized and experienced. One may ask most Americans, for example, to divide the "book" of their life into "chapters" as a way of getting at the important turnings, but the metaphor would not work in a non-literate society.

The focus that comes from employing a structured approach to life history research enhances observation, yet also constricts it. Each structure focuses on the life phenomena in a different way. To many scholars, the most inclusive and seemingly natural scheme for gathering and interpreting a life history would be that of the "life span," "life cycle," or "life course."[11] Data from this sort of developmental approach will undoubtedly overlap with data gathered using Mandelbaum's scheme, but there will be differences as well. Neither is inherently preferable. The choice of scheme-- Mandelbaum's or any other--should depend on the theoretical objectives of the research project and on the suitability of the approach to the people being studied. The skills and talents of the researcher also should be taken into consideration when making these methodological choices.

Even in a formal study, one may wish at some point to grope for themes in the relatively unstructured narratives of an informant. This takes us full circle to the problem of meaning in the lives of informants. In her study of identity in the lives of a sample of American women over 70, Kaufman (1981:55) defines life history themes in her informants' accounts as "cognitive areas of meaning . . . which explain, unify, and give substance to their perceptions of who they are and how they see themselves participating in social life." A researcher should expect a certain consistency in identifying themes, as they are the means by which coherence of self over time is maintained. Identifying themes is a process of discovery that can safeguard against pre-packaged interpretations and analyses that are too pat.

Finally, as Chris Fry has put it (personal communication, 1984), the life history can be used to "vacuum up all the variables that can't be gotten any other way" in conjunction with other research methods in the study of aging. It provides a common sense, naturalistic perspective for framing questions to reveal social processes and personal interpretations that otherwise might go unstated. The example she proposes is the question: "At the death of your parents, what happened?" For example, did property remain? If so, what became of it? Did siblings come together in a new way or drift apart? Did the only child now acquire a new identity as "old"? In sum, each life, depending on the culture or society, will have predictable points of crisis that may be tapped to add depth to our knowledge of aging.

NOTES

In this chapter we have drawn on Frank's experience with the life history method in American contexts and on Vanderburgh's with Canadian Indians. Much of the framework has been utilized from Frank's (1980) chapter in the first edition of this volume. The order of names on this article is alphabetical, reflecting the equal contributions of the co-authors.

1. This research was supported by the Canada Council (Grant S74-0105, 1974-75) and the Social Sciences and Humanities Research Council of Canada's (Grant 492-82-0010) Population Aging Programme (1982-83). As well, Erindale College, University of Toronto, has provided on-going support in the form of travel grants. The Ojibwa, Odawa (Ottawa), and Potawatomi are related linguistically as speakers of mutually intelligible Algonkian dialects. At one time they shared a similar ecological adaptation and religious system. Historically, they were linked in the Three Fires Confederacy of the seventeenth century (Hunt 1968; Wallace 1972) and, during the nineteenth-century removal of Indians from Michigan, Illinois, and Wisconsin, Canada became a refuge area for thousands of Anicinabe refugees who refused removal across the Mississippi. See Clifton (1975) for a description of the Potawatomi migration to Canada.

2. Currently life histories are being used to investigate the information-transmitting aspect of Anicinabe elderhood for Vanderburgh's study "Tomorrow's Elders." Four women, each of whom has had significant experiences in socialization by traditional elders, were chosen. The traditional elders who helped raise these four women are known to the investigator and most have contributed life history material of their own.

3. See Fischer (1978) for a critical review of the modernization theory of aging.

4. For a discussion of the genealogical method in life-history collecting, see Langness and Frank (1981:57).

5. For a discussion of interviewing with photographs, see Collier (1967:46-66) and Greenhill (1981).

6. See Dethlefsen (1969, 1981) and Dethlefsen and Jensen (1977) for interesting perspectives on graveyard demography.

7. For a review of ethical issues, see Langness and Frank (1981:117-54).

8. Vanderburgh (1977:209-10)

9. With computers and word processors, texts can be indexed by beginning paragraphs with key words that serve as flags for future compilation. Such software programs as "Ethnograph" and "Super Sort" can facilitate the grouping of notes on a topical basis and, in turn, the content analysis of a large corpus of data.

10. This review chronology can later be used as the basis for a chronological chart for publication, as in Vanderburgh (1977:16-17). See also Frank (1984:642-43).

11. See, for example, the critical review articles by Riegel (1974) and Rossi (1980).

BIBLIOGRAPHY

Allport, Gordon. 1942. The Use of Personal Documents in Psychological Science. New York: Social Science Research Council.

Briggs, Jean L. 1970. Never in Anger: Portrait of an Eskimo Family. Cambridge: Harvard University Press.

Butler, Robert. 1968. "The Life Review: An Interpretation of Reminiscence in the Aged." In Middle Age and Aging, ed. Bernice Neugarten. Chicago: Unviersity of Chicago Press.

Clifton, James A. 1975. A Place of Refuge for All Time: The Migration of the American Potawatomi into Upper Canada 1830 to 1850. Ottawa: National Museum of Man Mercury Series.

Collier, John, Jr. 1967. Visual Anthropology: Photography as a Research Method. New York: Holt, Rinehart & Winston.

Cornelison, Ann. 1976. Women of the Shadows: A Study of the Wives and Mothers of Southern Italy. New York: Random House.

Crapanzano, Vincent. 1977. "The Life History in Anthropological Field Work. Anthropology and Humanism Quarterly 2(2-3): 3-7.

Dethlefsen, Edwin S. 1969. "Colonial Gravestones and Demography." American Journal of Physical Anthropology 31(3):321-34.

____. 1981. "The Cemetery and Cultural Change: Archaeological Focus and Ethnographic Perspective." In Modern Material Culture, the Archaeology of Us, ed. R. A. Gould and M. B. Schiffer. New York: Academic Press, pp. 137-59.

Dethlefsen, Edwin S., and Kenneth Jensen. 1977. "Social Commentary from the Cemetery." Natural History 76(6): 32-39.

Deutscher, Irwin. 1970. "Words and Deeds: Social Science and Social Policy." In Qualitative Methodology: Firsthand Involvement with the Social World, ed. William J. Filstead. New York: Rand McNally, pp. 27-51.

Dollard, John. 1935. Criteria for the Life History. New Haven, Conn.: Yale University Press.

Edgerton, Robert B., and L. L. Langness. 1978. "Observing Mentally Retarded Persons in Community Settings: An Anthropological Perspective." In Observing Behavior, Vol 1: Theory and Applications in Mental Retardation, ed. Gene P. Sackett. Baltimore: University Park Press, pp. 335-48.

Featherman, David L. (1983). "Life-Span Perspectives in Social Science Research." In Life-Span Development and Behavior, Vol. 5, Baltes and Brim (eds.) New York: Academic Press, pp. 1-59.

Fischer, David Hackett. 1978. Growing Old in America, expanded ed. New York: Oxford University Press.

Frank, Gelya. 1979. "Finding the Common Denominator: A Phenomenological Critique of Life History Method." Ethos 7(1): 68-94.

_____. 1980. "Life Histories in Gerontology: The Subjective Side to Aging." In New Methods for Old Age Research: Anthropological Alternatives, ed. C. Fry and J. Keith. Chicago: Loyola University Center for Urban Policy, pp. 155-71.

_____. 1984. "Life History Model of Adaptation to Disability: The Case of a Congenital Amputee." Social Science and Medicine 19(6): 639-45.

_____. 1985. "'Becoming the Other': Empathy and Biographical Interpretation." Biography 8(3): 189-210.

Greenhill, Pauline. 1981. So We Can Remember: Showing Family Photographs. Ottawa: National Museum of Man Mercury Series, No. 36.

Heidegger, Martin. 1962. Being and Time. New York: Harper & Row.

Honigmann, John J. 1970. "Sampling in Ethnographic Field Work." In A Handbook of Method in Cultural Anthropology, ed. Raoul Naroll and Ronald Cohen. Garden City, N.Y.: Natural History Press, pp. 266-81.

Hunt, George T. 1940. The Wars of the Iroquois. Madison: University of Wisconsin Press.

Kaufman, Sharon. 1981. "Cultural Components of Identity in Old Age: A Case Study." Ethos 9(1): 51-87.

Kluckhohn, Clyde. 1945. "The Personal Document in Anthropological Science." In The Use of Personal Documents In History, Anthropology, and Sociology, by Louis Gottschalk, Clyde Kluckhohn, and Robert Angell. New York: Social Science Research Council, Bull. 53, pp. 79-176.

____. 1949. "Needed Refinements in the Biographical Approach." In Culture and Personality, ed. S. Stansfeld Sargent and Marian W. Smith. New York: The Viking Fund, pp. 75-92.

____. 1962. "The Limitations of Adaptation and Adjustment as Concepts for Understanding Cultural Behavior." In Culture and Behavior, ed. R. Kluckhohn. Glencoe: Free Press, pp. 255-64.

Kuper, Hilda. 1978. Sobhuza II, Ngwenyama and King of Swaziland: The Story of an Hereditary Ruler and His Country. New York: Africana.

Langness, L. L. 1965. The Life History in Anthropological Science. New York: Holt, Rinehart & Winston.

Langness, L. L., and Gelya Frank. 1981. Lives: An Anthropological Approach to Biography. Novato, Calif.: Chandler & Sharp.

Levy, Robert I. 1973. Tahitians: Mind and Experience in the Society Islands. Chicago: University of Chicago Press.

Linde, Charlotte. 1985. "Explanatory Systems in Oral Life Stories Folk Models: The Cultural Part of Cognition, ed. Naomi Quinn and Dorothy Holland. Cambridge University Press.

Mandelbaum, David G. 1973. "The Study of Life History: Gandhi." Current Anthropology 14(3): 177-206.

Mintz, Sidney. 1979. "The Anthropological Interview and the Life History." Oral History Review, pp. 18-26.

Myerhoff, Barbara. 1978. Number Our Days. New York: E. P. Dutton.

____. 1980. "Telling One's Story." The Center Magazine XIII (2): 22-40.

Myers, Fred R. 1979. "Emotions and the Self: A Theory of Personhood and Political Order among Pintupi Aborigines." Ethos 7(4): 343-70.

Paine, Robert, ed. 1970. Patrons and Brokers in the Eastern Arctic. Toronto: University of Toronto Press.

Pelto, Pertti J., and Gretel H. Pelto. 1978. Anthropological Research: The Structure of Inquiry, (2d ed.). Cambridge: Cambridge University Press.

Press, Irwin, 1969. "Ambiguity and Innovation: Implications for the Genesis of the Culture Broker." American Anthropologist 71(2): 205-17.

Riegel, Klaus F. 1974. "Adult Life Crises: A Dialectic Interpretation of Development." In Life-Span Developmental Psychology: Normative Life Crises, ed. N. Datan and L. H. Ginsberg. New York: Academic Press.

Rivers, W. H. R. 1910. "The Genealogical Method of Anthropological Inquiry." Sociological Review 3:1-12.

Rosaldo, Michelle Z. 1980. Knowledge and Passion: Ilongot Notions of Self and Social Life. Cambridge: Cambridge University Press.

Rosaldo, Renato. 1976. "The Story of Tukbaw: 'They Listen as He Orates.'" In The Biographical Process: Studies in the History and Psychology of Religion, ed. F. Reynolds and D. Capps. The Hague: Mouton, pp. 121-51.

Rossi, Alice S. 1980. "Life-Span Theories and Women's Lives." Signs: Journal of Women in Culture and Society 6(1): 4-32.

____ (ed.). 1984. Gender and Life Course. Hawthorne, NY: Aldine.

Spradley, James P. 1969. Guests Never Leave Hungry: The Autobiography of James Sewid, A Kwakiutl Indian. New Haven, Conn.: Yale University Press.

Vanderburgh, R. M. 1977. I Am Nokomis, Too: The Biography of Verna Patronella Johnston. Don Mills, Ontario: General Publishing.

____. 1982. "When Legends Fall Silent Our Ways Are Lost: Some Dimensions of the Study of Aging among Native Canadians." Culture 2(1): 21-28.

Wallace, Anthony F. C. 1972. The Death and Rebirth of the Seneca. New York: Vintage Books.

Watson, L.C., and Maria-Barbara Watson-Franke. 1985. Interpreting Life Histories. New Brunswick, NJ: Rutgers.

9
Measuring Morale and Life Satisfaction

CORRINE N. NYDEGGER
Medical Anthropology Program
University of California, San Francisco

Gerontologists have used the terms "morale," "life satisfaction," and "well-being" interchangeably to refer to the subjective aspect of quality of life. Although doing injustice to their differing antecedents and referents in other contexts, the usages now are so well established that efforts directed towards terminological clarity are fruitless. However, continued efforts directed towards conceptual clarity are necessary, for despite the long history of gerontological study of morale, researchers still use a multiplicity of techniques to measure it. The critical questions, then, are: How do the measures differ? How are we to choose among them? Which are most useful to anthropologist?

HOW DO THE MEASURES DIFFER?

In devising life satisfaction indices, researchers have tapped various overlapping domains and have referred to them by a confusing number of terms. Lawton warns, "let us not be fooled, however, by the proliferation of terms used to describe other scales; they both are and are not the same as morale, to our utter confusion" (1977:6).

The core notion gerontologists hope to tap is fairly clear: an individual's maintenance of a positive state toward himself and his life. Thereafter, nothing is clear. How much of this state is captured by items restricted to one's current life and how much by items assessing the past? Should "currently" refer to the past year or the past week? How are self and life satisfactions to be distinguished? Is helplessness or anomie an aspect of morale, or is it causally implicated? Is it better to include explicitly such situationally induced factors as retirement satisfaction, loneliness, or perception of health status? Are intrapsychic or psychosomatic symptoms integral to the concept or do they represent distinct domains? These and other questions like them have bedeviled the field.

During the 1970s, the construct of morale, its related domains, and their measurement came under critical scrutiny, and I recommend study of the Gerontological Society's special publication

Measuring Morale (Nydegger 1977), which contains thoughtful critiques of measures and their uses by a number of experienced gerontologists. I will briefly summarize only a few of the points they made, so that I can explore more fully the anthropological issues of central concern here.

Lawton (1977) classified moralelike instruments in terms of a set of constructs they attempt to measure, distinguishing among measures of happiness, mood, continuity of self, positive self-concept, self-rated health, and so forth. He has listed popular measures, their apparent construct referents, and their psychometric properties (see Table 9.1). The work of George and Bearon (1980) is another valuable resource for measures of a wide range of constructs related to life satisfaction.

I have developed another scheme to classifiy measures (and constructs), according to which of the following questions they address: How does R feel about his life? How does R feel about himself? How does R feel about his relation to the world? I have listed the simplest and shortest measures in Table 9.2. They are the most reliable and best validated, but I must point out that many appear simply because there are no alternatives; few of the measures have received serious psychometric attention, as Table 9.1 indicates. (Symptom scales have been excluded, since factorial studies show that morale is distinct from psychopathology).

But no classification can be altogether satisfactory. Concepts shade subtly into one another and overlap; delimitation of related concepts is often arbitrary. When possible, the parameters of constructs are best established not by common sense or intuitively but on the basis of factorial analyses. Lawton and Sherwood, who pioneered this work, cite several references (1977), and others are beginning to appear in the literature (e.g., Lohmann 1980). Therefore I have marked with an asterisk the constructs in Table 9.2 which are proving to be distinct from the core meaning of morale or life satisfaction. That is, scores on these dimensions do correlate significantly with other morale scale scores, but demonstrate relative independence in factorial analyses.

HOW ARE WE TO CHOOSE AMONG THEM?

Even if we were to develop more factorially "pure" measures, the criterion of choice is not purity, but appropriateness: the decisive question is why we want to measure well-being or morale at all. What do we intend to do with the data we obtain? Thus, choice of measures is based on design questions first; only then do psycho-metric quailities become relevant (the discussions by Carp [1977], Sherwood [1977] and George [1979] are particularly valuable in regard to design issues).

For example, if we wish simply to "establish" a distribution of our respondents along a broad, general life satisfaction dimension, we should use a measure which samples a number of constructs to yield the most reliable overall estimate. The Neugarten Life Satisfaction Index A or the revised Philadephia Geriatric Center Morale Scale (depending on respondents' abilities to comprehend) are the instruments of choice: they are broad in scope and have had the most extensive psychometric evaluations.

Some researches prefer to let respondents do their own averaging and have relied on single items such as the ubiquitous Bradburn (1969) happiness measure: "How would you say you are these days--very happy, pretty happy, or not too happy?" This is a tempting solution since the question appears to be straight-forward, lets respondents decide what is important to them, and has demonstrated respectably high correlations with some multiple-item indices. For anthropologists, it has the further advantage of being readily translatable except for the midterm "pretty happy," whose meaning is unknown even in English. However, considered psychometrically, single items are notoriously unreliable, and the user should be ready to defend the choice on other grounds.

On the other hand, if what we want to determine is the *relationship of factors* such as health to morale, we must avoid measures that include health items. Including portions of the dependent variable in the independent variable does yield gratifying significant correlations, but they are spurious. Because it is essential in such research to use the "purest" measures available for unambiguous interpretation, the factorial studies referred to earlier are especially valuable guides, as they are to anyone daring enough to use morale as an independent variable (dissatisfaction can be a powerful motivator).

The more global indices (such as those mentioned above) contain a number of long time-span items, many relating to the entire life span. And, as has been pointed out, they average across many constructs. Thus scores on the more global indices can be expected to be relatively stable over time and only moderately responsive to fluctuations in the immediate environment or to recent life events. Therefore they are not the measures of choice for *evaluating effects of interventions or life changes,* despite the frequency with which they are used for this purpose.

More accurate estimates of change will be obtained by instruments designed to tap satisfaction with specified targets of the interventions (i.e., satisfaction with health, with housing, and so forth) or by measures that emphasize current mood (such as the Bradburn Affect Balance Scale). Unfortunately, we know little about the generalizability of the specific satisfaction scales that have been used, and the validity of the Affect Balance Scale is not yet well established for older populations. However, as increasing numbers of researchers work with them, we can expect these deficiencies to be remedied.

Because the global indices contain life-span and age-specific items, they are inappropriate for *comparisons across age groups*. Statements such as "I am just as happy as when I was younger" have very different meanings to a 20-year-old and to an 80-year-old, and items pertinent to old age are simply meaningless for the young. Those life satisfaction measures discussed here that were designed specifically for older people cannot adequately assess the life satisfaction of all age groups.

This is relevant to a design issue of some importance for anthropologists: in cross-cultural research, we should *avoid measuring life satisfaction only among the elderly*. Even when age differences are not the focus of study, the lack of comparative age data renders many results inconclusive. For example, if we are told only that the aged among tribe X show a high level of life satisfaction, we do not know to what degree this characterizes other age groups in tribe X. The conclusion then begs a number of questions and adds little to our knowledge. Obtaining distributions of scores across age groups provides sounder bases for cultural comparisons: this strategy reduces the dangers of intercultural instrument incommensurability and provides more meaningful data on the relationship of age and life satisfaction.

A problem is posed by those measures which include *"age attitude"* items (such as "Old people are often sick"). Scores can be depressed by accurate responses to such items. Thus, though the respondent may succeed in discounting discouraging facts and actually have high morale, the measure can seriously underestimate it. For this reason, it is best to avoid those so-called attitudinal items that reflect cognitive content rather than affect. This conclusion is buttressed by the finding that they comprise a factorially distinct domain (Pierce & Clark 1973: Lawton 1975).

Finally, we may find, upon critical scrutiny of our research design, that we do not need a life satisfaction measure at all. We may be able to *operationalize variables more precisely using other measures*; or morale/life satisfaction, as such, may not be what we are really after. Studies frequently can be improved by using alternative constructs.

In particular, let me caution very strongly against further studies that do no more than estimate level of life satisfaction for some particular group. My classic horrible example is a study of elderly, chronically disabled, black, female welfare recipients, which triumphantly concluded that they had lower morale than middle-class whites in the literature! We know that health and income account for the lion's share of the variance in such scores, and this study adds nothing: it is trivial and informants rightly should feel abused. We should *need* to know something about morale to justify measuring it.

But despite numerous objections over the years, the seemingly endless flow of life satisfaction studies continues. Often measures are inappropriately or gratuitously included in studies, apparently because measures are ready to hand and a kind of morale tropism has been established among gerontologists. In final warning, let me quote from Taylor's provocative essay (1977:33):

> I ask you to take the time to look at some studies which have used morale as a variable and decide whether or not leaving out that variable does violence to the *major* understandings provided by the research. If a person . . . lives in a neighborhood where forced entry and rape are common, the fact that she is unhappy about it is one of the last things that might occur to you. If she worries whether her Social Security check will come on time next month, the fact that it makes her unhappy seems almost impertinent. If there is an accumulation of adrenachrome coursing through her system because of frequent stress situations, the fact that she is unhappy is just excess data.

WHICH ARE MOST USEFUL TO ANTHROPOLOGISTS?

This question is a tough one, for today's anthropologist is at least as likely to be found in a New York City hospital ward or a San Diego Tenderloin as in the New Guinea Highlands. No set of measures can be sufficiently protean to adjust to this range of settings. Although this does not mean that we cannot measure life satisfaction, it may mean that the only solution is to translate the concept into culture-specific domains and devise measures appropriate for each cultural setting. However, then the issue of cross-cultural comparisons becomes problematic.

We may get by with present measures in the United States and Europe, though ethnic minorities cannot be taken for granted. But when we move into the exotic populations traditionally studied by anthropologists, problems multiply: usually forced-choice instruments are hopelessly inappropriate; direct item translations are likely to produce absurdities; the concept of morale itself, as we know it, may prove culture-bound and meaningless. For at the core of the morale/life-satisfaction notion is a conscious comparison of present well-being with the level of well-being experienced in another state. This may be an experience some time in the past, or it may be a future or optimum state that has never been or never can be, actually experienced.

Just what standard a respondent is using to answer our questions is unclear in most of the current morale studies and poses a major difficulty for interpretation. Does R report relative satisfaction with his life because he sees it as good in some absolute sense? Because he sees it as good when compared to his neighbor's life? When compared to his own life at some earlier period? Or because he sees it as good "given my age" or situation? People discount, reduce their expectations according to the normative "facts of life." To what extent morale measures reflect these varying referents is unknown. Moreover, as Gubrium and Lynott (1983) point out, the image of life implicit in measures necessarily structures, limits, and perhaps distorts respondents' experience.

Westerners are addicted to taking their emotional pulse and apparently can read phenomenal sense into the instruments we use. But what if this conscious monitoring of emotional states is not a habit of all groups we study? There is good reason to think that it is not. In some modes of Eastern thought, such comparisons are prima facie evidence of spiritual immaturity: for drought-stricken Africans, happiness is summed up by today's full belly and life satisfaction is a redundant notion. In many settings, to use terms like morale or life satisfaction may be seriously misleading. For example, we may design a measure to obtain respondents' satisfaction with their lives. But their answers may be based on cognitive appraisals of success in relation to others rather than feelings and aspirations. Then our measure reflects accuracy of social perception, not the intrapsychic mood-tone of self and life appraisal that we expected to tap. This is simply a variant, in an exotic setting in which cognitive content is reflected rather than effected (as noted above).

This suggests the most basic question for cross-cultural research: to what extent is the morale or life-satisfaction concept, *as we know it,* a viable phenomenal construct in other cultures? Or are feelings about oneself and one's life so firmly tied to cultural contexts that the terms should not be extrapolated beyond our own? Investigations of some magnitude would be required to settle this issue, and I doubt if the effort could be justified, much less funded, solely on these grounds. However, a body of relevant data would be generated if anthropologists, in their diverse settings, could devise comparable techniques to address this question in addition to their primary concerns. At the very least, we then would know what constitutes well-being, life satisfaction, or morale across a range of cultures, including our own--no mean accomplishment.

To return to the issue of measurement as such in traditional settings, it seems to me the best solution is to try to measure life satisfaction by culturally flexible alternatives to the structured scales most commonly used today. There are two basic approaches: one continues to rely on self-reports as basic data, the other relies on alternative sources of data--sources other than the self.

Self-Report Data

The most intuitively appealing measure is the Cantril Self-Anchoring Scale (Cantril 1965). This is a vertical nine- to eleven-rung "ladder" whose extremes are determined by the respondent, who is asked to think of the best possible and worst possible life for him. A rung is selected to represent his actual life satisfaction in relation to these personal endpoints. (In essence: "I'd give it a nine."). Traditionally, three rankings are obtained: five years ago, currently, and five years in the future. Initially designed for a large cross-cultural study, this measure's unique advantage is its lack of imposed substantive content. It is virtually culture-free, at least for populations which experience little difficulty comprehending the simple ladder graphic.

One caution, however: the rankings "are anchored within an individual's own reality world" (Cantril 1965:25). That is, endpoints and rankings are individual and subjective; therefore, if two persons provide the same rank, it does not imply they both feel the same level of satisfaction in any absolute sense. Rather, they are both satisfied to the same relative degree in terms of their own aspirations and fears.

This ladder technique lends itself to any number of variations. For anthropologists, it is probably best used not as a single, global rating of life satisfaction, but in one or more of the following variations:

1. More focused questions (e.g., satisfaction with income, with kin relations) reduce ambiguity in comparisons of endpoints and rankings;

2. Narrowed or expanded time frames tailored to the question pinpoint critical changes in people's lives;

3. Multiple rankings for more than one aspect of the question facilitate comparisons.

For example, I have used these ladders to trace the life histories of men's relationships with each of their children and the resulting graphs agree well with assessments based on intensive interviews. Graphing over time spurs reminiscence, highlights change, and (at least in our society) elicits richer data than simple questions.

I also strongly recommend recording and analyzing the content of the respondent's endpoints and reasons for his choice of rank (Cantril's codes may be helpful here). This not only clarifies the task for the respondent, but elicits major values and fears, i.e., the emic bases of his satisfaction judgments. Indeed, knowing what people worry about, and the likelihood of their fears being realized, adds another dimension to quality of life: scores can be devised to reflect potential stability or risk.

Bortner and Hultsch (1973) demonstrated the value of adding two dimensions to this scale: perceived opportunity (the obverse of risk) and efficacy. Efficacy is simliar to locus of control, but the latter taps an ideological level--essentially a philosophical stance or cognitive style--whereas efficacy taps the empirical level: can I, by my own efforts, move toward a desired state? Interest in this empirical notion of control is increasing, and new measures are being developed, such as the Tripartite Scale (Levenson 1974) and the Desired Control and Expectancy Scales (Reid & Ziegler 1980). In general, perceived control appears to intervene between situational determinants and the sense of well-being. For cross-cultural use, and especially in homogeneous groups, measures of this empirical level of control are likely to show more variation than the broadly normative traditional locus of control measures. I recommend adding efficacy rankings to satisfaction ladders; it is a simple way to measure a probably important explanatory variable.

A very different solution is the substitition of *researcher ratings* for respondent answers to scale items. For example, Munnichs (1966) and Maas and Kuypers (1974) had judges rate interview protocols on scales designed to encompass major morale dimensions: zest vs. apathy, resolution and fortitude, congruence between desired and achieved goals, self-concept, and mood.

If the anthropologist has not already devised a technique for isolating the cultural dimensions of life satisfaction, usually a wealth of relevant data is available from which it is possible to estimate likely dimensions, to be further refined through discussions with informants. He can then develop a set of open-ended questions to systematically elicit data relevant to these dimensions and scales on which to rate the respondents. However, it is important to report the criteria for the endpoints and at least some intermediate points in sufficient detail so that others can replicate the ratings (discussed later) or judge the appropriateness of the scales for their populations and, it is hoped, experiment with them. Again, a major advantage of rating interview data is flexibility, for this approach lends itself readily to specifying various distinct content areas.

How do we develop guides to elicit adequate data for rating? Basically this is just good ethnographic technique. But there is some pertinent literature, for this idea of opening up heavily "psychometrized" concepts for informant validation and context specification is beginning to attract support. Jessor, for example, reports (1968:298) that an open-ended format for locus-of-control ratings produced less social desirability bias than the standard forced-choice format. And Lefcourt has even gone as far, psychometrically speaking, as to offer a sample open-ended interview guide to encourage researchers to derive more specific, goal-relevant control measures (1976: Appendix 9). This is an encouraging attempt to tie a construct more firmly to reality in a typical anthropological manner.

Alternative Data Sources

A completely different approach suggested by Bloom (1977) is to limit self-report instruments and rely more heavily on unobtrusive and nonreactive measures. This apppproach has an immediate appeal to most anthropologists, who use these techniques regularly. Such objective. indices could supplement, if not replace, self-reports; they also offer potential for validation of more traditional measures. However, they are not without their own inherent pitfalls, not the least of which is incommensurability, as Rosow points out (1977), for most are ipsative. But they are certainly worthy of serious consideration and experimentation, especially for intervention and follow-up studies wherein individuals can function as their own controls.

Another innovation has been tested in a typically anthropological setting: the Brittons' 1972 study of the elderly in a rural U.S. hamlet capitalized on the potential for combining commununity-study methods with survey and clinical techniques. The Brittons asked a panel of community members to rate elderly residents (well known to all) on dimensions similar to those found in esteem scales, such as respect and number of friends. This method of acquiring ratings suggests a valuable supplement to the usual observational/interview database for esteem scores. And, by modifying the dimensions, such a panel could function as an independent group of judges to rate morale of elders, to corroborate observational data, and to validate unobtrusive and self-report measures.

RELIABILITY

Reliability of measures refers to the same basic notion we use every day when we speak of reliability: Does the yardstick give me the same length when I repeat a measurement? Can I depend on it? Obviously, reliability is a necessary, though not sufficient, condition for validity. Ideally, when a new population is being measured, reliability should be reestablished. However, although it is simple to check the dependability of a yardstick, it is far more difficult to determine the dependability of a set of items intended to capture a state of mind.

Psychometricians have developed a number of techniques to assess reliability, and many excellent texts are devoted to this topic. But for the measures discussed here, in anthropological settings we are limited realistically to reliability over time, that is, test-retest reliability. Admittedly, replication can cause such awkwardness in field situations that one may have to forgo this nicety. However, if acceptable reasons can be given in the field for redoing tasks, by all means do so with at least a subsample of respondents, preferably about a month apart (Pearson's r can be computed by hand in the field for immediate feedback).

For ratings or coding of interview data, reporting reliabilities is *essential*: it offers the only evidence of the researcher's objectivity and of the solidity of the data. Since this is easily carried out, there is no excuse for the scarcity of such reports. Indeed, it is advantageous, for subjecting oneself to the discipline of setting out rating criteria early on invariably clarifies data requirements, sharpens interview questions, and greatly reduces missing or ambiguous data.

Whenever data are rated or coded by the researcher, at least a sizable subsample of the ratings should be duplicated by at least one other person. Reliability between raters is easily computed: the most common method is the number of agreements over the total decisions made. It is preferable to have hypothesis-testing data rated "blind," that is, by raters who are not aware of the hypotheses or from whom significant "biasing" information about respondents can be withheld. Sometimes reliabilities can be obtained in the field, but simultaneity of ratings is not necessary: reliability of ratings based on a corpus of interviews, observations, and the like can be obtained upon return from the field.

VALIDITY

Most of us are quite content to use a measure if it "looks good"-- if it has so-called face validity. But opinion is not validation. Psychometricians demand evidence that an instrument does measure what it purports to measure. Their concern is well-founded: we should be more concerned than we are about the validity of our measures. But how do we validate an internal state like morale? How can we demonstrate that our measure captures life satisfaction?

Opinion is divided: on the one hand, cautious experts like Lawton reject validation by agreement with self-reports on similar measures and hold out for validation by independent, external judgments on the same dimensions. Others are willing to accept self-reports as appropriate data for subjective-state convergent validation. Carp (1977) and Gubrium and Lynott (1983) have expressed additional concerns about content validity: are the dimensions of our measures truly comprehensive, capturing fully what we are after?

For the most part, we can sit back and let the experts argue, test, and settle these issues for us. But if we develop or modify measures ourselves in the field, then *we* are the experts. Whatever validation is done, we are the only ones who can do it. And if our analyses rely heavily on measures of questionable validity, be assured our conclusions will be questioned.

Now I do not expect that many anthropologists could take the time to mount a full-scale validation of all the measures they have developed or modified. But this does not imply wholesale rejection of these measures. It does mean we should negotiate a reasonable midground that allows flexibility, yet does not flout basic psychometric principles. On the positive side, we should remember that we do not measure anonymous, random strangers. We measure people we know, people we observe frequently in a variety of settings throughout months and even years. We are really in a much stronger position to develop a systematic body of validating data than the psychometrician, who typically deals with faceless, contextless, one-shot data.

First and foremost, validity is a common sense issue: if a measure yields results that are at odds with your own observations and the opinions of others who should be knowledgeable, it is unlikely that the measure is valid. So one way of establishing a first, crude validation of a measure is to examine preliminary results in these terms: do presumed experts agree with the scores? One or two good local informants can be asked to rate a few respondents on the dimensions presumably measured (or very similar ones), and direct comparisons made. If the results are encouraging, a panel can be chosen for a more thorough validation of a larger sample. Although comparisons of the extreme scorers will show the level of agreement most dramatically, it is best to use the full range of scores for validations. The greatest difficulty is likely to be in obtaining judges' understanding of the abstract concepts involved in many measures and often this may prove impossible. But for a number of constructs (e.g., agitation, depression, sastisfaction with income), neighbors and relatives can be excellent sources of validation.

If judges' ratings cannot be obtained, select a subset of the sample you can expect will cover the full range of the dimension involved, and establish a file on these individuals: observations, comments about them, their own comments, and relevant unobtrusive indices. When you have collected a reasonable amount of information, rate these data yourself and formally compare the results with the measure scores. If in-the-field reliability or subsequent reliability between raters is good and if the pooled ratings accord well with the measure scores, you will have provided a respectable validation.

If neither of these strategies is manageable, it is still worthwhile to approximate them by maintaining relevant materials in a file for even a small subset of the sample, especially if a wide range of levels can be included. Normative, group data--however accurate--will not do, for it cannot validate individual measurement instruments. But we should not be afraid to use our own good judgment and ingenuity to obtain validating evidence. An astonishing amount of research relies on so-called "face validity" without evidence of any other. Given the breadth and depth of our knowledge of our respondents, their communities, and their lives, we can do better.

Acknowledgements

The author gratefully acknowledges the support of NIA Grant AG00097 in preparation of this chapter.

Table 9.1 Scales Related to Morale: Basic Information

Authors	Name of Scale(s)	Apparent Content	No. of Items	Scaling Method	Standardization Group(s) Subjects	N	Reliability	Validities
Bradburn & Caplowitz (1965) Bradburn (1969)	Affect Balance Scale positive affect negative affect	happiness/mood intrapsychic symptoms	10 5 5	cluster-analytic	national sample, 21-59	± 4850	re-test: .76 .83 .76	gamma, self-reported happiness = .48 .36
Brodman et al. (1949)	Cornell Medical Index	psychophysiological & somatic symptoms intrapsychic/psychophysiological symptoms	144 51	none	medical out-patients, 21+	179	n.r.[a]	concordance with medical history, 95%
Burgess et al. (1949)	Chicago Attitude Survey happiness section	several domains happiness	56 7	item-analytic	urban residents 65+	100 + 168 + 98	test-retest = .72 n.r.	independent judgments, total, r = .53 n.r. for happiness section alone
Cumming & Henry (1961)	Cumming & Henry Morale Index	satisfaction/status quo	4	rational	urban, 50+	211	n.r.	median rho (N = 10), 4 judges, = .68
Kutner et al. (1956)	Kutner Morale Scale	life satisfaction	7	Guttman	NYC, 60+	500	n.r.	concurrent validities
Langner (1962)	22-item screening inventory	intrapsychic/psychophysiological symptoms	22	item-analytic	NYC, 21+	1,660	n.r.	patients vs. non-patients
Lawton (1972) Lawton (1975)	Philadelphia Geriatric Center Morale Scale PGC Morale Scale (revised)		22 17	item- and factor-analytic	institution & housing, 65+ housing 62+	199 828	K-R = .81 test-retest = .80	independent judgments, r = .47
Morris & Sherwood (1975)	HRCA Morale Scales agitation (tranquility) attitude-own aging (satisfaction-life progression) lonely dissatisfaction	intrapsychic symptoms age-related morale loneliness/life satisfaction	17 6 5 6		institution & housing applicants 60+ (?)	n.r.	alpha = .57 alpha = .71 alpha = .73	
National Health Survey (1970)	(not named)	psychophysiological symptoms	10	item-analytic	national sample 18+	6,672	K-R = .70	item phis with self-reported "nervous breakdown" = .17–.31
Neugarten et al. (1961)	Life Satisfaction Index A Life Satisfaction Index B	life satisfaction life satisfaction	20 12	Item-analytic Item-analytic	Urban, 50+ Urban, 50+	177 177	n.r. n.r.	Independent judgments, r = .39 .47
Adams (1969)	LSI-A mood tone zest for life congruity	happiness age-related morale continuity (?)	6 6 3	item- and factor-analytic	small town, 65+	508	internal consistency	no new validity determination

Table 9.1 (Continued)

Author (year)	Scale / subscale	Subscale description	No. items	Method	Sample	N	Reliability	Validity
Pierce & Clark (1973)	Pierce-Clark Morale Scale	intrapsychic/life satisfaction		cluster-analytic	urban normals, psychiatric patients, 60+	264	n.r.	pts. vs. normals
	depression-satisfaction		7	psychiatric		171		
	(social accessibility)	(interviewer ratings)	(3)					n.r.
	negative age	age-related morale	5					n.r.
	equanimity	intrapsychic symptoms	7					pts. vs. normals
	social alienation	attitudes	2					n.r.
	will to live	age-related morale (?)	3					pts. vs. normals
	physical decline	self-rated health/ psychophysiological	3					n.r.
	positive age	attitudes	4					n.r.
Schooler (1970)	Morale Scales			factor-analytic	national sample, 65+	3,996	n.r.	many concurrent validities
	transient response to external events	intrapsychic symptoms	7					
	anomie	attitudes	4					
	age-related morale	age-related morale	7					
	sustained unhappiness	life satisfaction	6					
Srole (1956)	Anomie Index	attitudes	5	Guttman	urban, ages 16-69	401	n.r.	n.r.
Thompson et al. (1960)	satisfaction with life	life satisfaction	3	Guttman	retired & nonretired USA. 64-66	1,159	n.r.	concurrent validities
	dejection	intrapsychic symptoms (mixed)	3	Guttman				
	hopelessness		3	Guttman				
Wood et al. (1969)	Life Satisfaction Index Z	life satisfaction	13	item-analytic	rural. 63+	100	alpha = .79	r = .57, judges' ratings (independent?)
Zung (1965)	Zung Depression Scale	intrapsychic symptoms	20	item-analytic	psychiatric pts., all ages	58	n.r.	depressives vs. other diagnoses
Morris et al. (1975)	agitation	intrapsychic/psycho-physiological	9	factor-analytic	mental hosp. pts., 20+	89	about .86	
	self-satisfaction	life satisfaction	8				about .81	

[a]Not reported in original publication.

Table 9.2 Life-Satisfaction Constructs

1. How does R feel about his life?

    Global   Life-Satisfaction Index A (Neugarten et al.
                           1961) Revised Philadelphia Geriatric Center
                           Morale Scale (Lawton 1975)
                           MUNSH Happiness Scale (Kozma & Stones
                           1980)
                           Self-Anchoring Ladder (Cantril 1965)

    Current   Agitation Scale and Lonely Dissatisfaction
                              Scale (PGC)
                           Depression-Satisfaction Scale (Pierce &
                              Clark 1973)
                           Affect Balance Scale (Bradburn 1969)

    *Age-Related**   Negative Age Scale (Pierce & Clark 1973)
                           Attitude Toward Own Aging Scale (PGC)

2. How does R feel about himself?

    *Health**   Self-Assessed (e.g., Maddox & Douglass 1974)
    Self-Concept   Semantic Differential (Back 1974)
                              Evaluation Factor *and* Activity Factor*
                           Self-Esteem Scale (Rosenberg 1965)

3. How does R feel about his relation to the world?

    Loneliness   Lonely Dissatisfaction Scale (PGC)

    Locus of   Revised Rotter Scale for Elderly (Hunter
       *Control**   1980)
                           Tripartite Scale (Levenson 1974)
                           Expectancy Scale (Reid & Zeigler 1980)
                           Efficacy Scale (Bortner & Hultsch 1973)

    *Anomie**   Anomie Scale (Srole 1956)
                           Social Alienation Scale (Pierce & Clark 1973)

    Specific   To be developed (e.g., satisfaction with
       *Satisfaction**   housing, Carp 1976)

*Factorially distinct from core life-satisfaction measures.

BIBLIOGRAPHY

Back, K. 1974. "Transition to Aging and the Self-Image." In Normal Aging (vol. 2), ed. E. Palmore. Durham, N. C.: Duke University Press.

Bloom, M. 1977. "Alternatives to Morale Scales." In Measuring Morale, ed. C. Nydegger. Washington, D.C.: Gerontological Society, pp. 23-29.

Bortner, R., and D. Hultsch. 1973. "Patterns of Subjective Deprivation in Adulthood." Mimeo. Available from D. Hultsch, Pennsylvania State University.

Bradburn, N. 1969. The Structure of Psychological Well-Being. Chicago: Aldine.

Bradburn, N., and D. Caplovitz. 1965. Reports on Happiness. Chicago: Aldine.

Breytspraak, L. 1974. "Achievement and the Self-Concept in Middle Age." In Normal Aging, (vol. 2), ed. E. Palmore. Durham, N. C.: Duke University Press.

Britton, J., and J. Britton. 1972. Personality Changes in Aging. New York: Springer.

Cantril, H. 1965. The Pattern of Human Concerns. New Brunswick, N. J.: Rutgers University Press.

Carp, F. 1976. "User Evaluation of Housing for the Elderly." Gerontologist 16:102-11.

____. 1977. "Morale: What Questions Are We Asking of Whom?" In Measuring Morale, ed. C. Nydegger. Washington, D.C.: Gerontological Society, pp. 15-22.

George, L. 1979. "The Happiness Syndrome: Methodological and Substantive Issues in the Study of Social-Psychological Well-Being in Adulthood." Gerontologist 19:210-16.

George, L. and L. Bearon. 1980. Quality of Life in Older Persons. New York: Human Sciences Press.

Gubrium, J. F., and R. J. Lynott. 1983. "Rethinking Life Satisfaction." Human Organization 42:30-38.

Hunter, L., et al. 1980. "Discriminators of Internal and External Locus of Control Orientation in the Elderly." Research on Aging 2:49-60.

Jessor, R. 1968. Society, Personality, and Deviant Behavior. New York; Holt, Rinehart & Winston.

Kozma, A., and M. J. Stones. 1980. The Measurement of Happiness: Development of the Memorial University of Newfoundland Scale of Happiness (MUNSH). Journal of Gerontology 35:906-12.

Lawton, M. P. 1975. "The Philadelphia Geriatric Center Morale Scale: A Revision." Journal of Gerontology 30:85-89.

_____. 1977. "Morale: What Are We Measuring?" In Measuring Morale, ed. C. Nydegger. Washington, D.C.: Gerontological Society, pp. 6-14.

Lefcourt, H. 1976. Locus of Control. Hillsdale, N. J.: Erlbaum.

Levenson, H. 1974. "Activism and Powerful Others: Distinctions within the Concept of Internal-External Control." Journal of Personality Assessment 38:377-83.

Lohmann, N. 1980. "A Factor Analysis of Life Satisfaction, Adjustment, and Morale Measures with Elderly Adults." International Journal of Aging and Human Development 11:35-43.

Maas, H., and J. Kuypers. 1974. From Thirty to Seventy. San Francisco: Jossey-Bass.

Maddox, G., and E. Douglass. 1974. "Self-Assessment of Health." In Normal Aging (vol. 2), ed. E. Palmore. Durham, N. C.: Duke University Press, pp. 55-63.

Munnichs, J. M. A. 1966. Old Age and Finitude. Basel: Karger.

Neugarten, B., R. Havighurst, and S. Tobin. 1961. "The Measurement of Life Satisfaction." Journal of Gerontology 16:134-43.

Nydegger, C., ed. 1977. Measuring Morale. Special Publication No. 3. Washington, D.C.: Gerontological Society.

Pierce, R., and M. Clark. 1973. "Measurement of Morale in the Elderly." International Journal of Aging and Human Development 4:83-101.

Reid, D., and M. Ziegler. 1980. "Validity and Stability of a New Desired Control Measure Pertaining to Psychological Adjustment of the Elderly." Journal of Gerontology 35:395-402.

Rosenberg, M. 1965. Society and the Adolescent Self-Image. Princeton, N.J.: Princeton University Press.

Rosow, I. 1977. "Morale: Concept and Measurement." in Measuring Morale, ed. C. Nydegger. Washington, D.C.: Gerontological Society, pp. 39-45.

Rotter, J. B., 1966. "Generalized Expectancies for Internal versus External Control of Reinforcement." Psychological Monographs 80.

Sherwood, S. 1977. "The Problems and Value of Morale Measurement." In Measuring Morale, ed. C. Nydegger. Washington, D.C.: Gerontological Society, pp. 34-38.

Srole, L. 1956. "Social Integration and Certain Corollaries. American Sociological Review 21:709-16.

Taylor, C. 1977. "Why Measure Morale?" In Measuring Morale, ed. C. Nydegger. Washington, D.C.: Gerontological Society, pp. 30-33.

10
Network Methodologies in the Study of Aging

JAY SOKOLOVSKY
Department of Sociology
University of Maryland (Baltimore County)

The growing interest in maintaining elderly segments of our population in the community as well as humanely dealing with their
problems has greatly stimulated research interest in social networks that can serve as "natural" systems of support. In 1970 Alvin
Wolfe anticipated this by suggesting that network analysis might
eventually play the role in studies of modern societies, that
genealogy has played in tribal studies (p. 227). This prediction has
been born out by a converging stream of work not only in
anthropology (Mitchell 1969; Wolfe 1970; Barnes 1972; Boissevain &
Mitchell 1973; Boissevain 1978; Sokolovsky & Cohen 1981b, 1983) but
in most of social science.[1] For the interdisciplinary field of
sociocultural gerontology, the aged's social interaction has always
been a key issue, crucial to theory and practice. However, it is
only in the last decade that "network analysis" has been transformed from a mere buzzword to an important research strategy
employed in studies of aging.

Nevertheless, acolytes of this perspective on examining personal relationships seldom have considered the dilemmas involved in
gathering information that accurately portrays the real world.
More of an effort has gone into designing computer programs to
manipulate numbers and create dichotomous variables once data
has been collected (Holland & Leinhardt 1979; Project in Structural

231

Analysis 1981; Burt and Minor 1982). Contrastingly, this chapter seeks to examine the key methodological problems in gathering accurate and qualitatively salient information on the dimensions of social networks. In doing this I hope to show how anthropological research is relevant to applying a network approach to the study of gerontology.

NETWORK ANALYSIS, ANTHROPOLOGY, AND GERONTOLOGY

Network analysis has emerged in anthropology as a means to deal analytically with the dynamics of behavior, especially in settings where social action is not readily subsumed within overarching institutional structures such as corporate kin groups or age sets. An anthropological approach to examining networks involves not only ethnographically defining the transactional nature of personal linkages but also defining the cultural meaning they hold for social actors. Researchers in the anthropology of aging have frequently recognized at least tacitly the importance of such a methodological strategy. Simmons, in his watershed comparative work, appropriately notes that

> social relationships have provided the strongest securities to the individual, especially in old age. With vitality declining, the aged person has to rely more and more upon personal relations with others, and upon the reciprocal rights and obligation involved. . . . To withstand the strain of obligations, social ties have had to be continuously revitalized, and for the aged the surest move to this end has been continued execution of socially useful work. (1970:177)

This statement highlights the importance of a network approach in studying the adaptation to old age in preindustrial societies, where, even given the existence of corporate kin groups or age sets, the need to socially negotiate the size, viability, and support capacity of networks still exists. A good example of this process is found in Curley's book on the Longo of Nigeria where elders form flexible age-peer coalitions called *etogo*, which link old men of different clans in reciprocal exchanges of ritual performance (1973:51-66).

The concern for understanding and measuring social interaction is scarcely an anthropological monopoly, as is seen by noting that some notion of social participation has always been a central issue in the development of general gerontological theory. First with activity (Maddox 1963; Lemon, Bengtson & Peterson 1972; Schmitz-

Scherzer & Lehr 1976; Knapp, 1977) and disengagement theories (Cummings & Henry 1961; Havighurst, Neugarten & Tobin 1968; Hochschild 1975), and more recently with exchange (Dowd 1975, 1980; Emerson 1976) and ecological models of adaptation (Lawton & Nahemow, 1973; Kahana 1980), each broad perspective has demanded in one way or another data on the nature, extent, and change of friendship, kinship, and other personal ties.

Also pertinent to an anthropological contribution to the aging field has been the recent general concern for "natural" support systems, recognizing the importance of social rather than bureaucratic relationships in meeting the needs of old people, even in postindustrial society (Lieberman 1978; Kahn 1979; Cantor 1980; Wagner & Chapman 1980; O'Brien & Wagner 1980; Johnson & Catalano 1982; Antonucci & Depner 1982). Indeed a growing number of studies relating health states (especially mental illness) to networks indicate "the buffering effect of social support to moderate the relationship between acute stresses . . . and criteria for well being" (Kahn 1979:85). (See especially Dean & Lin 1977; Sokolovsky et al. 1978; Pattison, Llamas & Hurd 1979; Snider 1981; Pilsuk and Minkler 1981; Wan 1982.)

Probably the most dramatic indication of the prophylactic effect of network involvement comes from the study of Berkman and Syme (1979) who showed that over a ten-year period, in a general age population, age-adjusted mortality is reduced among those who have good network support. For the elderly, reported consequences of relatively weak interpersonal support systems include mental health problems (Lowenthal & Haven 1968); poor adjustment to widowhood (Lopata 1979); a greater likelihood of institutionalization (O'Brien & Whitelaw 1973); a diminished sense of well-being (Tannenbaum 1975); and difficulty in reacting to problems associated wih diminished health (Cohen & Sokolovsky 1979b). Unfortunately, in many of these studies a major problem lies in assessing the comparability of network variables.

NETWORKS AS VARIABLES

Most anthropologists taking a network approach to research have focused on ego-centered sets of social linkages and their interconnections, called "personal networks," to not only interpret the social behavior of the persons involved (Mitchell 1969:2) but to analyze the basis of strategic "mobilization of people for specific purposes under specific conditions" (Whitten & Wolfe 1973:720). In this latter sense, personal networks are frequently discussed in practical terms as a "support system" involving "an enduring pattern of continuous or intermittent ties that play a significant part of maintaining the psychological and physical integrity of the individual over time" (Caplan 1974:7). As the notion of "support systems" is generally construed, a distinction is often made between "informal" support marked by personal or non-bureaucratic ties selected from among kin, friends, neighbors and co-workers versus the "formal" support engendered by bureaucratic, administrative, client formal-caregiver (e.g., shaman-patient) ties. Here informal support systems are the equivalent of personal networks, and it should be noted that the bureaucratic nature of a tie does not prevent such a link from becoming a personal one if the relationship goes beyond the bounds of exchange performed in professional caregiving or work relationships.

Another important distinction is that between actual, direct linkages and potential networks, ties involving perhaps what Boissevain calls "friends of friends" (1978; see Katz [1966] for a discussion of actual vs. potential networks). I would propose, for practical methodological purposes, that we focus on behaviorally active linkages for empirical comparison, while not ignoring the cultural meaning of potential networks for understanding adaptation to old age.

Graphically, personal networks should be familiar to any ethnographer who has traced a genealogy or analyzed the social links required to carry out a religious ritual. The notion of social network actually subsumes such measures of cultural phenomena, partial sets of linkages bounded by various criteria such as social category (e.g. patrilineally linked males), specific goals, what Mayer (1966) calls "action sets" (e.g., politically recruited supporters), or role systems (e.g. age-set systems). Networks can also generally be bounded *behaviorally*--by including only those persons who are interacted with on a weekly basis, or *cognitively*--by deriving from respondents lists of those persons whom they consider important to themselves.

In fact, the methodological bounding of networks can be achieved in an almost limitless manner. If one attempts to consider networks in relation to the life course, as Sanjek notes, "In a total sense the temporal bounds of a network are set by an individual's birth and death; the spatial bounds are set by his movements" (1974:589). To capture this sense of movement, Kahn and Antonucci use the term "convoy of social support' to represent changing network structure in the process of aging and other life-course changes (1981). However, Sanjek suggests that from a life-span perspective the total behavioral content or the cognitive organization of networks can never be studied (1974). Other than extensive longitudinal studies, an attempt to deal with this problem is to derive equivalent cross-sectional network data by age segments and at least grossly approximate the changes in networks over time (Hess 1972; Shulman 1975; Lowenthal 1975; Stueve & Gerson 1977; Cubbitt 1978; Fisher 1982:179-90). As we will observe, the most basic methodological dilemmas in network studies are (1) bounding the nature of social relationships, and (2) securing quantitative and qualitative data comparable between both respondents in a sample and between societal groups.

Dimensions of Networks

Before deciding how to approach these two problems it is necessary to consider briefly the basic dimensions of networks: member attributes; linkage attributes; and network attributes (Leveton et al. 1979).[2] Member attributes involve the sociodemographic features of each variable, such as sex, age, occupation, ethnicity, residential location. Linkage attributes include all those features that demarcate the nature of transactions that flow from a respondent to a given network member. Measures of linkage attributes have been typically discussed as "interactional criteria" (Mitchell 1969; Boissevain 1978:28-35) which can focus on the following factors:

1. Context of recruitment: Under what circumstances was an alter incorporated into ego's networks? For example, principles of descent, fictive kinship, job interaction, ritual procedure.

2. Activity field: The institutional sector of society now occupied by a link (household, extended kin sector, co-worker).

3. Frequency of interaction: How often does interaction occur?

4. Duration: Time since the inception of the relationship.

5. Temporal fluctuation: Short-term variations (diurnal, monthly, seasonal) in contact.

6. Content: The resources that are flowing in the dyadic transaction. Deriving a cross-culturally valid specific list of contents may be undesirable, as the nature of perceived resources, especially affective ones, will obviously be shaped by emic perceptions. As I will suggest later, in discussing "network profiles," key areas of resource exchange and the appropriate questions to elicit them must be developed through participant observation (see Keith, chap. 1 in this volume). However, general categories of content areas that seem to have universal applicability include socializing; exchange of goods, money or services; exchange of knowledge;

generalized reinforcers (Dowd 1980:38), such as deference, approval, and recognition; and affective/emotional valence--expression of emotional attachment.

7. Directionality: The preponderant direction in which transactions flow "instrumentally" from ego to another; "reciprocally" between ego and another; or "dependently," from another to ego.

8. Magnitude: Relative level of exchange within the context of a given content (a loan of one dollar vs. one thousand dollars).

9. Intensity: Mitchell defines this as "the degree to which individuals are prepared to honor obligations, or feel free to exercise the rights implied in their link to some other person" (1969:27). He goes on to note that this is a highly subjective question, the answer to which must rely on the assessment of the fieldwork. Whitten and Wolfe, however, suggest that a cross-culturally valid measure of intensity may in fact be impossible to attain (1973). At this point I am inclined to go along with this statement, but I suggest that the subjective importance of a given relationship should be ascertained. The salience of this was seen in my network study of inner-city elderly, where kin ties, although having few content areas of ongoing exchange and extremely low frequency of interaction, were likely to be considered very important, and this network variable was signifcantly related to measures of mental health.

10. Uniplex-multiplex: Links to a given network member may be single-stranded (uniplex), comprising a single transaction (e.g, casual conversation) or multiplex, involving multiple content (e.g., talking, visiting, reciprocal food exchange) and most likely involving multiple roles (e.g., cousin, employee, friend). The anthropological notion of multiplexity has usually stressed counting role involvements (Gluckman 1955; Boissevain 1978). I believe it more fruitful to take the tack of Mitchell in focusing on counting context areas (1969:22). In my own network research (Sokolovsky et. al. 1978) with a New York City inner-city aged population who have exited out of most of our society's recognized roles, understanding the complexity of their social bonds by talking about conjugal, co-worker, or even friendship roles became irrelevant. There was found to be an important distinction between minimally multiplex links, with only two types of content, and those of greater complexity, involving three or more types of transactions. A crucial cross-cultural factor in successful adaptations of aging may be the manipulation of these various levels of multiplexity in the process of network building.

Finally, the dimension of Network Attributes refers to the morphological nature of the network as a configurational entity. Network attributes that may have social implications for the elderly include the following:

1. Size: Total number of behaviorally active network members.

2. Spatial distribution: How network members are distributed spatially in relation to ego.

3. Homogeneity: The similarity of network member attributes (e.g., age, class, ethnicity).

4. Density: Ratio of actual to potential interconnections among members of a respondent's first order zone. $D = 100 \times n_0 (N/2(N-1)\%)$ (where Na equals the number of actual interconnections and N is the size of the first order zone). Note that any analysis using this variable must control for size of the network.

5. Degree of connection: The average number of relations each person has with others in the same network ($De = (2 \times Na)/N$).

6. Number of social clusters (also called plexus groups): Number of segments of a network that have high-density interaction.

7. Dispersion: The ratio of actual to potential number of activity fields from which network members are drawn.

8. Multiplexity: The proportion of network members who have multiplex relations with ego.

9. General morphology: How networks as a whole are structually distinct.[3]

NETWORK METHODOLOGIES: RIGOR VS. RELEVANCE

Despite the large number of studies now done on social networks, a methodological dilemma has persisted in articulating ethnographic studies of networks with relevant models developed to explain behavior. As Heckathorn notes, "Field studies typically generate huge volumes of data which cannot be accommodated within existing formal models; and formal models may demand enormous volumes of data which are nearly impossible to gather in the field"

(1979:223). This quandry of rigor vs. relevance (Roistacher 1975:2) is especially apparent in the gerontological work discussed previously, where theories requiring detailed data on social linkages have often been tested with typically superficial measures of social interaction, the behavioral validity of which can often be called into question.

In the following section I will discuss a variety of means for eliciting data on the network dimensions just discussed, especially those which have been used in studying aged populations. Each will involve certain compromises between rigor and relevance. This entails trading off, to varying degrees, the ability to observe through participant observation all relevant behavior, with interview techniques which would hopefully elicit data approximating actual behavior.

Sociometrics

The eliciting technique most often used in studies of elderly social interaction and associated with mass survey sociological research is generally referred to as "sociometrics." This may involve either limited choice questions: "Who are your three best friends?" "Name the three relatives whom you see most often" or enumerative questions: "How many relatives did you see last week?" "How many good friends do you have?" In either case research based on these methods generally has been used without the benefit of ethnographic field techniques, which could help validate the behavioral veracity of responses and could provide a basis for asking meaningful questions within given societal contexts. Thus studies (Rosow 1967; Rosenberg 1968; Lowenthal & Haven 1968) trying to assess comparatively the level of sociability or the degree of social isolation of the aged using some kind of enumerative "friendship" index (based usually on the question, "How many friends did you see in the last week?") generally ignore the variable meaning of friendship even within sampled populations.

In such studies, having (or claiming to have) friends is equated with a high degree of sociability, conversely a claimed absence of "friends" is equated with isolation. Lowenthal herself, who used such methods in studying the link of social isolation to mental illness among the aged, recognized a crucial difficulty with friendship studies: even within our society there is a wide disparity in perception of friendship networks and the definitions of friends, by sex, socioeconomic status, and geographic location (1975). This difficulty would be amplified in applying the technique cross-culturally, especially in societies where the notion of "friends" is poorly developed.

A more sophisticated approach to large-scale survey network study has been to request enumeration of persons associated with structural features of social life (see especially Babchuk 1978; Cantor 1980; Lopata 1979; for applications to elderly populations). One such interview technique developed by McCallister and Fisher (1978; see also Fisher 1982:267-350) elicits names of persons associated with key activities or types of problems. Data on member attributes and some linkage and network attributes for a portion of the total network is then obtained by having the subject fill out a short questionnaire on these individuals. It is claimed that this method can provide data on up to 30 network members in a twenty- to thirty-minute interview. Yet, as Fisher himself states, "in pretesting . . . interviewees had surprisingly poor recall of the people they knew, and in the absence of extensive probing they were likely to forget important persons" (1982:286). Thus, while such techniques may provide samples of a thousand or more, the data collected seldom illuminate the complexity of social interaction and may inaccurately portray actual behavior (see especially Bernard, Fillworth and Sailer 1981).

Sociability Indices and Interactive Scales

Sociability indices and interactive scales are designed to elucidate the subject's interaction based on a variety of parameters that purportedly encompass the total field of interaction. While such measures make important strides in focusing on the behavioral aspects of networks, a basic problem has been the over emphasis on the quantitative features of interaction, while excluding important linkage attributes such as content and intensity.

The studies by Townsend (1957) in England and by Clark and Anderson (1967) in California are good examples of this approach. Townsend's behavioral approach toward a British elderly sample entailed scaling interaction on the basis of social contact per day (social contact score). This was facilitated through the use of genealogies and diaries over a two-week period, with certain types of contacts (those in one's household) receiving a higher score for daily contact, while other types of contact received a lower score (contact with postman). While this differential value of contact seems justified, the weighting of contacts is not related to linkage attributes in a fashion that lends itself to complex cross-cultural comparison.

Clark and Anderson, anthropologists who carried out a monumental study of aging and stress (especially mental illness) in San Francisco, developed a "social interaction level" scale (1967). The scale, abstracted from interviews with respondents, entailed five levels of interaction: (1) participation in business, cultural, charitable, religious or political affairs; (2) attendance at social functions or visits with friends and/or relatives; (3) visits from friends and/or relatives living outside household; (4) social activity with other household members; (5) less than above or no social contact. While this is not a direct network approach, it incorporates much of the information that can be extracted from network data. While these levels combine personal, economic, and cultural activity, nonetheless, as the authors note, "no effort was made to distinguish them on the basis of the duration, content or frequency of the social interaction" (Clark & Anderson 1967).

Ethnographic Aproaches: Network Serials and Network Profiles

The anthropological perspective on networks can potentially deal with many methodological problems by its emphasis on holistic analysis, ethnographic description, and a concern for the emic meaning of behavior. In trying to effectively bridge the gap between rigor and relevance it is suggested that an anthropological approach to social networks should attempt to accomplish the following: (1) empirically define the total behaviorally active personal network for meaningful samples; (2) elucidate the qualitative aspects and cultural meaning of interactional and structural network characteristics; and (3) establish the broad dimensions of structural change of networks.

Yet since the beginning of anthropological concerns for analytically rather than metaphorically researching networks, a constant dilemma has been investigating the behavior and cultural complexity of linkage and network attributes for more than a few individuals. One approach to this problem has been to focus on "action sets" (Mayer 1966) or "partial networks" (Kapferer [1969]), where ethnographic attention could be focused on a given field of interaction (e.g. the workplace) to allow meticulous examination of network dimensions (see especially Kapferer 1969). Such an approach might be applicable to studying, say, the household networks of the elderly, but would be unwieldy if one's concerns extended to contacts in all relevant activity fields and the interconnections among them.

Thorough applications of an ethnographic approach to studying the total networks of the aged have been rare. The best examples are Francis's (1984) comparison of Jewish elderly in Cleveland and England and the study by Wentowski (1982) of a heterogeneous urban population. Both researchers employ participant observation, life histories, genealogies, and informal interviews to probe networks as support systems. Francis's methods are based on a comprehensive set of semistructured questions ("aide memoire") centering around practical (transportation, shopping, money, etc.) and emotional (advice, attending ritual, visiting, etc.) services. In Wentowski's study, questions did not systematically focus on areas of support, but were elicited as events occurred, especially when behavior conflicted with expectations of help. Both studies achieve impressive levels of qualitative analysis, but each has different limitations. While the Francis's study generates a relatively small sample (twenty-two women), Wentowski's methods make the task of empirical analysis and comparison difficult. Two types of solutions to these problems have been developed. One approach focuses on reported interaction over a specified short time period, the other seeks lists of all significant ties by organizing interviews around salient activity fields and content areas.

Network-Serial Method

The former method, as developed in Roger Sanjek's urban fieldwork in Accra, Ghana (1978), elaborates on the work of Epstein, who analyzed urban networks through the written accounts of Chanda, a Zambian clerk-typist (1961). Through this record, Epstein recreates Chanda's network ties activated over five days (noncontinuous) in a variety of nonwork settings. In his own work Sanjek combined Epstein's strategy with Harris's notion of the "multi-actor scene," centering on a "full record of sequence, activity, place, and actors present" (Sanjek 1978:258). The network-serial method then involves the "documentation of an actor's spatial movements and interactions over a relatively short sample period of time".

After about four months of fieldwork, during which knowledge of daily activities and likely scenes of activities were developed, the Sanjek husband and wife team used intensive interviewing to extract the four-day network-serial of forty persons (twenty males, twenty females). Interviews were conducted in two parts, each recording two days (total timeframe: two weeks and a weekend) and detailing in narrative the settings of social behavior (e.g. ego's workplace, church; twenty settings in all, divided into work/public, residential, leisure settings) as well as the characteristics of network actors. Sanjek's methods are similar to other diary approaches, such as those of Boswell (1975), Kapferer (1973), who combines interviews, participant observation, and what she calls a "structured diary" kept by each respondent for a week. The only application of a similar method to studying the elderly that I know of is the work of Jonas and Wellin (1980), which focuses on the extent of health care aid exchanged over a two-week period among public-housing residents in Milwaukee. While the network-serial approach nicely centers data around the behavioral aspects of networks, the environmental context of social action, and attributes of network members, this method does not typically provide a notion of the total network in either size or general structure. Further, as Sanjek himself notes, the representative nature of a four-day network serial is problematic and it would be helpful to ascertain for the population studied the nature of variability in terms of interaction over a year's time.

Network Profiles

In an effort to elucidate the total extent of personal ties an individual may have, fieldworkers have often attempted to obtain lists of such relationships. Most often this has been accomplished through extensive interviewing entailing various levels of structured questions. Boissevain, in trying to assess the relative impact of entire networks on personality in rural vs. urban Malta, asked respondents to list all persons they knew and then to provide data on a variety of member and linkage attributes (social background, activity field, frequency, content) (1978:97-146). The networks derived were so large (1,751 and 648 persons) that this cognitive bounding ("Who do you know?") provided a sample of only two. While Boissevain concedes this does not provide the basis for comparative research, structuring questions around network variables generates an incredible amount of information about the social linkages involved.

This methodological approach is also seen in the classic work of Bott on the relation of conjugal roles to network morphology (1982:6-24, 231-37). Bott, in a semistructured interview, organized questions around three informal activity fields--relatives, friends, and neighbors--and in the process of a series of interviews with each couple, researchers asked questions pertaining to all three network dimensions I discussed previously.

Knowledge about each household (which was the "anchor" of each network) was derived by having respondents keep a diary, and by asking questions on decision making, financial support and management, housework, child care, and recreation. Information was based almost exclusively on this questionnaire technique rather than on participant observation. In this way networks generated by twenty conjugal pairs were studied, requiring about twelve hours per case. It is not entirely clear how Bott bounded the networks collected; on the one hand she included all kin known, and on the other included all persons respondents *cared* to list as friends. However, what is important in her methods is the ordering of questions by network sector (activity field) and behavioral components of linkage attributes. This provided a fairly comprehensive picture of interactional and structural network variables which could be compared for more than just a few cases.

Various researchers, including myself, have elaborated on this approach as a means of generating characteristics of the significant bonds that directly link individuals to their social world. Both Pattison (a community psychiatrist) and I have referred to such methods as "network profiles" (Sokolovsky et al. 1978; Pattison 1975, 1977). For Pattison, elaboration of what he calls the "psycho-social kinship system" was determined by asking respondents to list the *subjectively important* people in their life, under the categories of family, relatives, friends, co-workers and social organization" (1977:230). Each contact was then rated by variables of interpersonal relations: degree of interaction (relatively high-frequency contacts); emotional intensity (relationship involving positive emotion); instrumental base (concrete assistance); symmetrical reciprocity (relationships where there is an "affective and instrumental quid pro quo" [ibid]). Finally, the subjects drew a diagram of all the social connections that existed between all the people they listed.

The network profile that I developed in studying released mental patients and the elderly living in Manhattan single-room-occupancy (SRO) hotels does not depend on the initial importance. Instead, it is based on behaviors within specified activity fields. I found in my work that comparable data among respondents was facilitated by discussing the aspects of "importance" or "intensity" *after* the behavioral aspects of the relationship were established. It is crucial to note that like types of interaction were accomplished only after about four months of fieldwork. I am convinced that it is necessary to ethnographically establish informed knowledge of typical categories of behavior to ask meaningful questions about personal networks.

In the case of the hotel elderly, who prize autonomy so highly, initial questions about who was "important" to them led to active denial of any important relationships, although, through observation and later use of the network profile, relationships crucial to their very physical and psychological survival were elicited.

Using a Network Profile

Figure 10.1 represents a page from the network profile I used in my research in Manhattan. It shows the hotel-resident sector of interaction. The total network profile included two other activity fields of the informal support system--outside (non-hotel resident), nonkin, and kin ties--as well as two sectors of formal ties to hotel staff and health/welfare personnel (doctors, social workers). It was found that the most consistent way to elicit accurate responses about networks, which were also comparable between respondents, was initially to frame questions around each sector of interaction, e.g., "Let's talk about the people you have contact with in the hotel." Questions then proceeded to inquire about the three dimensions of each social matrix.

Member Attributes. The simplest data to obtain are member attributes. Here direct questions are asked about the age, sex, address, race/ethnicity, and occupation of a given alter. This information will be used in the contruction of network attribute variables, such as size, homogeneity, and spatial distribution.

In studying the SRO elderly I included only links active within the prior year (known for at least a month) with a minimum frequency of once a month for hotel residents and every three months for nonresidents, and once a year for kin. It was determined that network members with less contact than this in a given activity field were generally of little practical or cultural/psychological meaning to SRO residents. It should be noted that the network profile elicited in certain cases what many would consider "weak" or "nominal" relationships, either because with acquaintances interaction might be by conversation only, or with kinfolk contact might involve only a letter once a year. This was necessary, as it was discovered that such links were an important pool of potentially more significant social linkages, transactions with whom could be intensified in times of crisis. For other elderly populations, with relatively large networks (say averaging more than fifteen members), it may not be advisable to record "nominal" ties.

Linkage Attributes--Interactional Features. Queries next sought to establish the simple interactional and environmental basis of linkage attributes by asking: "When did you first meet X?" "How did you first meet X?" "When did you last talk with X?" "Would you say you see or talk to X each day or several times a week?" "When are you most likely to see X . . . during the day or at night, or is there any special time of the month or year when you talk more often to X, or are *not* likely to see or hear from X?" These last questions are linked to others establishing the environmental context of contact: "Where do you see each other, in the lobby, nearby park, or cafeteria?" "How often do you get together in each other's room?"

This part of the profile derives some information on network flux, a crucial gerontological issue, but perhaps the most difficult to handle methodologically. While we found the daily, monthly, and seasonal activation of ties important in the lives of the hotel elderly, this information was elicited with difficulty and inconsistency throughout the sample. Larger changes were determined in two ways: (1) after the profile was completed, respondents were asked about any significant persons whom they had lost contact with in the prior two years; (2) as part of obtaining background information on each respondent, we used an adult "social isolation index" (Granick & Nahemow 1961), a structured enumerative questionnaire based on a measure of contacts in a person's prior job career, marital arrangement, kinship connections, friendships, and organization activity. Obviously, an ideal situation would allow for a longitudinal design. Here, however, one can anticipate special coding problems when, inevitably, at time 2 interviews, additional network members are remembered who should have been included at time 1.

Linkage Attributes--Exchange Content. Next, the exchange content of the linkage is established, beginning with more tangible types of transactions: "When you get together, what types of things do you talk about?" "What kinds of advice do you give each other?" "When money runs low at the end of each month, how much do you loan each other?" "When in your room or sitting together in the park or a bar, do you ever share a drink or buy rounds for each other?" "How often do you share hot-plate meals, or exchange leftovers, or go out to the same place to eat?" What other places do you go to together or meet each other (parks, movies, senior center, etc.)?" Questions then proceed to less tangible, affective elements of the relationship: "When you are feeling down or you see X feeling down, how does X help you/how do you help X?" "What kinds of personal thoughts/feelings (fears about getting older, family problems) do you share with each other?" "In terms of how important a person could be to you, how do you feel about X--not important; important; very important; or most important?" "There are many types of relationships that a person can have; how do you regard X in terms of friendship--not a friend; a friend, a good friend; a best friend?"

Several things are important to note here. I strongly feel that questions should be asked in as positive and concrete a manner as possible. "When you are not feeling well, how does X help you? is preferable to "Does X give you any medical aid?" Some people will not understand the latter question, and others will take the easy way out and simply respond "no," irrespective of the reality of the situation. Additionally, in carrying out the interview with respect to content areas, there was often no set order in which the type of transaction was explored. There are at least two reasons for this. First, as the interview is done in a conversational manner, respondents often spontaneously discuss particularly important aspects of the relationship (e.g., feelings of intimacy), and I encourage them to expand on that point as necessary. Secondly, by varying the order of questions, boredom is reduced for both researcher and interviewee, a significant factor in long interview situations (the network profile took from one to six hours to complete). The key point, always kept in mind is that certain minimal data must be gathered about all network variables, irrespective of the order in which they are asked.

Thus, in charting a tenant's contacts with each network member, the extent of content of the relationship is delineated, as is the frequency, duration, intensity, and directional flow of the link.

The content of linkage attributes is typically the crucial component of network studies of the aged. It is the reality of which support systems are composed, and the data that help one understand the divergent cultural meanings of networks. But it is difficult to organize this data without grossly distorting its meaning. Coding schemes should be developed that avoid conversion of this complex data into simple dichotomous variables (e.g., absence/presence). At the point of recording information from interviews, provision should be made to capture the distinction between, say, loans of money that are given reciprocally, frequently, and in significant amounts, from a petty money exchange provided unilaterally once over the last six months. This will be crucial in the creation of additive or multiplicative variables derived from separate network dimensions.

Network Attributes. Network attributes are conceptual representations of a social matrix as a whole, dynamic phenomenon. These variables are either constructed in aggregate (e.g., size) or ratio (e.g., multiplexity) form from member and linkage attributes, or derived by questions about the linkage of network members with one another. In deriving measures of density, degree, and network morphology, it is first necessary to either ask directly about interconnections or to present a diagram of all contacts and have respondents connect those network members who have some level of communcation with each other. This is also an appropriate time to probe group dynamics among highly interconnected clusters of a network.

However, among the SRO elderly, knowledge about interconnections between nonresidential linkages was very inconsistent; it was usually impossible to verify by observing or questioning the dispersed network personnel outside the hotel walls. This may not be such a dilemma in different settings, such as in an isolated Mexican village I studied. Here not only did 90 percent of an elder's social linkages live in the community but there was also a great degree of knowledge about the activities of network members. (Sokolovsky and Sokolovsky 1985)

The validity of network data is always a problem. Although observational checks could not be systematically done, in certain cases data could be doubled-checked when profiles were done on persons whose social linkages overlapped. Especially in cases where few network members were initially noted, we used Sanjek's network-serial approach and reviewed the respondent's activities over a one- to five-day period.

SUGGESTIONS FOR A CROSS-CULTURAL NETWORK PROFILE

It is not the intention of a network-profile approach to provide researchers with a precoded protocol, but rather to help develop within varied ethnographic contexts accurate means for collecting network data. Developing a profile would probably best be done after completing what Keith (chap. 1 in this volume) calls phase 1 of participant observation, which establishes a basic cultural map of the research setting. To facilitate intersocietal comparison, I would like to propose a flexible network form that might be used in different cultural contexts. Figure 10.2 shows a general format for the community/locality nonkin activity field.

The following are suggested guidelines for the cross-cultural use of the network profile:

1. Primarily, include only persons with a minimum frequency of once a month; secondarily, include individuals who are interacted with less frequently over a year's time if contact has either behavioral or cognitive importance.

2. Include persons who exchange, at a minimum, informal conversation and one other content.

3. Attention should be given to appropriate sampling by sex and age, especially taking into consideration important transition periods within the "aged spectrum" (e.g., healthy/frail).

4. In collecting data on linkage attributes, pay attention not only to the frequency, direction, and relative magnitude of exchange, but also to the meaning the exchange has for the respondent, especially how it relates to the perception of one's own aging (e.g., does the degree of dependency imply a perception of being old).

5. Questions dealing with particular content areas should be based as concretely as possible on culturally relevant occurrences.

6. Reconstruct a network serial for two days of the preceding week.

7. Once a network profile is completed, use the information as a baseline for comparison to the period just before entering a culturally defined stage of old age. That is, using current extant contacts, one can--through the linkage variable of duration--trace network ties backwards and ask simple questions about gross changes in the linkage and network attributes. This certainly will not be easy, but we may be deceiving ourselves if we do not attempt to collect such data.

FIGURE 10.1. Network Analysis Profile

NAME:_____   Code:_____

(Use direction/frequency codes for contents)
Directionality Code: 1. ego to other   Frequency Code: 0. None
                      2. other to ego   1. 1 per month
                      3. reciprocal   2. less

	Hotel Sector	Contact #1
	Contact Name, Sex, Address; Age	Eva, P.; F; Rm 304; 64
	Race (1-white; 2-black; 3-hispanic; 4-other;9-na)	2
	Occupation (1-works; 2-soc sec; 3-ssi; 4-welfare; 9-na)	2
	Length of Link (years)	6
	Context of Link (1-work; 2-friend; 3-kin; 4-hotel; 5-random; 6-center; 7-other; 9-na)	4-"Just met in hotel lobby"
	Last Saw (1-yesterday/today; 2-few weeks; 3-past month; 4-past 6 mos.; 5-past yr.; 6-over year; 9-na)	1
	Contact Frequency (1-daily; 2-few weeks; 3-once/week; 4-once/month; 5-twice/year; 6-once/year; 7-once/five yrs; 8-less)	
	Telephone/Letters (Same code as above)	0/0
	Time of Contact (1-day; 2-night; 3-day/night; 9-na)	0
	Monthly/Seasonal Change	Times when away for a week
	Visit Room	3/1
	Meet in Lounge	3/1
	Informal Conversation	3/1
	Advice	3/1-"We give each other advice about keeping healthy"
	Money/loans	3/1-small loans for food, drink, about $2-5/week
	Drinking/Drugs	3/1-every week they drink (beer) in ego's room
	Food Aid	3/1-cook for each other & share left-over snacks
	Medical Aid	3/2-twice in last year cared for each other when sick
	Other Aid	2/2-give each other emotional support, mostly other to ego.
	Eat out together	0
	Other social outings	0
	Sexual interaction	0
	Jobs	0
	Global Importance (1-not import.; 2-very import; 3-very import.; 4-most import; 9 na)	4-"She is the only one I can really depend on when in trouble or when I feel crazy"
	Friendship (1-not a friend; 2-friend; 3-good friend; 4-best friend; 9-na)	4-"She is the only one I would call a friend in this place"
	Do you share intimate thoughts?	3/1-"We don't hold anything back from each other"

Member Attributes

Interactional Features

LINKAGE ATTRIBUTES

Exchange Content

FIGURE 10.2. Proposed Cross-Cultural Network Analysis Profile

PROPOSED NETWORK ANALYSIS PROFILE — ACTIVITY FIELD D: COMMUNITY/LOCALITY NON-KIN

NAME _____

CODE NUMBER _____

Frequency Code
0. = No content
1. ≤ 1 x/month
2. Less of ten
9. Not ascertained

Directionality Code
1. Ego to other
2. Other to ego
3. Reciprocal

LINKAGE ATTRIBUTES

MEMBER ATTRIBUTES

Interconnections Write Activity field letter person number	Name, Sex 1. Male 2. Female AGE Relationship	Location (Note approximate distance to ego's house) Ethnicity/Occupation	Duration (Length of link in yrs.)	Context of Link 1. Kin principles 2. Ritual kin 3. Ritual Procedure 4. Work 5. Voluntary Assoc. 6. Introduced thru contact 7. Bureaucratic setting (e.g. clinic) 8. Other	Frequency of Contact 1. Often/daily 2. Once a day 3. Several per wk. 4. weekly 5. monthly 6. 4 x/yr. 7. 1 x/yr. 8. less often (Note whether physical or not)	Fluctuation (Note any important fluctuations on mo., seasonal basis

LINKAGE ATTRIBUTES

Socializing

Informal Conversation (in public space)	Visiting	Eating or Recreational drinking/ drug use	Sexual Contact	Social Outings	Other

Figure 10.2. (Continued)

LINKAGES ATTRIBUTES

Goods, Money, and Service Exchange							Knowledge Exchange/Advise				Generalized Reinforcers	Affect/Emotional Valance
Loan of money/substitute goods	Gifts	Food Preparation	Work/ Service	Medical/ Therapeutic Care	Ritual Procedure/ Activity	Child Care	Ritual/ Religious	Family Matters (social)	Economic Matters	General Comportment/ Values	Note type of deference, approval, recognition	Note perception of overall affect/ emotional importance

NOTES

The author would like to acknowledge the support and aid of Dr. Carl Cohen of the New York University Medical Center, especially in helping to develop the Network Analysis Profile discussed in this chapter. The research in this chapter was supported by NIA grant AG00097. The author also is indebted to Dr. Linda George for her critical review of an earlier version of this chapter.

1.   The interdisciplinary nature of concern for studying social networks is seen in a recent anthology edited by Samuel Leinhardt (1977), which brings together classic articles from many different disciplines. See especially the work of Whitten and Wolfe (1973), Wolfe (1978), and Foster (1979), for a discussion of the development of the network approach in anthropology.   As for other disciplines; sociology (Craven & Wellman 1973; Fisher et al. 1977; Wellman 1980; Warren 1981; Burt 1982; Fisher 1982; Marsden & Lin 1982); psychology (Caplan 1974; Erickson 1975; Pattison 1977; Hirsh 1979; Turkat 1980; Gottlieb 1981); social work (Patterson 1974; Collins & Pancoast 1976; Swenson 1979; Froland 1981); public health (Kaplan, Cassel & Gore 1977; Garrison 1981); and communication studies (Rodgers & Kincaid 1980).

2.   For a more thorough discussion of linkage attributes and network attributes, see Mitchell (1969:1-50) and Boissevain (1978:24-48).

3.   In analysis of network data based on inner-city elderly in New York City, the following categories of general network morphology were used: Cluster--at least 75 percent of persons in ego's network were in contact with each other; Diffuse--no interactions occured between members of ego's network; Diffuse/Cluster--interaction existed between at least two network members, but less than 75 percent of members were in contact with each other; Kin Cluster/Diffuse--at least 75 percent of members were in contact with each other, but nonkin had no interaction among themselves.

BIBLIOGRAPHY

Antonucci, T., and C. Depner. 1982. "Social Support and Informal Helping Relationships." In Basic Process in Helping Relationships, ed. T. A. Willis. New York: Academic Press.

Babchuk, N. 1978. "Aging and Primary Relations." International Journal of Aging and Human Development 9:137-51.

Barnes, J. A. 1972. Social Networks. Addison-Wesley Module in Anthropology, No. 26. Reading, Mass.: Addison-Wesley.

Berkman, L. F., and S. L. Syme. 1979. "Social Networks, Host Resistance and Mortality: A Nine-Year Follow-Up Study of Alameda County Residents." American Journal of Epidemiology 109:186-204.

Bernard, H. R., P. Killworth, and L. Sailer. 1981. "Summary of Research on Informant Accuracy in Network Data on the Reverse Small World Problem." Connections 4:18-25.

Boissevain, J. 1978. Friends of Friends. Oxford: Basil Blackwell.

Boissevain, J., and J. C. Mitchell, eds. 1973. Network Analysis: Studies in Human Interaction. The Hague: Mouton.

Boswell, D. 1975. "Kinship, Friendship and the Concept of a Social Network." In Urban Man in Southern Africa, ed. C. Kileff and W. C. Pendleton. Signal Mountain, Mambo Press.

Bott, E. 1982. Family and Social Network. New York: Free Press.

Burt, R. S. 1982. Toward a Structural Theory of Action: Network Models of Social Structure, Perceptions and Action. New York: Academic Press.

Burt, R. S., and M. Minor, eds. 1982. Applied Network Analysis: Structural Methodology for Empirical Social Research. Beverly Hills: Sage.

Cantor, M. 1980. The Informal Support System: Its Relevance in the Lives of the Elderly, ed. E. Borgatta and N. McClusky. Beverly Hills: Sage, pp. 131-44.

Caplan, G. 1974. Support Systems and Community Mental Health. New York: Behavioral Publications.

Clark, M., and B. Anderson. 1967. <u>Culture and Aging: An Anthropological Study of Older Americans</u>. Springfield, Ill.: Charles C. Thomas.

Cohen, C., and J. Sokolovsky. 1978. "Schizophrenia and Social Networks." <u>Schizophrenia Bulletin</u> 4:546-60.

____. 1979a. "Clinical Use of Network Analysis for Psychiatric and Aged Populations.: <u>Community Mental Health Journal</u> 15:203-13.

____. 1979b. "Health Seeking Behavior and Social Networks of the Aged Living in Single Room Occupancy Hotels," <u>Journal of the American Geriatric Society</u>, VXXVII (6):270-78.

Collins, A., and D. Pancoast. 1976. <u>Natural Helping Networks</u>. Washington: National Association of Social Workers.

Craven, S., and B. Wellman. 1973. "The Network City." <u>Sociological Inquiry</u> 43:57-88.

Cubbitt, T. 1973. "Network Density among Urban Families." In <u>Network Analysis</u>, ed. J. Boissevain and J. C. Mitchell. The Hague: Mouton, pp. 67-82.

____. 1978. "Friends, Neighbors and Kin: Development of Social Contacts with Special Reference to Stages in the Life Cycle and Class Factors." <u>Connections</u> 1:42.

Cummings, E., and W. Henry. 1961. <u>Growing Old: The Process of Disengagement</u>. New York: Basic Books.

Curley, R. 1973. <u>Elders, Shades and Women</u>. Berkeley: University of California Press.

Dean, A., and N. Lin. 1977. "The Stress-Buffering Role of Social Support." <u>Journal of Nervous Mental Disorders</u> 165:403-17.

Dowd, J. 1975. "Aging as Exchange: A Preface to Theory." <u>Journal of Gerontology</u> 30:584-94.

____. 1980. <u>Stratification among the Aged: An Analysis of Power and Dependence</u>. Monterey: Brooks-Cole.

Emerson, R. M. 1976. "Social Exchange Theory." In <u>Annual Review of Sociology</u> (vol 2), ed. A. Inkeles, J. Coleman, and N. Smelser. Palo Alto: Annuals Reviews.

Epstein, A. L. 1961. "The Network and Urban Social Organization." Rhodes-Livingstone Journal 29:129-62.

Erickson, G. 1975. "The Concept of Personal Network in Clinical Practice." Family Process. 14:487-98.

Fisher, C. S. 1982. To Dwell among Friends: Personal Networks in Town and City. Chicago: University of Chicago Press.

Foster, B. 1979. "Formal Network Studies and the Anthropological Perspective" Social Networks 1:241-57.

Francis, D. 1984. Will You Still Need Me, Will You Still Feed Me, When I'm 84? Bloomington: Indiana University Press.

Froland, C. et al. 1981. Helping Networks and Human Services. Beverly Hills, Calif: Sage.

Garrison, J. 1981. "Clinical Construction of Action Social Networks" International Journal of Family Therapy 3:258-67.

Gluckman, M. 1955. The Judicial Process among the Barotse of Northern Rhodesia. Manchester: Manchester University Press.

Gottlieb, B., ed. 1981. Social Networks and Social Support in Community Mental Health. Beverly Hills: Sage.

Granick, R., and L. Nahemow. 1961. "Preadmission Isolation as a Factor in Adjustment to an Old Age Home." In Psychopathology of Aging, ed. P. Hoch and J. Zubin. New York: Grune & Stratton, pp. 285-392.

Havighurst, R., B. Neugarten, and S. Tobin. 1968. "Disengagement and Patterns of Aging." In Middle Age and Aging, ed. B. Neugarten. Chicago: University of Chicago Press, pp. 161-72.

Heckathorn, D. 1979. "The Anatomy of Social Linkages." Social Science Research 8:222-52.

Hess, B. 1972. "Friendship." In Aging and Society (vol. 3), ed. M. W. Riley et al. New York: Russell Sage Foundation. pp. 357-93.

Hirsch, B. J. 1979. "Psychological Dimensions of Social Networks: A Multimethod Analysis." American Journal of Community Psychology 7:263-77.

Holland, P., and S. Leinhardt, ed. 1979. Perspectives on Social Network Research. New York: Academic Press.

Hochschild, A. R. 1975. "Disengagement Theory: A Critique and a Proposal." American Sociological Review, 40:553-59.

Johnson, C., and D. Catalano. 1982. "Childless Elderly and Their Family Supports." Gerontologist 21:610-18.

Jonas, K., and E. Wellin. 1980. "Dependency and Reciprocity: Home Health Aid in an Elderly Population." In Aging in Culture and Society, ed. Christine Fry. New York: J. F. Bergin, pp. 217-38.

Kahana, E. 1980. "A Congruence Model of Person-Environment Interaction." In Aging and the Environment: Directions and Perspectives, ed. M. P. Lawton, P. Windley, and T. Byerts. New York: Garland STPM.

Kahn, Robert. 1979. "Aging and Social Support." In Aging from Birth to Death, ed. M. W. Riley. AAAS Selected Symposia Series. Boulder, Colo.: Westview, pp. 77-91.

Kahn, R., and T. Antonucci. 1981. "Convoys of Social Support; A Life-Course Approach." In Aging: Social Change, ed. S. Kiesler, J. Morgan, and V. K. Oppenheimer. New York: Academic Press. pp. 383-405.

Kapferer, B. 1969. "Norms and the Manipulation of Relationships in a Work Context." In Social Networks in Urban Situations, ed. J. C. Mitchell. Manchester: Manchester Univesity Press, pp. 181-245.

Kaplan, B., J. C. Cassel, and S. Gore. 1977. "Social Support and Health Care." Medical Care 15(5), supp.:47-58.

Katz, E. 1966. "Social Participation and Social Structure." Social Forces XLV:299-321.

Knapp, M.. 1977. "The Activity Theory of Aging." Gerontologist 17(6).

Knoke, D., and J. Kuklinski. 1982. Network Analysis. Beverly Hills: Sage.

Lawton, M. P., and L. Nahemow. 1973. "Ecology and the Aging Process." In Psychology of Adult Development and Aging, ed. C. Eisdorfer and M. P. Lawton. Washington, D.C.: American Psychological Association, pp. 619-74.

Leinhardt, Samuel, ed. Social Networks: A Developing Paradigm. New York: Academic Press.

Lemon, B., V. Bengtson, and J. Petersen. 1972. "An Exploration of the Activity Theory of Aging: Activity Types and Life Satisfaction among In-Movers to a Retirement Community." Journal of Gerontology 27:511-23.

Leveton, L. et al. 1979. "Social Support and Well-Being in Urban Elderly." Paper presented at the Gerontological Society Meetings.

Lieberman, G. L. 1978. "Children of the Elderly as Natural Helpers: Some Demographic Difference." American Journal of Commmunity Psychology 6:489-98.

Lopata, H. 1975. "Support Systems of Elderly Urbanites: Chicago of the 1970's." Gerontologist 15:34-41.

____. 1979. Women as Widows. New York: Elsevier.

Lowenthal, M. F. 1975. "Life Course Perspectives on Friendship." In Four Stages of Life, ed. M. F. Lowenthal et al. San Francisco: Jossey-Bass, pp. 48-71.

Lowenthal, M., and C. Haven. 1968. "Interaction and Adaptation: Intimacy as a Critcal Variable." American Sociological Review 33:20-30.

McCallister, L., and C. S. Fisher. 1978. "A Procedure for Surveying Personal Networks." Sociological Methods and Research 7:131-48.

Maddox, G. L. 1963. "Activity and Morale: A Longitudinal Study of Selected Elderly Subjects." Social Forces 42:195-204.

Marsden, P., and N. Lin, ed. 1982. Social Structure and Network Analysis. Beverly Hills: Sage.

Mayer, A. C 1966. "The Significance of Quasi-Groups in the Study of Complex Societies." In The Social Anthropology of Complex Societies, ed. M. Banton. London: Tavistock, pp. 97-122.

Meyers, J. M., and C. Drayer. 1979. "Support Systems and Mental Illness in the Elderly." Community Mental Health Journal 4:277-86.

Mitchell, J. C. 1969. Social Networks and Urban Situations. Manchester: Manchester University Press.

O'Brien, J., and D. Wagner. 1980. "Help Seeking by the Frail Elderly: Problems in Network Analysis." Gerontologist 20:78-83.

O'Brien, Jr., and N. Whitelaw. 1973. "Analysis of Community Based Alternatives to Institutional Care for the Aged." Final Report to Oregon State Program on Aging and AOA. Washington, D.C.: U. S. DHEW.

Patterson, S. 1974. "Older Natural Helpers: Their Characteristics and Patterns of Helping." Public Welfare, Fall: 45-50.

Pattison, E. 1977. "A Theoretical-Empirical Base for Social Systems Therapy." In Current Perspectives in Cultural Psychiatry, ed. E. Foulkes et al. New York: Spectrum, pp. 217-53.

Pattison, E., R. Llamas, and G. Hurd. 1979. "Social Network Mediation of Anxiety." Psychiatric Annals 9:56-67.

Pattison, E., et al. 1975. "A Psychosocial Kinship Model for Family Therapy." American Journal of Psychiatry 132:1246-51.

Pilsuk, M, and M. Minkler. 1981. "Supportive Networks: Life Ties for the Elderly." Journal of Social Issues 36:95-116.

Project in Structural Analysis. 1981. "STRUCTURE: A Computer Program Providing Basic Data for Analysis of Empirical Positions in a System of Actors." Computer Program 1. Berkeley: Uni- versity of California, Survey Research Center.

Rodgers, E., and D. L. Kincaid. 1980. Communication Networks: Toward a New Paradigm for Research. New York: Free Press.

Roistacher, R. 1975. "Acquisition and Management of Social Network Data." Paper presented at the Mathematical Social Science Board Advance Research Symposium on Social Networks, September 17-21.

Rosenberg, G. 1968. "Age, Poverty and Isolation from Friends in the Urban Working Class." Journal of Gerontology 23:533-39.

Rosow, I. 1967. Social Integraton of the Aged. New York: Free Press.

Sanjek, R. 1974. "What is Network Analysis, and What Is It Good For?" Reviews in Anthropology 1:588-97.

____. 1978. "A Network Method and Its Uses in Urban Ethnography." Human Organization 37(3):257-68.

Schmitz-Scherezer, R., and U. Lehr. 1976. "Interaction of Personality, SES and Social Participation in Old Age." In The Developing Individual in a Changing World (vol. 2), ed. Klaus Riegel and John Meacham. Chicago: Aldine, pp. 621-27.

Shulman, N. 1975. "Life Cycle Variation in Patterns of Close Relationships." Journal of Marriage and the Family, November: 813-21.

Simmons, L. 1970. The Role of the Aged in Primitive Society. London: Archon Books.

Snider, E. 1981. "The Role of Kin in Meeting Health Care Needs of the Elderly." Canadian Journal of Sociology 6:325-36.

Sokolovsky, J., and C. Cohen. 1981a. "Being Old in the Inner-City: Support Systems of the SRO Aged." In Dimensions: Aging, Culture and Health, ed. Christine Fry. New York: J. F. Bergin, pp. 163-84.

____. 1981b. "Measuring Social Interaction of the Urban Elderly: A Methodological Synthesis." Aging and Human Development 13:233-44.

Sokolovsky, J., and C. Cohen. 1983. "Networks as Adaptation: The Cultural Meaning of Being a 'Loner' among the Inner-City Elderly." In Growing Old in Different Societies: Cross-Cultural Perspectives, ed. J. Sokolovsky. Belmont, Calif.: Wadsworth, pp. 189-201.

Sokolovsky, J., et al. 1978. "Personal Networks of Ex-Mental Patients in a Manhattan Hotel." Human Organization 37:5-15.

Stueve, C. A., and K. Gerson. 1977. "Personal Relations across the Life Cycle." In Networks and Places, ed. C. Fisher. New York: Free Press, pp. 79-98.

Swenson, C. 1979. "Social Networks, Mutual Aid and the Life Model of Practice." In Social Work Practice: People and Environments, ed. Carel Germain. New York: Columbia University Press, pp. 213-38.

Tannenbaum, D. 1975. People with Problems: Seeking Help in an Urban Community. Toronto: Center for Urban and Community Studies, University of Toronto.

Townsend, P. 1957. The Family Life of Old People: An Inquiry in East London. London: Routledge & Kegan Paul.

Turkat, D. 1980. "Social Networks: Theory and Practice." Journal of Community Psychology 8:99-109.

Wagner, D., and N. Chapman. 1980. "Informal Group Interaction, Informal Supports and Neighborhood Environment: Perspectives on the Frail, Urban Elderly." Networks for Helping: Illustrations from Research and Practice. Proceedings of the Conference on Networks. Portland, Ore.: Regional Research Institutes for Human Services.

Wan, Tom. 1982. Stressful Life Events, Social Support Networks, and Gerontological Health. Lexington, Mass.: Lexington Books.

Warren, D. 1981. Helping Networks: How People Cope with Problems in the Urban Community. Notre Dame, Ind.: Notre Dame Press.

Wellman, B. 1980. "A Guide to Network Analysis." Mimeo. Working Paper No. 1A, Structural Analysis Programme, Department of Sociology, Unversity of Toronto.

Wentowski, G. 1982. "Reciprocity and the Coping Strategies of Older People: Cultural Dimensions of Network Building." Gerontologist 21:600-09.

Whitten, N., and A. Wolfe. 1973. "Network Analysis." In Handbook of Social Cultural Anthropology, ed. J. Honigmann. Chicago: Rand-McNally, pp. 717-46.

Wolfe, A. 1970. "On Structural Comparisons of Networks." Canadian Review of Sociology and Anthropology 7(4)226-44.

_____. 1978. "The Rise of Network Thinking in Anthropology." Social Networks 1:53-64.

Worach-Kardas, H. 1979. "Family and Neighborly Relations: Their Role for the Elderly." In Family Life in Old Age, ed. G. Dooghe and J. Helander. The Hague: Martinus Nijhoff, pp. 39-47.

11

Ethnicity: Its Significance and Measurement

LINDA E. COOL
Department of Sociology & Anthropology
University of Santa Clara

Increasingly, ethnicity has gained the attention of social scientists and policy planners. As a result, great strides have been made in understanding the relation of ethnicity to other forms of social stratification and interaction. For example, many researchers are now discarding the simplistic notion that ethnic categories or groups may be defined as reified units of a social structure solely in terms of a listing of shared cultural traits (Nagata 1976:244). We are also moving away from preconceptions that ethnic groupings must be stable and enduring even though the larger society of which they are a part is marked by continual change. In spite of such progress, however, our understanding of ethnicity has not advanced as rapidly as one could hope. Even the definition of the concept itself remains hazy, leading Cohen to suspect that the term "ethnic" has now come to be used for what anthropologists once called "tribal" or "cultural" (1978).

Anthropologists interested in examining the relationship of aging and ethnicity thus face a twofold problem: (1) defining two variables that are apparently well known to all (and therefore remain undefined); and (2) demonstrating their mutual interference and reinforcement. However, I believe that basic research in the area of ethnicity and aging can both advance the study of ethnicity and lend broader theoretical significance to the anthropology of aging itself. In order to illustrate the ways that anthropologists may combine the study of ethnicity and aging, I will briefly examine the concept and definitions of ethnicity, the possible significance of ethnicity for older people, and some methodological problems that must be considered when using ethnicity as a variable in a study of the aging process.

THE CONCEPT OF ETHNICITY

Ethnicity refers to socially significant characteristics of an aggregate of people within a larger sociocultural context (van den Berghe 1970:10), while an ethnic group is the set of individuals who interact with each other on the basis of these shared characteristics. Although various researchers emphasize different aspects of ethnicity, I believe that most would agree that six criteria constitute aspects of a working definition of the concept:

1. a past-orientation, which emphasizes distinctive origins (whether real or putative);
2. a concept of current social and cultural distinctiveness;
3. an extension of loyalties beyond the face-to-face interactions of a kin or locality grouping;
4. the presence of a larger, contrastive social context;
5. the situational nature of ethnicity whereby ethnic phenomena arise from other conditions of the social environment (including ecological, economic, and political factors); and
6. the subjective nature of ethnicity, which gives rise to different interpretations of its significance by individuals, both those who share the ethnic characteristics and those who do not.

We must not overlook the fact that ethnicity is multidimensional, with at least three factors demanding research attention: cultural, behavioral/organizational, and personal.

The Cultural Component

The first step in using ethnicity as a variable is defining those special characteristics that set their holders apart. These characteristics may include race, common origins, religion, language, or some other shared understanding that permits one to distinguish one's own from other categories of people. However, relying solely on overt cultural forms or markers for the identification of an ethnic group may lead researchers astray. Gelfand and Kutzik have rightly identified the fallacy of insisting that the vitality of an ethnic group must be measured according to the extent to which its members retain their comparatively few and fading "foreign" components (1981:358). Each successive generation of ethnic members redefines its ethnic designation by virtue of ancestral and personal identification. In the course of time, some traditional cultural forms characterizing a particular ethnic group may well be discarded without irreparable harm to the group's ongoing collective identity. Distinctive clothing styles, for example, are often the first external ethnic sign to disappear (Cronin 1970). In this sense, ethnic groups are constantly being created and recreated.

Barth revolutionized the study of ethnicity when he emphasized how and why boundaries are maintained between groups rather than what constitutes ethnic cultural content per se (1969). According to Barth, ethnic boundaries are often more social (perceptions of distinctiveness) and psychological (feelings of loyalty and identification) in nature than material or geographical. In fact, the group's enumeration of distinctive attributes comes as a result of both ascription from within and stereotyping from without. It is this sense of being different that is important, not the particular material forms that the difference takes or the historical validity of the group's claims to being distinctive.

The Behavioral/Organizational Component

Such feelings of belonging to a special category of people give rise to a "social identity," which helps to establish who a person is and how he or she will respond to a given social situation (Brim 1960: 144). The behavioral component of ethnicity includes distinctive values, beliefs, and norms that lead to actions and serve as the bases for social interaction and the rise of an ethnic group per se. Ethnic groups themselves exhibit a degree of social organization ranging from relatively loose interpersonal networks, based on a sense of shared origins and history, to formal corporate associations whose economic and political institutions are clearly defined by membership lists and articulated goals.

The larger social context strongly influences the kind of social organization exhibited by a particular ethnic group. In fact, ethnicity can be as much created by outsiders (through their stereotypes and resultant actions) as by members (through self-labeling). An ethnic group's continued survival depends on its ability to create a social environment in which its members can find satisfaction for their instrumental, emotional, and cognitive needs without having to participate in the larger society (Francis 1976:250). In this sense, it is even possible for an ethnic group to exist in the absence of obvious cultural differences with the larger society, so long as the group continues to fulfill the perceived needs of its members for social interaction and normative frameworks. Such a perspective helps explain the interest that many Americans have in asserting their northern European "heritage" by attending ethnic events even though they have no overt cultural markers (language, customs, etc.) with which to prove their identity.

The Personal Aspect

The molding of a personal identity, a sense of self, derives at least partly from the roles one assumes or is allowed to assume. According to Royce, individuals take their personal ethnic identity from two different sources: "one being the ethnic group itself [what defines the group to itself], the other the sense of solidarity that devolves upon groups that find themselves different from other groups or cut off from society [boundaries]. . ." (1982:7). However, ethnicity as personal identity and source of group membership does not automatically accrue to a person because of descent or place of birth. Even individuals who apparently have a legitimate claim to ethnic identity or membership must work toward substantiating that claim, i.e., they must act appropriately. Corsican ethnic identity in the context of the larger French society, for example, seems to be a belonging that is at once ascribed and achieved. Those individuals born on the island to two Corsican parents (who, in turn, were born on the island) are immediately recognized as Corsicans. However, these people may lose their ethnic status in the eyes of their peers if they adopt French posturings and attitudes: lack of interest in Corsica and her problems, association with other Frenchmen more than with Corsicans, failure to return to the island to visit, or failure to aid other Corsicans. In a similar manner, individuals of more dubious ancestry (those not born on the island and/or those who have only one parent who is Corsican) can "prove" their ethnicity by adopting Corsican values and attitudes, by joining ethnic organizations, by learning the language, or by being very vocal in the defense of the island and fellow Corsicans.

Little (1966), Nagata (1974), and Cool (1980) have emphasized the individual's ability to compartmentalize his or her ethnic identity and membership by "turning them on and off" in order to make appropriate responses to different social situations. It is highly likely that an individual can ignore and/or disguise ethnic membership at times when he or she is occupied with other roles (such as raising a family or making a living) and yet still revitalize the membership at a later date, when he or she has lost or modified these interim roles and identities.

ETHNICITY AND AGING

The National Urban League (1964) first coined the term "double jeopardy" to indicate the special problems of the minority aged: they are old (a devalued status in the United States) and they are members of a minority group (which has suffered discrimination at the hands of the larger society). Since its creation, the validity and importance of the concept of double jeopardy have been a focus for continuing debate among gerontologists. For example, Dowd and Bengston (1979) attempted to test the validity of the double-jeopardy hypothesis by empirically examining the situation of older blacks, hispanics, and whites to see whether, with age, the differences among them increase (positive evidence for double jeopardy) or diminish (evidence that old age acts as leveler of differences). The results were inconclusive: some variables (income and self-assessed health) showed increased differences, while others (tranquility, optimism, and frequency of social interaction) did not differ greatly with increasing age. At best, it seems that double jeopardy is not a theory per se, but rather a description of existing conditions (Gelfand 1982:39).

IDENTITY AND THE ELDERLY

As individuals grow older, they carry with them their distinctive ethnic culture, derived from group interactions and early socialization. In this respect, an ethnic value system can support older people by providing them a continuing place in the social system. And to the extent that older ethnic members remain committed to such a distinctive world-view and normative order, they should be better able to avoid the internalization of the larger society's negative attitudes toward them as older persons. This does not mean, of course, that ethnicity is a fail-safe investment against the negative self-perceptions that threaten many elderly people in industrialized nations. However, its presence does provide an additional basis for continuing self-identification and communal belonging at a time in life when the older person begins to experience the diminution of his or her conventional identities formed on age, sex, or occupation. Barth's point (1969:17) that ethnic identity is a form of status recognition that is superordinate to most other statuses, is therefore well taken.

SOCIAL INTERACTION AND THE ELDERLY

One advantage of ethnicity is that it can provide informal support networks to people of all ages who claim to be ethnic (Gelfand 1982:105). In fact, Cohen reports that a hypothesis deserving of research efforts is that "the greater the participation in ethnic group activities, the less persons feel alienated in contemporary society" (1978:401). Cohen believes that this hypothesis helps to explain why ethnicity continues to be valued in the face of powerful assimilative forces in the larger society. But it also provides a clue as to the importance of ethnicity to older ethnic members.

As Burgess perceived, the elderly are left out of meaningful social activity; their condition is a "roleless role" (1960). Ethnic group membership offers the possibility of interaction in informal networks based on this shared identity, as well as participation in more formal organizations or ethnic clubs (Cool 1980; Cuellar 1978; Myerhoff 1978). In addition, one of the keys to high morale in old age may be not only the amount or type of social activity, but also (and perhaps more important) people's acceptance of the community in which they live (and vice versa) as the focus for their social and personal identification. In fact, recent research among elderly members of a French ethnic group, the Corsicans, and among elderly Portuguese-Americans indicates that ethnicity does lead to identity maintenance and network participation for older members (Cool 1980, 1981). These older people are actively engaged in manipulating their identities and roles and generally creating a niche for themselves in their ethnic networks, and consequently in the larger society.

While ethnicity may constitute an important variable in the aging process, we have only begun to appreciate the complex nature of the relationship between ethnicity and older ethnic members. In a recent book, Gelfand (1982:34) argues that in order to understand a contemporary cohort of ethnic aged people we must focus on a number of aspects:

1. the general social and cultural characteristics of the people themselves;
2. the relationship between these characteristics and attitudes toward growing older that are held by older (and younger) members; and
3. the relationship between ethnically specific charcteristics and the satisfaction of ethnic aged people with their present life (including their ability to manipulate, or create, support networks.

In short, we need to know how people view and use their own

ethnicity and how this changes for an individual over time and for an ethnic group in succeeding generations. Such a focus will lead to an emphasis on the heterogeneity of ethnic populations and on the generational differences within them—a useful corrective to the image of the stable, homogeneous ethnic group that is often presented in the literature on ethnicity.

ETHNIC MEASUREMENT AND AGING RESEARCH

At least three general problems confront the researcher interested in examining the relationship of ethnicity and aging. First is the matter of delimiting the ethnic category to be studied and finding individuals who will serve as the research population. Next is the difficulty of using and measuring ethnicity as a variable. The measurement of ethnicity is crucial but complex, for "social borders are not simply present or absent in different settings, they exist in many degrees of definition" (Ross 1975:53). Finally, the researcher must confront the most difficult (and important) problem of all—that of measuring an individual's ethnicity and relating it to his or her aging experience. Individuals may have varying emotional and practical attachments to their ethnic membership and identity at different stages of their life cycle. Once again, the researcher must be aware of the fallacy of assuming that ethnic identity is stable or that it necessarily constitutes an all-or-nothing variable.

Delimiting the Ethnic Category

The first step of ethnic research must be to define the parameters of the ethnic group and to determine whether individuals are in fact members of the group. All too often, studies of ethnicity begin with individuals who are already defined as ethnic and then proceed to measure just how strong those individuals' indentification is. This, however, already represents a relatively advanced stage of the research endeavor.

The method of participant observation[1] is very useful in initially defining the boundaries of an ethnic group. Here the researcher acquires a first-hand experience in the group's characteristic networks and social organization, its self-definition as presented to the outside world, and the value system that serves to differentiate it from the larger society. Participant observation is particularly useful as a methodological tool, for it allows the researcher some access to the life that is lived "backstage" (to borrow and expand upon Goffman's usage of the term). In this way, an anthropologist may come to grips with the differences between ideal and real behavior.

M. Estellie Smith (1974), for example, has contributed an interesting study of insiders' and outsiders' perceptions of Portuguese-Americans in several New England communities. In brief, Smith has found that behavioral reality is not consonant with beliefs about Portuguese-Americans held by both the Portuguese themselves and by members of the larger community. The consensus of both insiders and outsiders is that physical and social boundaries are clearly drawn and carefully observed between Portuguese and non-Portuguese. And both Portuguese and non-Portuguese explain this separation as due to Portuguese traditionalism and reluctance to accept American values. However, Smith finds that a push to become American permeates the Portuguese community:

> Older women want to Americanize their houses, their dress, their life style generally; adult males admire men who don't behave like "Greenies" [new immigrants] . . . . Contrariwise, people who are disliked or who for some reason are the object of ridicule are called "dumb Portygees"--with the emphasis on "Portygees" (a highly derogatory term) rather than "dumb" (Smith 1974:83).

In the end, Smith argues that the Portuguese immigrants have been neither more nor less willing than other groups to accept new cultural patterns. "The aura of traditionalism--accepted even by the Portuguese-Americans as part of their identity--is spurious but is one of the devices which . . . insures the continuance of boundaries between Portuguese and non-Portuguese" (1974:89).

Even though a researcher engaging in participant observation may provide detailed information and personalized accounts of the ethnic group, he or she must never lose sight of the fact that the researcher's perspective is still essentially that of an outsider, albeit (perhaps) a privileged one. Therefore, some awareness and use of the techniques of cognitive anthropology[2] are also extremely helpful in the early stages of research on ethnicity. Cognitive anthropology, with its emphasis on language and insider's perceptions, leads to a model of how the informant conceives of the social world, how the informant divides up that world into categories, and how and where the informant places himself or herself. To define the boundaries and membership of an ethnic group, the perceptive researcher must combine an outsider's stereotypic and often exaggerated notions with the insider's firsthand and often emotional judgments. The definition of the ethnic group and its boundaries must be clearly stated early in the research, for this definition will determine the researcher's pool of ethnic informants.

STRATEGIES AND PROBLEMS IN CLASSIFYING ETHNIC MEMBERS

Ethnicity is a multidimensional phenomenon. It requires multiple measurement strategies that are sensitive to differences of degree, not just absolute differences of kind. The following will highlight some of the issues with which a researcher must come to grips in analyzing ethnicity and its relationship to the aging process. Although clear differences among the cultural, behavioral, and personal components of ethnicity were set out earlier in this chapter, the three overlap and the researcher must be careful to indicate the mutual interference of these aspects of ethnicity.

Measuring the Cultural Aspect of Ethnic Identity

Parental or ancestral location of origin and even family names are frequently employed as markers of ethnic belonging. Although they do provide a starting point for selecting informants, a major problem with this approach is that it assumes that a person's origin or kinship lines automatically define his or her personal identity. This, obviously, is not always the case; one has only to look at the many individuals who have changed their family names in order to hide their origins to see the difficulties with the tactic. Another difficulty with this approach lies in its claims to objectivity. While questions such as "Where was your father born?" and "Where was your mother born?" seem to require answers that are straightforward and verifiable, inconsistencies can appear quite easily. For example, how does a researcher determine the country of origin (and, accordingly, a person's ethnicity) for an informant when his or her ancestors are from different countries or regions? Also, the distinction between "objectivity" and "subjectivity" (or "cultural" and "personal" dimensions of ethnicity as they have been defined in this chapter) is often a fine one. For example, Plax (1972) includes in his interview schedules questions that ask an informant to make personal decisions about national origin without any precise reference to actual place of birth: "Since we're talking about your background, let me ask your *feelings* about it. Sometimes our nationality backgrounds make us think of ourselves not only as Americans, but as related to other countries, and we call ourselves French, or English, or Swiss. Thinking of your background, *what would you call yourself*?" (emphases mine). This kind of question more rightly serves as an example of the elicitation of the insider's personal perspective than of any concrete or cultural statement of national origin. Researchers must be careful to make this distinction when analyzing and presenting their data.

In addition to these kinds of methodological problems, the question still remains as to how much the informant's place of birth or ancestry can tell a researcher about his or her ethnicity. In my own research among the Corsicans of France, I found that many young people who were born in Paris and who had spent very little time with their families on the island still considered themselves to be Corsicans. However, some individuals who were born on the island of Corsican parents refuse to recognize themselves as anything but "true Frenchmen." Some people who claim Corsican ethnicity on the basis of ancestry and place of birth are said by their fellow islanders to be no longer Corsican (this is particularly true of certain highly placed individuals in Paris who have not supported Corsica in the manner or to the degree that other islanders expect). Finally, some people who were not born on the island and who are not of Corsican ancestry but who now make their home on the island believe that they are Corsican because of their chosen homeland. Thus, relying solely on ancestry or place of birth is a poor indicator of self-perceived ethnicity or ethnic membership.

An additional method of selecting ethnic informants that is easily combined with the elicitation of ancestry and location of birth centers on behavioral aspects of ethnic membership: food and dress preferences, language spoken, membership and participation in ethnic organizations. Such indices of ethnicity have the advantage of being rather easily observed and compared: Does a person speak the language in question? How often and why does a person participate in an ethnic organization or club? However, behavioral indicators of ethnicity must be approached with some caution, especially when dealing with older ethnic members. For example, people behave in certain ways as a method of impression management. Researchers must take care that the behaviors they observe are in fact deemed to be important as ethnic indicators by members of the ethnic group in question and that the people they observe are acting in a typical manner (i.e., they are not engaging in "front-stage" behavior solely to impress the researcher). I found, for example, that not all people who claim to be Corsican or who participate in Corsican friendship and kinship networks speak the Corsican language. This is particularly true for younger people. Among the older ethnic members, those who no longer claim knowledge of the language are usually the people who have deliberately dropped their Corsican identity. In my sample of elderly Corsicans in Paris, 69 percent indicate that to be "true" Corsican, one must know the language because it is the Corsican "soul." One might also note that this percentage conforms closely to the percentage of informants who actually do know the language (77 percent of the sample). Obviously, older Corsicans who value their ethnicity but who do not know the language are not going to claim a linguistic capability that they themselves do not have as an important marker of ethnic membership.

Researchers who attempt to measure social activity levels and network involvement as indicators of ethnicity and ethnic membersip face particular problems in dealing with older informants. Proponents of the activity and disengagement theories in gerontology have been arguing for decades about the significance of older peoples' participation in social-interaction networks and roles. The gerontological researcher must come to grips with the general issue of interpreting the significance of activity and roles before addressing the issue of the ethnic involvement of older people.

Measuring Personal Ethnic Identity

Various identification scales have been used to measure the degree to which an individual identifies himself or herself as an ethnic member. Some of these scales have been created for use with a particular ethnic group and have little or no validity for other groups (Uyeki 1960; Segelman 1967; Masuda, Matsumoto & Meredith 1970), while others are transethnic in approach and are designed to be used for comparative work (Pavlak 1976; Driedger 1976; Plax 1972). The scales also differ as to the kind and number of dimensions measured as well as the number of questions used to measure a particular dimension. Plax (1972), for example, attempts to measure "passive identification" by asking such questions as "Do you ever think of yourself as being a __?" or "How important was being a __ in your family? Is it important to you now?"

Social-distance scales have also been used to measure this subjective factor of ethnicity. Mitchell, for example, measured social distance by administering a formal, self-completed questionnaire to 329 male Zambian students. The students were asked whether they would willingly engage in close relationships (marriage, work, visiting, etc.) with individuals from twenty different ethnic categories. The answers were tabulated and statistically analyzed into a "hierarchical clustering of perceptions of social distance between categories" (Mitchell 1974:6).

The individual's self-identification as ethnic is undoubtedly crucial. However, one must exercise caution in using the kind of scale mentioned above. One problem is whether the scales actually measure what they are supposed to measure. Are such scales and the categories they set out meaningful to the informants in the research? Careful anthropological fieldwork must be carried out prior to the construction and use of such scales. Another problem is that the subjective experience is vague, shifting, and largely unconscious. Is it possible to accurately measure a situationally dominated variable with one scale administered under formal, artificial circumstances at a single point in time?

Measuring Ethnic Participation

The kinds of social organization available to and employed by older or younger individuals who claim ethnic membership can range from informal friendship and kinship networks to formal associations.[3] The types of social structures found within an ethnic group depend on the group's relation to the larger society and on the individual member's manipulation of existing opportunities.

The most informal kind of ethnic group is the friendship and/or kinship network based on place of origin. This network seems to approach Mayer's definition of an "interactive quasi-group" (1966). According to Mayer, this type of group is ego-centered in the sense that it depends on existence of a specific individual as the focal point of the group. The actions of any member of the group are relevant only insofar as they are interactions between him or her and ego or ego's intermediary (Mayer 1966:97-98).

A slightly more formalized grouping based on ethnicity is a quasigroup that depends mainly on the participants' common interests and the availability of a central meeting place. Mayer has called this type of quasigroup "classificatory". Common interests and needs lie at the base of participation in this group to the extent that the participants' shared interests and styles of behavior lead these individuals to interact and possibly to create formal associations at any time (Mayer 1966:97).

Finally, the most highly structured ethnic organization is the ethnic club. This group has set meeting dates, formal membership lists, elected leaders, and clearly articulated goals.

Membership and participation in these kinds of ethnic networks are not mutually exclusive. In fact, the strength of a person's evaluation of himself or herself as a "true" ethnic member (and conversely, the evaluation made of him or her by others--both members of the ethnic group and of the larger society) is closely correlated with the extent to which he or she makes use of all the available types of ethnic networks and with the degree to which ethnic networks as such comprise the majority of an individual's social interaction. Thus, to measure ethnicity using the behavioral component, the researcher must know the kinds of ethnic networks that exist, the extent to which a given person makes use of any or all of them, and the extent to which this ethnic participation represents the majority or totality of that person's social interaction. Thus, to a certain extent, the researcher can rank individuals according to their ethnic involvement by comparing the amount of participation in ethnic groups (both frequency of interaction and kinds of different networks employed) and the extent to which this ethnic social activity is their only link to the world outside their immediate families. In addition, one could logically assume that the individual who has the strongest subjective ethnic identity (as measured by identification or social-distance scales) would be the individual who also would participate the most frequently in the widest variety of ethnic networks available. How this identification and participation affect the individual's perceptions of and reactions to the aging process can then become the subject for research by employing one or more of the measures of morale in old age (see Nydegger, chap. 6 in this volume).

In my own research, I have combined the various approaches mentioned above in attempting to determine the effect of ethnic membership on older Corsicans in France (1980, 1981). To locate Corsican informants in Paris, I employed contacts that I had made during my fieldwork on the island (friends and relatives of the people with whom I lived and worked on Corsica); I asked these people to suggest other people (the "snowball" technique); I frequented Corsican-owned restaurants, cafes, and other meeting places); I obtained the list of members of the formal Corsican clubs in Paris; and, on occasion, I even resorted to using the telephone book to find a variety of people who illustrated the range of Corsican ethnic styles in Paris. These styles ranged from "joiners" (people who participated in all three of the kinds of ethnic networks just described) and "nonjoiners" (individuals who participate in friendship-kinship networks and quasigroups but who refuse to participate on more than a provisional basis in the ethnic club) to "drop-outs" (people who deny ethnic membership).

By means of participant observation and techniques suggested by cognitive anthropology, I attempted to determine what it means to be a Corsican in Paris. Finally, I assigned individuals an "ethnic score" based on their answers to a social-identification scale, their claims to use ethnic cultural symbols (and my observation of their actual behavior), and their claims to participate in ethnic organizations and networks (and my observation of their actual behavior). Finally, I administered the Life Satisfaction Index A of Neugarten,

Havighurst, and Tobin (1961) and compared informants' self-assessed life satisfaction scores with the ethnic scores that I had assigned them.

CONCLUSION

One of the contributions which the anthropology of aging may make to studies of ethnicity in general lies in our focus on the individual and his or her ethnic membership. Surely this will lead us away from simplistic notions of homogeneous ethnic groups and the idea that people may be easily fitted into ethnic slots according to externally defined characteristics (last name, physical characteristics, place of origin). Also, by focusing on individual adaptation, we may gain a better understanding of historical changes in the use of ethnic symbols and sentiments and the growth and development of the ethnic group itself. Finally, by working with older ethnic members we may gain some perspective on the general debate concerning the relation of social class and ethnicity. Is it ethnicity per se that makes a difference for people in hierarchical societies or is it a social-class phenomenon, wherein ethnicity is merely a labeling device for placing certain individuals in disadvantaged economic positions? Bengtson (1979) is correct in stressing that we must focus on a multiple-hierarchy model of stratification, which considers socioeconomic class, ethnicity, sex, and age as separate but interrelated aspects of social inequity. The longitudinal and cross-sectional approaches that often characterize anthropological research with older populations ought to help define the relative effects of ethnicity and class. A comprehensive methodological approach will include different age cohorts of the ethnic population (with particular focus on middle-aged and elderly members) as well as representatives from all income levels found in the group. Does the elderly person living in an urban working-class housing tract view and use ethnic membership in the same way as his or her counterpart living in a suburban middle-class subdivision? I doubt that ethnicity will ever stand alone as the explanatory variable for all the attitudes and actions of elderly ethnic members. But by adopting ethnicity as the prime variable and by viewing social-class variations as situational manifestations of it, we should gain a better understanding of the complex relationship of aging, ethnicity, and social class.

There is no single method of studying ethnicity. The perspective described here emphasizes the changing situational and personal nature of ethnic involvement. Yet in spite of the difficulties of such research, it must be undertaken. Ethnicity may well be one of the major variables that not only determines a person's attitudes toward the whole experience of growing older, but also affects his or her personal identity and possibilities for social interaction. We must never lose sight of the fact that older people, like their younger counterparts, are manipulators of their particular social context.

NOTES

1. For a detailed discussion of this approach and its application to the study of older people, see Keith, chapter 1, in this volume.

2. For a discussion of cognitive anthropology, its goals and methods, see Fry, chapter 5, in this volume.

3. My definition of the kinds of social organization available to ethnic members overlaps considerably with an earlier categorization proposed by Ross (1974). In the earlier work, Ross (1975:54) distinguishes what she calls "degrees of the definition of borders between groups": the category (common shared status is noted), the collectivity (norms are shared and a sense of collective responsibility appears), intensive contact (members interact with each other more than they interact with outsiders), and the formal association (corporate groups appear).

BIBLIOGRAPHY

Barth, Fredrik. 1969. Ethnic Groups and Boundaries. Boston: Little, Brown and Co.

Bengtson, Vern. 1979. "Ethnicity and Aging: Problems and Issues in Current Social Science Inquiry." In Ethnicity and Aging, ed. D. Gelfand and A. Kutzik. New York: Springer, pp. 9-31.

Brim, Orville G., Jr. 1960. "Personality as Role Learning." In Personality Development in Children," ed. Ira Iscoe and Harold Stevenson. Austin: University of Texas Press.

Burgess, W. E. 1960. Aging in Western Societies. Chicago: University of Chicago Press.

Cohen, Ronald. 1978. "Ethnicity: Problem and Focus in Anthropology." Annual Review of Anthropology, ed. Bernard J. Siegel, 7:379-403.

Cool, Linda E. 1980. "Ethnicity and Aging: Continuity through Change for Elderly Corsicans." In Aging in Culture and Society, ed. Christine L. Fry. New York: J. F. Bergin, pp. 149-69.

____. 1981. "Ethnic Identity: A Source of Community Esteem for the Elderly." Anthropological Quarterly 54(4):179-89.

Cronin, Constance. 1970. The Sting of Change. Chicago: University of Chicago Press.

Cuellar, Jose. 1978. "El Senior Citizens Club: The Older Mexican-American in the Voluntary Association." In Life's Career--Aging: Cultural Variations on Growing Old, ed. Barbara Myerhoff and Andrei Simic. Berverly Hills: Sage, pp. 207-30.

Dashefsky, Arnold. 1975. "Theoretical Frameworks in the Study of Ethnic Identity: Toward a Social Psychology of Ethnicity." Ethnicity 2:10-18.

Dowd, J., and V. Bengtson. 1978. "Aging in Minority Populations: an Examination of the Double Jeopardy Hypothesis." Journal of Gerontology 33(3):427-36.

Driedger, Leo. 1976. "Ethnic Self-Identity: A Comparison of Ingroup Evaluations." Sociometry 39:131-41.

Francis, E. K. 1976. Interethnic Relations: An Essay in Sociological Theory. New York: Elsevier.

Gelfand, Donald E. 1982. Aging: The Ethnic Factor. Boston: Little, Brown & Co.

Little, Kenneth. 1966. West African Urbanization. Cambridge:
Cambridge University Press.

Masuda, M., G. H. Matsumoto, and G. M. Meredith. 1970. "Ethnic
Identification in Three Generations of Japanese Americans."
Journal of Social Psychology 81:199-207.

Mayer, Adrian C. 1966. "The Significance of Quasi-Groups in the
Study of Complex Societies." In The Study of Complex Societies,
ed. Michael Banton. London: Tavistock.

Mitchell, J. C. 1974. "Perceptions of Ethnicity and Ethnic
Behaviour: An Empirical Exploration." In Urban Ethnicity, ed.
A. Cohen. London: Tavistock.

Myerhoff, Barbara. 1978. "A Symbol Perfected in Death:
Continuity and Ritual in the Life and Death of an Elderly Jew."
In Life's Career--Aging: Cultural Variations on Growing Old, ed.
Barbara Myerhoff and Andrei Simic. Beverly Hills: Sage, pp.
163-202.

Nagata, Judith. 1974. "What Is A Malay?" American Ethnologist
1:331-50.

_____. 1976. "The Status of Ethnicity and the Ethnicity of Status."
International Journal of Comparative Sociology 17(304):242-60.

National Urban League. 1964. Double Jeopardy: The Older Negro
in America Today. New York: National Urban League.

Neugarten, Bernice, Robert Havighurst, and Sheldon Tobin. 1961.
"The Measurement of Life Satisfaction." Journal of Gerontology
16:134-43.

Pavlak, T. J. 1976. Ethnic Identificaton and Political Behavior.
San Francisco: R & E Research Associates.

Plax, Martin. 1972. "On Studying Ethnicity." Public Opinion
Quarterly 36:99-104.

Ross, Jennie-Keith. 1975. "Social Borders: Definitions of Diversity." Current Anthropology 16:53-61.

Royce, Anya Peterson. 1982. Ethnic Identity: Strategies of Diversity. Bloomington: Indiana University Press.

Segelman, R. 1967. "Jewish Identity Scales: A Report." Jewish Social Studies 71:92-111.

Smith, M. Estellie. 1974. "Portuguese Enclaves: The Invisible Minority." In Social and Cultural Identity: Problems of Persistence and Change. Southern Anthropological Proceedings, No. 8, ed. Thomas K. Fitzgerald. Athens: Southern Anthropological Society.

Smith, Tom W. 1980. "Ethnic Measurement and Identification." Ethnicity 7:78-95.

Uyeki, Eugene S. 1960. "Correlates of Ethnic Identification." American Journal of Scoiology 65(5): 468-74.

van den Berghe, Pierre. 1970. Race and Ethnicity. New York: Basic Books.

12
Treatment of the Aged in Nonindustrial Societies

ANTHONY P. GLASCOCK AND SUSAN L. FEINMAN
Department of Anthropology
University of Wyoming

An absence of systematic comparative studies of the role and treatment of the aged in nonindustrial societies has led to analyses within anthropological gerontology that are largely descriptive and nonanalogous. Generalizations and/or propositions concerning the treatment of the aged are primarily developed from the study of single examples and, in many cases, are inappropriate when applied outside this one society. This general lack of a comparative framework within anthropological gerontology has opened the field to the charge that it can never accomplish anything more than the mere description of the behavior of the aged in isolated societies or social groups. In this chapter we will challenge this view by presenting a series of hologeistic propositions concerning the treatment of aged individuals. In addition, a series of suggestions as to the type and scope of data needed for the development of a systematic comparative study of old age, along with possible measurement techniques to be utilized in the analysis of these data, will be presented.

Hologeistic analysis "is a research design for statistically measuring the relationship between two or more theoretically defined and operationalized variables in a world sample of human societies" (Rohner et al. 1978:128). The method relies on the analysis of previously collected ethnographic data and in the majority of cases utilizes the Human Relations Area Files (Naroll 1970; Rohner 1977). A confusion exists as to the proper terminology to be applied to multicultural comparative research. For many years the terms "cross-cultural," "holocultural," and "hologeistic" were used interchangeably, but during the 1970's a distinction was made between the three terms. "Cross-cultural" now refers to studies of two or more societies that do not use one of the recognized holocultural samples (Murdock & White 1969; Naroll, Michik & Naroll 1976). (Some examples of cross-cultural aging studies are Hippler 1969; Lopata 1972; Press & McKool 1972; Shanas 1973; and Townsend 1973.) "Holocultural" and "hologeistic" now refer to studies that use samples from the HRAF. (Examples of holocultural or hologeistic aging studies are Simmons 1945a, 1945b; Silverman & Maxwell 1978; Maxwell 1977; Lee & Kezis 1981.)

The strengths and weaknesses of hologeistic analysis are often misunderstood, and as a result the approach has been little used in the analysis of aged individuals. The strength of hologeistic analysis rests in its interdependence with ethnographic and cross-cultural approaches. These three approaches are related to each other in a cyclical manner. Ethnographic monographs yield data, which can be used in the construction of hologeistic hypotheses. Hologeistic analyses, in turn, yield new, untested propositions, which can then be tested by ethnographic fieldwork and in cross-cultural studies of a limited number of societies. Through these methods of testing, a hypothesis can be refined and the cycle begun anew. (For more extensive discussion of this relationship, see Glascock & Feinman 1981).

Weaknesses of the hologeistic approach are twofold. First, the approach does not lend itself to the analysis of intracultural variation. That is, the nature of the approach does not allow for the detailed analysis of variations in behavior in a single society. Although the careful application of the hologeistic approach allows for the elucidating of some behavioral variation within a single society, its strength lies in comparison among a large sample of societies and the development and testing of broad generalizations. A second weakness of the hologeistic approach is not inherent in the approach itself but is found instead in the use made of its conclusions. The generalizations of propositions that result from hologeistic analysis are not proven laws. Instead, the conclusions are statements of relationships that must be tested through additional research in specific social settings. The acceptance of the conclusions of hologeistic analysis as definitive and proven gives the approach a role that is both unwarranted and unwanted. Properly used, hologeistic analysis is not the endpoint but actually only one part of the research cycle.

The goal of the present work is to stimulate the cycle by suggesting a series of hologeistic propositions concerning the aged that can be systematically tested with data from new fieldwork. The propositions focus on two major interrelated areas: (1) the treatment accorded the aged in nonindustrial societies, and (2) the differentiation of old people into more than one age category in nonindustrial societies.

These propositions have been developed over the last four years at the University of Wyoming by the systematic analysis of a sample of nonindustrial societies.

A standard hologeistic methodology was employed in the development and testing of the hypotheses concerning the treatment of old people (for more complete discussion of the methodology utilized, see Glascock & Feinman 1980). Five categories from the Human Relations Area Files provided the data base from which the codes were constructed: age stratification, old-age dependency, senescence, activities of the aged and status and treatment of the aged. Twelve codes were developed concerning the treatment of old people. Since separate entries were made for males and females, the final coding procedure contained twenty-four distinct elements. Raoul Naroll's HRAF Probability Sample Files were selected as the sample of societies for final analysis (Naroll, Michik & Naroll 1976).

Seven propositions were developed through the systematic analysis of the ethnographic data for the sixty societies comprising the Probability Sample Files. Three of these propositions concern the treatment accorded the aged; three concern the differentiation of old persons into more than one age category; and one concerns both. The consideration of each of these seven propositions is divided into two sections. The first section discusses each of the propositions incorporating the hologeistic evidence that led to the development of the proposition, and additional ethnographic evidence that both illustrates and contributes further substantiation to the propositions. The second section discusses the means by which the propositions can be used and tested in fieldwork.

SEVEN HOLOGEISTIC PROPOSITIONS

Proposition 1

Behavior. Our first proposition is that in nonindustrial societies there is often a difference in the attitude stated by individuals toward the aged and the treatment accorded the aged. This difference is frequently overlooked by the anthropologist, leading to the confusion of attitude and behavior. The problems associated with this confusion are discussed by Fry, Keith, and Nydegger (chaps. 5, 1, and 6 in this volume) in specific contexts; it is an issue that the gerontological anthropologist must face continually in the research setting.

Our findings contradict a commonly held belief that old people in most societies are primarily given supportive treatment and that the prolongation of life is sought (Cowgill 1971, 1972; Myerhoff & Simic 1977; Simmons 1960; Maxwell 1977). The results of our analysis indicate that nonsupportive treatment of the aged is a more frequent occurrence than supportive behavior (58-42 percent). This is the case even though in each and every one of the societies in which nonsupportive behavior is found, the attitude toward the aged is one of respect. The recording of the attitude of respect as positive "treatment" would have led to dramatically different conclusions for the present study and to a skewing of the data toward supportive treatment of the aged.

This confusion of attitude and behavior and the resultant skewing of findings toward the occurrence of supporting treatment is found in all research areas of anthropological gerontology: ethnographic, cross-cultural and hologeistic. It especially occurs in comparative studies when prestige, respect, and often reverence expressed by younger people toward the aged are equated by the researcher with positive and supportive treatment.

Proposition 2

Variation in treatment. Our second proposition is that there are a limited number of possible treatments accorded to the aged in nonindustrial societies. Nine treatment codes emerged from the analysis of our data:

1. supportive treatment;
2. nonspecific nonsupportive treatment;
3. old people insulted;
4. old people regarded as witches;
5. old people forsaken;
6. old people's property taken;
7. old people living apart from the main social group;
8. old people abandoned;
9. old people killed.

These nine treatment categories accounted for all the data present on the PSF societies. They appear to encompass the range of treatment patterns directed at the aged in nonindustrial societies.

To increase the efficiency of the nine-code scale, it was converted from a nominal to an ordinal scale and statistically grouped by t-test to form three major groupings:

1.   supportive treatment;
2.   treatment not hastening death, comprised of nonspecific, nonsupportive treatment, insulting, regarding as a witch, taking property, living apart (defined as nonsupportive treatment that does not lead directly to death); and
3.   treatment hastening death, comprised of forsaking, abandoning, and killing (defined as nonsupportive treatment that leads directly to death of the aged person).

It is our contention that treatment behavior observed by ethnographers will be classifiable within one of the nine original treatment codes. Thus, treatment of older adults can subsequently be classified into one of the three broad original categories, which will facilitate comparative analyses. Use of these classificatory schemes should not result in the perversion of data or the forcing of data into pigeonholes. Instead, it should allow for the clarification and standardization of concepts, without which there is little hope that anthropological gerontology will improve beyond the descriptive noncomparative nature of the discipline that exists at present.

Proposition 3

Multiple treatments. In nonindustrial societies it is common to have multiple treatments accorded the aged within one social group. Distinctions of primary, secondary, and tertiary treatment made during our hologeistic analysis proved to be relevant. Treatments for a given sex in a given society were ranked by a combination of how often the treatment was mentioned and how much emphasis was placed upon the treatment by ethnographers.

Prevalence of more than one form of treatment in nonindustrial societies is indicated by the fact that over two-thirds of the societies (68 percent) in the PSF made use of at least two types of treatment. Two brief examples illustrate the frequency of multiple treatments accorded the aged. Supportive treatment is the most frequent single category, occurring 35 percent of the time. However, supportive treatment alone occurred in only 16 percent of the societies in which treatment could be coded. In the remaining instances, supportive treatment was found in conjunction with at least one nonsupportive treatment. Killing of the aged was the second most prevalent treatment, occurring 19 percent of the time. Killing alone, however, occurred in only five instances (4 percent); the remaining occurrences linked killing with another treatment.

Proposition 4

Nonsupportive treatment. Our fourth proposition is that non-supportive treatment of the aged is found frequently in non-industrial societies (nonsupportive treatment is behavior that can be classified in either grouping 2 or 3 outlined under proposition 2). Astoundingly, 84 percent of the societies with data concerning the treatment of the aged had some form of nonsupportive treat-ment. In particular, death-hastening behavior appears to be present in the societies studied by anthropologists much more often than has previously been assumed, as over one-third of the societies in the PSF had some form of death-hastening behavior.

It is our contention that most nonsupportive treatment of the aged has gone unnoticed by anthropological gerontologists for three reasons. First, there has been a confusion between the attitudes of society members toward the aged and treatment accorded the aged. Second, since nonsupportive treatment of the aged goes against values that the anthropologist may hold, it is often hidden from the anthropologist by society members. Third, nonsupportive treatment is almost always part of a multiple-treatment pattern and therefore the anthropologist may be able to discern one type of treatment but be unable to see beyond the primary treatment to secondary and tertiary treatments.

Proposition 5

Differentiation in the category "old." In nonindustrial societies there is a differentiation of the aged into at least two groupings. The existence of such a distinction within the old-age category was first suggested by Simmons (1945a:62, 1945b:42, 1960:87). Further evidence for the existence of such a differentiation is found in the work of Bernice Neugarten (1974, 1975; Neugarten & Hagestad 1976). Neugarten's work has been focused on American society, but her arguments for the existence of a distinction between the young-old and the old-old support the idea that such groupings exist in all societies.

In our analysis, the terms selected for the two groupings within the old-age category are "intact" and "decrepit." Intact refers to individuals who are old but who are still capable, however that may be defined by members of a particular society. "Decrepit," following Simmons, refers to individuals who are incapacitated to a degree that they are "living liabilities." Almost one-third of the societies in the PSF (eighteen societies--32 percent) distinguished different groups of elderly people. Of these, almost all (fifteen societies--26 percent of all PSF societies) made the distinction between young or intact old, on the one hand, and old or decrepit old, on the other.

The existence of the intact/decrepit distinction in only 26 percent of the PSF societies does not appear to offer convincing evidence to anthropological gerontologists of the validity of our fifth proposition. Nevertheless, it is our contention that the intact/decrepit distinction is found in many more societies than has been reported. A brief example illustrates this point. The !Kung were part of a pretest sample of societies that was used in the development of our codes. After analyzing all available data on the !Kung, the coders concluded that the !Kung made no distinction within the old-age category. Since this coding, a recent ethnographic report on aging among the !Kung by Megan Biesele and Nancy Howell (1981) indicates the existence of at least two categories of old individuals: "old" and "nearly dead." This more recent research on the !Kung by anthropologists who are interested in issues of aging found just the anticipated distinction. The implication is clear: gerontological researchers should explicitly look for these groupings within the old age category. They may be extremely subtle as the !Kung data indicates; but they are present, we argue, in the majority of nonindustrial societies.

Proposition 6

People. In nonindustrial societies in which the intact/decrepit distinction is made, multiple treatments accorded the aged will be present. Of the fifteen societies in which the intact/decrepit distinction is made, only one accords old people a single treatment. All societies but this one accord old people multiple treatments, of which at least one component is nonsupportive.

The gerontological researcher who finds that the aged are grouped into more than one category should find multiple treatments accorded to the aged. Supportive behavior should be found for individuals who are defined as intact and some form of nonsupportive behavior should be found for those who are defined as decrepit. One additional factor, though, makes the observation of the intact/decrepit distinction and associated treatments difficult.

Aged individuals who are defined as decrepit may in some

societies show no change in physical appearance or physical or mental capabilities during the transition from intact to decrepit. Instead of changes in aged people, there may be changes in the physical and social surroundings, which bring about a change in the position of the aged. The situation in which the aged find themselves changes: drought occurs, the social group moves, the food supply changes, there is an intrusion of outside cultures, etc. These changes may precipitate the transition of the aged individuals from useful society members to burdens.

Consequently, the category of decrepit old and associated nonsupportive treatments may not be present at all times but may only occur for short periods of time at widely scattered intervals. This makes the actual observation of the distinction and associated nonsupportive behaviors a matter of timing.

Proposition 7

Societal characteristics. Our final proposition is that there is a relationship between the treatment behavior directed at the aged, the intact/decrepit distinction, and certain societal charac-teristics. This proposition is the most general, since the results of the hologeistic study indicate that these proposed relationships are extremely complex. Some patterns, though, do emerge from the analysis. Nonsupportive treatment and the intact/decrepit distinction tend to be present in societies that (1) are in harsh climates, in particular desert and tundra areas; (2) have no or only shifting horticulture; and (3) lack systems of stratification. Supportive treatment tends to be present in societies that (1) are in forest or temperate climates; (2) have intensive or advanced agriculture; (3) have systems of stratification; (4) possess political centralization; and (5) have a belief in active high gods. In other words, given the data available, nonsupportive treatment of the aged and the intact/decrepit distinction are found in societies in which the cultural development can best be described as simple: hunting-and-gathering societies, pastoral societies, and shifting horticultural societies. Societies with exclusively supportive treatment of the aged are more economically complex societies and tend primarily to be sedentary agriculturalists.

FIELD TESTING OF THE PROPOSITIONS

The seven propositions discussed here are designed to be used in the development of a comparative framework within anthropological gerontology by being evaluated through fieldwork. For these propositions to be tested, they must be put into testable forms, and, although this process will be somewhat different for each specific research endeavor, some broad guidelines can be given. These guidelines fall into three general processes: (1) the type and scope of data necessary to test the propositions; (2) the type of measurement schemata necessary to elicit variance within a culture; and (3) some suggestions as to the most appropriate method of gathering the data.

The first proposition, that there is often a difference between a society's stated attitudes toward the aged and that same society's treatment of the aged, is the most difficult to test. The difficulty is that we must distinguish between ideal and actual behavior--a task difficult in the best situations, but especially arduous when dealing with treatment of the aged. As shown in the hologeistic analysis, the confusion between attitudes about the aged and the treatment of the aged is common in the anthropological literature. Consequently, the anthropological gerontologist must carefully distinguish between verbalized attitudes about the aged and actual, concrete behavior directed toward the aged. The distinction does not mean that the researcher may ignore either type of data. Quite the contrary, the researcher must be careful to collect both types of data in order to discover what, if any, differences between ideal and actual behavior exist.

The scope of the data collected is also crucial to the testing of the first proposition. The problem of sampling is discussed in several chapters in this volume (see Sokolovsky, chap. 10; Keith, chap. 1; Frank and Vanderburgh, chap. 8; and Fry, chap. 5), and sampling is the key to testing all seven propositions. The sampling design utilized in the field will vary considerably from one situation to another, but certain factors should remain constant: male and female kin of the aged, friends, other community members who interact with the aged, and noncommunity members who either interact with or have authority over the aged should be interviewed and observed. In addition, care must be taken to observe a wide range of behavioral areas that affect the aged. For example, variations in health care, in taboos based on age, in authority, and in eating habits and types of foods must be measured and recorded.

The measurement of variations is critical to the testing of this first proposition, and in fact to the testing of all seven propositions. The variations indicated by the hologeistic study should be present in most, if not all, societies. In particular, it should be found in those societies in which the intact/decrepit distinction is present. These variations may be quite subtle and, in some cases, even transitory in nature, but their observation is necessary in order to test not only the first proposition but to understand the treatment of the aged in general. (Actual measuring techniques are considered more fully in the discussion of Proposition 2).

The means by which data on attitudes toward the aged can be collected will vary to a certain extent from one social setting to another; still certain anthropological methods appear to be more appropriate than others. The life-history technique when used with structured interviewing (see Frank and Vanderburgh, chap. 8 in this volume) is particularly suited to the elicitation of attitudes concerning the treatment of the aged. In conjunction with interviewing and the collection of life histories, a technique such as the card sort (see Fry, chap. 5 in this volume) can be utilized to elicit attitudes concerning the appropriate treatment of the aged from a relatively large sample of individuals. In particular, the subject of respect and status accorded the aged can be determined through the use of a card sort and possible variation between different groups of community members determined.

The observation and recording of actual treatment behavior directed toward the aged is best accomplished by a combination of participant observation and network analysis (for a fuller discussion of these methodologies see Keith, chap. 1; and Sokolovsky, chap. 10 in this volume). The nine treatment codes developed in Proposition 2 accounted for the treatment behaviors directed toward the aged for the data from the PSF societies, but the generality of these codes has yet to be tested in the field situation. This testing must commence by first viewing the codes as a set of variables applicable to the particular research setting. This transformation should focus the research on a set of relevant questions, such as the following: Are all aged individuals supported by the social group? If not, which aged individuals are supported; which ones are not? In what contexts are the aged supported, and by whom? What variation occurs in this support during the year? What factors appear to affect the scope and nature of this support? The next questions, or similar questions depending on the field circumstances, should be asked for each of the nine codes: Are all aged individuals insulted by members of the social group? If not all, which aged are insulted and in what contexts? Are the aged regarded as witches? And so on. By using these codes as a set of variables, the full range of actual behavior can be observed, and the reliance on informants' expressed attitudes can be lessened. Furthermore, the variations that may exist between different aged individuals and between different contexts can be determined and measured by this procedure.

One caution, though, is necessary in relation to testing of the second proposition: in some social settings the nonsupportive-treatment behavior may be extremely difficult to observe. If the second, third and fourth propositions are substantiated, nonsupportive behavior will be found alongside of supportive behavior and an attitude of increased respect for the aged. Consequently, the researcher must continually search for forms of behavior, in addition to supportive treatment, in a wide range of social contexts.

The third and fourth propositions--that multiple treatments occur in the majority of nonindustrial societies and that a high frequency of treatment behavior is nonsupportive can be tested in general by the use of the research techniques discussed in relation to the first two propositions. Additionally though, the gerontological researcher should be careful to attempt to observe and measure the full range of behaviors present in the particular social setting. The recognition that the aged are a heterogeneous category has led to the realization that a wide range of treatment behaviors can be found among a relatively small number of individuals. Therefore, the simple observation that multiple treatments occur is insufficient to answer important questions concerning treatment of the aged. These questions must focus on the variation that exists among aged individuals and the variation that may exist within the social network of a single individual. The hologeistic data indicate clearly that these variations exist, but the actual variations must be determined by detailed field studies.

The testing of the fifth and sixth propositions--that the intact/decrepit distinction exists and that this distinction is found in conjunction with multiple treatments toward the aged--requires the examination of a number of variables in addition to those already discussed. The gerontological researcher must once again approach the testing by clearly differentiating between the attitudes expressed concerning the groupings with the aged category and behavior directed toward individual members in the different groupings. A card sort appears to be the most useful technique by which the existence of these groupings can be derived and should be used in conjunction with interviewing a representative sample of community members.

The observation of behavior directed at individual members within the different groupings may prove to be somewhat difficult for two reasons. First, for reasons that have been discussed previously, nonsupportive treatment may be difficult to observe, but if the fifth and sixth propositions are substantiated, the behavior directed toward members of the decrepit category should be nonsupportive. Second, the differences in treatment behavior directed toward members of these two groupings may be extremely subtle and may vary with the context of the behavior. The researcher must therefore be careful to observe and record behavior between the aged and community members over as long a period of time as possible. Once again, the nine treatment codes developed in Proposition 2 function as a set of variables around which the research can be organized.

The actual measurement of decrepitude is an essential part of the testing of the fifth and sixth propositions, a measurement that may prove to be quite difficult. One possible research technique that may make this measurement easier is an extension of the procedure discussed by Beall and Eckert (chap. 2 in this volume) concerning the measurement of the functional capacity of the aged. The use of the measurement techniques that they discuss should provide an etic measure for the existence of more than one grouping within the aged category. Used in conjunction with the attitudinal measure and the concrete observational data, this etic measure could offer an effective test of the fifth and sixth propositions.

The testing of the seventh proposition, that there is a relationship between the treatment behavior directed at the aged, the intact/decrepit distinction and certain societal characteristics is, like the proposition itself, general in nature and broad in scope. It is, of course, necessary before beginning to test this proposition for the gerontological fieldworker to have determined the treatment patterns in his/her particular field site, measured the variance that may exist among the treatment patterns, and determined whether the intact/decrepit distinction exists (and, if so, the extent of its application). Once these factors have been determined and measured, the comparison with other societal features can be undertaken. This comparison, of course, will require that a wide range of data be collected, e.g., on the environment, the food supply--including fluctuation in food supply and types of food--caloric and nutritional data, the kinship system, the exchange system, the political structure, and the religious behavior of community members. Even after these data have been collected the comparison will not be a simple task. The existence of multiple treatment patterns and the slippery nature of the intact/decrepit distinction will require a more sophisticated analytical procedure than simple correlation. A procedure that incorporates some form of multiple-regression analysis or partial correlations should be effective in analyzing these relationships. In some cases, though, the most appropriate procedure may be painstaking comparison, on an individual-by-individual basis. It is in these cases that detailed network analyses will be the most beneficial to an understanding of the variations within social groups.

These suggestions as to the type and scope of data, the type of measurement schemata, and the most appropriate methods of gathering the data necessary to test the seven propositions are offered as general guidelines. Research into the variables associated with the seven propositions is absolutely necessary if a comparative framework for anthropological gerontology is to be developed. However, the propositions are not offered as definitive statements but only as one possible means of systematically testing a series of ideas concerning old people. It is anticipated that as fieldwork progresses, the number of propositions and the nature of the propositions will change, and a greater understanding of the treatment of the elderly cross-culturally will be gained as a result.

294 New Methods for Old-Age Research

BIBLIOGRAPHY

Biesele, Megan, and Nancy Howell. 1981. "The Old People Give You Life." In Other Ways of Growing Old, ed. Pamela T. Amoss and Stevan Harrell. Stanford, Calif: Stanford University Press.

Cowgill, Donald O. 1971. "A Theoretical Framework for Considerations of Data on Aging." Paper presented at the meetings of the Society for Applied Anthropology, Miami.

____. 1972. "A Theory of Aging in Cross-Cultural Perspective." In Aging and Modernization, ed. D. O. Cowgill and L. D. Holmes. New York: Appleton-Century-Crofts.

Glascock, Anthony P., and Susan L. Feinman. 1980. "A Holocultural Analysis of Old Age." Comparative Social Research 3.

____. 1981. "Social Asset or Social Burden: An Analysis of the Treatment of the Aged in Non-Industrial Societies." In Dimensions: Aging, Culture and Health, ed. Christine Fry. New York: J. F. Bergin.

Hippler, A. E. 1969. Fusion and Frustration: Dimensions in the Cross-Cultural Ethnopsychology of Suicide." American Anthropologist 71(6): 1074-87.

Lee, Gary R., and Mindy Kezis. 1981. "Societal Literacy and the Status of the Aged." International Journal of Aging and Human Development 12(3).

Lopata, Helena Znaniecki. 1972. "Role Changes in Widowhood: A World Perspective." In Aging and Modernization, ed. D. O. Cowgill and L. D. Holmes. New York: Appleton-Century-Crofts.

Maxwell, Robert J. 1977. "Information and Esteem: Cultural Consideration in the Treatment of the Aged." In Human Aging and Dying, ed. W. H. Watson and R. J. Maxwell. New York: Martin's Press.

Murdock, George P., and Douglas White. 1969. "Standard Cross-Cultural Sample." Ethnology 8:329-69.

Myerhoff, B. G., and A. Simic. 1977. Life's Career--Aging: Cultural Variations on Growing Old. Beverly Hills: Sage.

Naroll, Raoul. 1970. "What Have We Learned from Cross-Cultural Surveys?" American Anthropologist 72:1227-88.

Naroll, Raoul, Gary Michik, and Frada Naroll. 1976. Worldwide Theory Testing. New Haven, Conn.: HRAF Press.

Neugarten, Bernice L. 1974. "Age Groups in American Society and the Use of the Young Old." Annals of the American Academy of Political and Social Science 415:187-98.

_____. 1975. "The Future and the Young-Old." Gerontologist 15(1): 4-9.

Neugarten, Bernice L., and Gunhild O. Hagestad. 1976. "Age and the Life Course." In Handbook of Aging and the Social Science, ed. Robert S. Binstock and Ethel Shanas, New York: Van Nostrand.

Press, Irwin, and Mike McKool, Jr. 1972. "Social Structure and Status of the Aged: Toward Some Valid Cross-Cultural Generalizations." Aging and Human Development 3(4): 297-306.

Rohner, Ronald P. 1977. "Advantages of the Comparative Method of Anthropology." Behavior Science Research 12:117-44.

Rohner, Ronald P., et al. 1978. "Guidelines for Holocultural Research." Current Anthropology 19(1): 128-29.

Shanas, E. 1973. "Family Kin Networks and Aging in Cross-Cultural Perspective." Journal of Marriage and the Family 35(3): 505-11.

Silverman, Philip, and Robert J. Maxwell. 1978. "How Do I Respect Thee? Let Me Count The Ways: Deference towards Elderly Men and Women." Behavioral Science Research 13(2): 91-108.

Simmons, Leo W. 1945a, 1970. The Role of the Aged in Primitive Society. New Haven: Archon Books.

_____, 1945b. "A Prospectus for Field Research in the Position and Treatment of the Aged in Primitive and Other Societies." American Anthropologist 47:433-38.

_____. 1960. "Aging in Pre-Industrial Societies." In Handbook of Social Gerontology, ed. C. Tibbitts. Chicago: University of Chicago Press.

Townsend, P. 1973. "The Place of Older People in Different Societies." In Age with a Future. Proceedings of the Sixth International Congress of Gerontology. Philadelphia: F. A. David Co.

Index

Acclerometers, 37
Activities of aged, 283
Activities of Daily Living, 38; Measurement of, 30–40. *Also see* Physical functioning
Administration of research, xvii
Age: and componential analysis, 111–113; and role transitions, 142–147; as an index, 109; biological, 41–42; cultural definitions of, 57; cultural systems based on, 164–165; data from large populations, 59–64; data from small populations, 64–68; dimensions of, 109; elicitation frames, 111; estimating, 56–76; ethnosemantics & organization, 126; lexical markers, 110; life course, 110; life course transitions, 131–162; life stages, 110; measurement of, 57–76; need for measurement, 58; problems of measurement, 57–58; semantic domain of, 109–110; semantic organization of, 109–110; social, 142–143
Age categories: concensus in, 112–113; significatum, 112
Age class, 164
Age confounds, 149–150; age set societies, 150; historical & timetable interactions, 151; historical effects, 150–151; implications for anthropology, 150–151; problems of time defined variables, 149
Age differentiation: gender differences, 116
Age estimates: age calendars, 66; biased errors, 59; documents, use of, 68–70; evaluating quality of data, 59; evaluation of, 58–68; event calendar accuracy, 72; informants, 70–71; internal consistency of source, 73; need for demographer, 58; opportunistic methods, 68; physical evidence, 71; random errors, 59; sources of error, 59; special problems for very old, 72; techniques of making, 68–71
Age estimates, evaluation of: independent methods of, 66; need for multiple data sources, 64–66
Age grade, defined, 109
Age grades, 164
Age measurement problems: age heaping, 60–62; age rounding, 62; age vanity, 62–63; socially important ages, 62
Age pyramids: sex distribution, 63; subpopulational differences, 63–64
Age stratification, 283
Age transitions, 132–133; and chronological age, 132; role transitions, 132
Aging: cultural definitions, xix; cultural factors, xx–xxi; historical dimensions, 79; physical

aspects, xviii–xix; social networks, xx; subjectivity, xix–xx
Aging and ethnicity: definition of variables, 263; mutual effects on, 263
Analysis: cross-sectional data, 92; life course data, 91–95; life cycle ritual, 176–178
Analysis plans, xvii
Analysis of data. *See* Data analysis; appropriate for kind of data, 13; cluster analysis, 13; coding, 13; cross-tabulations, 13; fieldnotes, 13; multidimensional scaling, 13; recording & analysis, 14
Analysis of life course data: computerized retrieval system, 93; duration, 93; life-table approach, 94–95; repeatability of life events, 92; storage in computer files, 92
Analysis of life cycle ritual: cosmological control of humans, 177; gender definition, 177; model of changing relationship, 177; models of role sequences, 176–177; old age, 177; symbolism index, 177–178
Anthropological perspective: emics & etics, xxi; features of, xx–xxi; holism, xxii; qualitative research, xxii; real & ideal culture, xxii
Anthropological research: quantitative research, xxii
Attitude toward aged: difference in treatment, 283
Attitudes: differentiated from behavior, 291
Attitudes toward aged: measurement of, 290
Attributes of age: age profiles, 117; computerized manipulation, 117–118; discovery of combinations, 116–118; elicitation procedures, 113–115; informant manipulated combination, 117; ungrammatical combinations, 117–118

Behavior: real & ideal, 289
Biological age, measurement of, 42
Biological capacity: assessment of, 41–43; presentation of data, 43; reasons for objective assessment, 41
Biological change, age related, 23
Bradburn Affect Balance Scale, 215
Bradburn Happiness Measure, 215

Cantril Self-Anchoring Scale, 219–220
Card sort techniques: among literate populations, 120; among nonliterate populations, 121; coding of data, 122–123; definition of objects, 119–120; presentation formats, 120–121; protocols for, 121–122; social

297